The World of

JOSEPHUS

The World of

JOSEPHUS

G. A. Williamson

LITTLE, BROWN AND COMPANY · BOSTON · TORONTO

933
W

TO MY WIFE

Contents

Part Three

THE SEQUEL

Foreword

MANY BOOKS HAVE BEEN WRITTEN ABOUT JOSEPHUS; FAR MORE
about the world in which he lived. Is there room for yet another
book? I think that there is. It is an unfortunate fact that most of
the works that deal with the man himself are hard to come by,
and some of the most important are not available in our language.
Those that deal with his world deal with one half only: their
scope is limited either to Rome or to Palestine; or else they cover
the Empire as a whole and have room for only a passing glance at
the tiny country in which he spent the first half of his life. And as
there is no book that deals specifically with both the regions in
which he lived, so there is none that concentrates on the period
spanned by his three-score years. The present book has been
written in the hope that it will be helpful to those who have not
time or inclination to read many books, or to extract from
encyclopaedias and many-volumed histories the information
necessary if they are to form an intelligible picture of Josephus'
world. It is not written for experts, and I have taken nothing
more for granted than a very slight acquaintance with the regions
and the period to which Josephus belonged. Nor have I assumed
that his own writings have been studied; for most of them are
very rarely to be found on booksellers' shelves. If this book leads
any of my readers to obtain copies of at least the most important
of his works, so that they can form their own opinions on the
many controversial questions on which I have perforce expressed
my own, it will have been worth while.

But not only is it probable that many readers of these pages have
studied none of our author's own writings; it may well be that to
some Josephus is merely a name, a shadow without substance. It
would be somewhat bewildering to read lengthy descriptions of a
writer's world when totally unacquainted with the writer himself,
to whom that world is but the background, or if you will, the
setting. It is important to know at the outset something of the

man, who and what he was, what he did and what he left behind him. All this will be discussed in detail in the course of our study, from which I trust that a clear and truthful picture will emerge; but it will help those who are about to make Josephus' acquaintance for the first time if we run rapidly now over the essential facts that are known about him, postponing all the many doubts and problems for consideration later. With those facts in mind we shall be able to turn our attention to Josephus' world—the world that helped to make him what he was, the world of geography, of history, of religion, of thought, of circumstance.

Briefly then, Josephus was a Jewish priest, born in Palestine in the thirty-seventh year of our era. He received a varied education and showed himself an assiduous and very precocious pupil. In the year 64, when he was twenty-seven, he visited Rome. It is possible that he witnessed the burning of Rome and the consequent burning of Christian scapegoats: it is certain that the power and culture and sophistication of Rome made an immense impression on him. He returned to Jerusalem to find preparations in full swing for the fatal rebellion which broke out in 66 and led, most surprisingly, to his appointment as governor of Galilee and organizer of its defences against the expected Roman invasion. Those defences proved ineffective and a few months later the governor—whether by accident or by design we shall have to consider later—found himself the prisoner of the Roman commander-in-chief, Vespasian, and later the favoured dependant of Vespasian's son, Titus, destined like his father to be Roman emperor. From the Roman side he witnessed much of the war, which ended three years later in the ruin of Palestine and the total destruction of Jerusalem. From there he followed his patrons to Rome, where he settled down as their pensioner and began his career as a writer, a career which he was to pursue with the utmost diligence till his death, which occurred at about the end of the century.

How many books he wrote we do not know: four have come down to us. Two of them are important historical works. Much the longer of these two is *Antiquities*, a detailed history of the Jews from their first origins to the author's own lifetime; the shorter is *The Jewish War*, a much more readable work, and an invaluable source-book for both Jewish and Roman history. The other two are of lesser importance, and one of them, an autobiography known as *The Life*, is a very unsatisfactory composition. The other, generally referred to as *Against Apion*, is a well written defence of Jewish beliefs, customs, and behaviour. In the course of this book we shall draw on all these works, *The Jewish War* supplying far more information than the others put together. At the end we shall have something to say about the quality of Josephus' writing; but he is an author who is studied for his matter, not his style.

Anyone who writes on such a subject as this is bound to draw heavily on the fruits of other men's labours in the same field. In the pages that follow I have named a great many of those to whom I am indebted, chief of whom is the late Dr. St. John Thackeray, whose work on Josephus included the editing of the first five volumes of the Loeb bilingual edition, with their admirable introductions, translation, and notes, which all students of Josephus will find invaluable.

Of course I have drawn most heavily on the writings of Josephus himself, quoting constantly from all his four works. I have thought it better not to take all these quotations from the same translation, but for the greater interest of the reader to draw sometimes on Whiston, sometimes on Traill, and sometimes on my own translation of the *Jewish War* in Penguin Classics, which I have reproduced by courtesy of the publishers, Penguin Books Ltd. In the few cases where I have not named the translator his identity, I think, is obvious. I have also quoted a number of apposite and illuminating passages from Holy Scripture, following the example of Josephus, who made continual use of the books which form our Old Testament and Apocrypha. These passages I have as a rule quoted in their familiar if old-fashioned wording; but in a few cases a rendering into current English seemed more helpful, and this—greatly daring—I have ventured to provide myself.

Chronological Table

B.C.

63 Capture of Jerusalem by Pompey

48 Defeat of Pompey at Pharsalus; Julius Caesar supreme

47 Herod, governor of Galilee

44 Assassination of Julius Caesar

42 Defeat of Brutus and Cassius at Philippi

40 Herod, king of the Jews

37 Capture of Jerusalem by Herod and Sossius

31 Defeat of Antony and Cleopatra at Actium

29 Murder of Mariamme

20 Building of Temple begun

7? Births of John and Jesus

4 Death of Herod; accession of Archelaus, Antipas, and Philip

A.D.

6 Banishment of Archelaus

14 Death of Augustus; accession of Tiberius

26-36 Pontius Pilate, procurator of Judaea

30? Crucifixion, Resurrection, Ascension, and Pentecost

34 Death of Philip

37 Death of Tiberius; accession of Gaius (Caligula)
Birth of Josephus

39 Banishment of Antipas

41 Murder of Gaius; accession of Claudius

41-44 Agrippa I, king of Judaea

52-60 Felix, procurator

53 Agrippa II, king of Trachonitis and Ituraea

54 Murder of Claudius; accession of Nero

60-62 Festus, procurator

62-64 Albinus, procurator

64 Fire of Rome. Josephus in Rome

64-66 Gessius Florus, procurator

66 Jewish Revolt; defeat of Cestius; Josephus in Galilee

67 Arrival of Vespasian; Josephus a prisoner; subjugation of Galilee

68 Suicide of Nero; accession of Galba. Subjugation of Peraea

69 Murder of Galba; accession of Otho
Suicide of Otho; accession of Vitellius
Murder of Vitellius; accession of Vespasian

70 (March to September) Siege of Jerusalem by Titus

71 Josephus settled in Rome. 'Triumph' of Vespasian and Titus

73 Capture of Masada; end of Jewish War

75 Dedication of Temple of Peace

? Publication of *The Jewish War*

79 Death of Vespasian; accession of Titus

81 Death of Titus; accession of Domitian

93 Publication of *Antiquities*, followed at uncertain intervals by *Life* and *Apion Answered*

96 Murder of Domitian; accession of Nerva

98 Death of Nerva; accession of Trajan

The date of Josephus' death is unknown.

PALESTINE
in
Josephus' Time

Sidon

ABILENE

Damascus ·

Mt. Hermon

Caesarea Philippi

Tyre

PHOENICIA

ITURAEA

Gischala

Capernaum

Ptolemais

Tarichaeae

Julias (Bethsaida)

GALILEE

Tiberias

TRACHONITIS

Jotapata

Sepphoris

· Gamala

Mt. Tabor

DECAPOLIS

Caesarea

Mt. Carmel

Scythopolis

· Pella

SAMARIA

· Sebaste

R. Jordan

PERAEA

R. Jabbok

· Antipatris

Joppa

· Lydda

Philadelphia

Jericho ·

JUDAEA

Jerusalem ·

· Ascalon

Herodeion ·

DEAD SEA

Agrippeion (Anthedon)

· Hebron

· Machaerus

Engedi ·

Masada ·

IDUMAEA

A Preliminary Survey

EDUCATION, TO MANY OF US, DENOTES THE STUDY OF A VARIETY
of subjects, each under a different heading, each dealing with
different material. When we were at school the various subjects
were taught, maybe, in different classrooms, and by different
teachers, each of whom refrained from discussing any subject but
his own, whether for fear of trespassing on another man's pre-
serves, or because, as we suspected, he knew little about any
subject other than his own, and cared less. As we studied different
subjects in different rooms, so we stowed away our knowledge of
them in different compartments of our brain, knowledge which
neither pupil nor teacher made any attempt to co-ordinate. Of all
subjects the one most remote from the rest was Divinity or
Scripture Knowledge, completely isolated and hardly linked even
with Literature or History. We knew of course that the Bible
contained historical books; but their content was in no way
related to any history to be found in secular authors. We knew
that our Lord was born in the reign of Augustus, and that later
St Paul appealed to Caesar; but those links were tenuous indeed.
We knew that Pontius Pilate was a Roman governor; but that
his career and character could be studied from any other angle
than that of the evangelists did not occur to us. Herod the Great,
Archelaus, Antipas, and Herodias; the two Agrippas, Felix,
Festus, and Bernice; these were characters in the New Testament,
and we did not know that any of them could be read about elsewhere. And yet Herod's father had fought for Julius Caesar, and
he himself was the friend of Mark Antony and Octavian in turn;
Archelaus was made and unmade by Augustus, and Antipas was
the admirer and confidential agent of Tiberius. Both Agrippas
were brought up in Rome; the elder was imprisoned there by
Tiberius, to be released by Caligula and chosen by him to reign
as king over a domain even greater than his grandfather's. But he

was soon back in Rome, and when his crazy patron was murdered it was his mediation that induced the Senate to accept Claudius as his successor. The younger Agrippa spent all but seventeen years of his long life in Rome where, foreigner though he was and potentate though he had been, he served in the office of praetor. Finally Bernice, of whom St Luke allows us to catch but a glimpse, won the affections in succession of Vespasian and of his son Titus whose throne her enticements seriously endangered.

But it is not only of these remarkable personal links between sacred story and secular history that we have been left in ignorance; we have been allowed to think of the Jews as a tiny nation living in a diminutive country, keeping themselves to themselves, speaking their own language, holding aloof from all Gentiles and pagans, reading only their own scriptures, rigidly excluding all foreign influences, and unaffected by any wind of change. The truth, as we shall see later, was very different. Suffice it to say at this point that vast numbers of Jews lived outside the limits of Palestine: there were probably more in Alexandria than in Jerusalem itself, and they were to be found in Arabia, Armenia, and Mesopotamia; in Syria and Asia Minor; in Egypt, Libya, and Tunisia; in Cyprus, Crete, and Sicily; in Greece and Macedonia; in Rome itself; perhaps in South Russia and North India. Many of them could speak neither Hebrew nor Aramaic; many of them had absorbed much of the culture of the peoples among whom they lived. Even in the Holy Land itself it was probably only a small minority that was rigidly exclusive. The Greek language was used freely, Greek literature was read and enjoyed, Graeco-Roman customs were adopted, and the influence of Graeco-Roman ideas was evident on every hand.

But contacts between Jew and Gentile were not merely cultural: they were political as well. The Jews were subject to a foreign power, and that power was not Greece but Rome. For a proud people subjection was hard to bear, and when that subjection had lasted a hundred years, first while the Herods ruled by permission of Rome, and later when at least part of the country was under the direct control of Roman governors, an explosion occurred, and Palestine grappled with Rome in a struggle to the death. On the outcome of that struggle the destinies of both depended. The strands of Roman and Jewish history had long been intertwined; now they were indivisible. The clash was tremendous, and its consequences were tremendous. To the Jews it brought horror beyond measure; for them it spelt the end of an epoch, the destruction of a nation, the obliteration of what had seemed to be established for all time. But it was not only on Jewish history that the impact fell. Rome too felt the effects of the gigantic conflict. For Vespasian had begun the campaign as commander of the Roman army in Palestine; but as the direct result of his successes, which caused his delighted troops to hail him as *imperator*, he became the unchallengeable ruler of the Roman world. But for this fact the later history of that world would assuredly have been different.

Of that terrible struggle much will be said in the course of this book. It was a conflict between East and West; between a small but ancient people fighting for liberty and independence and a new but mighty empire bent on enforcing order and brooking no challenge to her domination of the world. On the one side was patriotism without limit and a religious fanaticism that no other nation could comprehend, on the other unrivalled discipline, the experience of centuries of warfare, the most efficient weapons of offence and defence, and superb equipment of every kind. On the one side was a motley host, torn by dissension and bloody strife, and led by rival self-appointed chieftains lusting for power, on the other a highly organized fighting-machine, devotedly loyal to a tried, cool-headed leader, sole and unquestioned commander-in-chief and a notable strategist, into whose shoes when he was called into a more exalted sphere a gifted and brilliant son was ready to step. The struggle was one to stir the emotions of all who after these many centuries still trouble to read its story, filled if ever a story was with breath-taking gallantry and heroic endurance, with revolting treachery and horrifying cruelty, with the extremes both of self-seeking and of self-sacrifice, with surging hopes and utter despair, with the exultation of victory and the agony of defeat. 'Then shall be great tribulation, such as hath not been from the beginning of the world until now, no nor ever shall be.'[1] No one who reads the story will dispute the accuracy of that prophecy.

For many years hostility between Jews and Romans had been mounting steadily towards this terrible culmination. During those same years something else had been happening, something that was to prove far more momentous to the world at large. The three years of intensive fighting coincided with the very middle of the life of the man whose world we are to explore in this book: he lived for thirty years before it began and for thirty years after it ended. Seven years before he was born there had been a very different birth, the birth of the Christian Church at Pentecost. Opposed, calumniated, and persecuted to the death, first by Jews and later by Romans, it had in the first of the thirty-year periods achieved a phenomenally rapid growth, its members multiplying at a rate which no one would have deemed possible, and bearing witness to their Founder, as He Himself had foretold, 'both in Jerusalem, and in all Judaea and Samaria, and unto the uttermost part of the earth'.[2]

In sober fact it spread, if not in the first thirty-year period, then certainly in the second, to every corner of the Roman Empire and beyond its boundaries. Wherever there were Jews, there communities of Christians were swiftly formed and carefully organized, and into them poured Gentile converts, various in race and speaking many languages, and everywhere including Roman citizens. In these communities Jews and Romans met and were united. And in the man who had done most to bring about this miracle—and had done it entirely within the limits of the first period—the 'chosen vessel',[3] the apostle who 'laboured more abundantly than they all',[4] the man whom the Fathers of the Church invariably meant when they wrote simply of 'the Apostle'; in him Jew and Roman were united indeed. 'Circumcised the eighth day, of the stock of Israel, of the tribe of Benjamin, a Hebrew of Hebrews',[5] in his enthusiasm for the religion of his fathers he had with the utmost vigour attempted to destroy the fledgling Church. But he had seen the light, and 'Saul, who

[1] Matthew xxiv. 21.   [2] Acts i. 8.   [3] Acts ix. 15.
[4] 1 Cor. xv. 10.   [5] Philippians iii. 5.

was also called Paul'[1] (a famous Roman name), travelled immense distances along the imperial highways, planting the banner of Christ in land after land within the wide domains of Rome. Was he not himself a Roman and proud of it? And did he not, when hounded by his own countrymen from Jerusalem, make that bold appeal to Caesar which was to carry him to Rome, and hand him over to the mercies of Nero himself? He had wanted to go to Rome, and though Rome meant prolonged bondage made more bitter by his rejection by his Jewish hearers, the release that seems to have been granted to him two years later did not prevent him from returning from his last missionary enterprise to the city where he was destined to die at the hands of that very Caesar to whom he had appealed. Little did Nero dream that the crazy religion which Paul had brought from Jerusalem was destined in eight more generations to conquer Rome herself!

It is evident then that in the first century of our era, and especially in the sixty years or so of which the writer whose name appears in the title of this book had first-hand knowledge, Jewish history, Roman history, and Christian history are inextricably intertwined, presenting us with a complex but enthralling story, which in the chapters that follow we must endeavour to unravel.

The integration of the history of Rome and Palestine in those crowded years has been made possible by this one man, a man whose life, split in two, as I have said, by the ghastly conflict between Roman and Jew, was spent, half in the land of his birth, half in the city of his adoption. In whichever of the two he might be, he kept himself fully informed of all that was happening in the other, and in addition understood perfectly the viewpoints of the opposing peoples and the feelings aroused in each by events that were of critical importance to them both. This 'paradox of a man', as he has been aptly called, was a Jew who of his own choice became a Roman; a priest of Jehovah who became at least half pagan; a politician, orator, and soldier who served on both sides in the same war; a man who began as Joseph ben Matthias and ended as Flavius Josephus; and a historian who, thoroughly aware of both the Roman and the Jewish strands in the history of

[1] Acts xiii. 9.

his time, and with some knowledge of the Christian strand also, employed the leisure years of his life to such good purpose that through his writings we know more of what happened in little Palestine than we know of the course of events in any of the great dominions of Rome in that, perhaps in any, century.

The bald facts of Josephus' life can be stated in a few words. He was born in A.D. 37; in 64 he paid his first visit to Rome; in 66 he became governor of Galilee, where he made elaborate preparations to resist the coming Roman invasion; the following summer he surrendered to the enemy in most astonishing circumstances, and put himself right with their commander by foretelling his future elevation to the imperial purple. From then on he assisted the Romans to the limit of his powers, and on the termination of hostilities accompanied the son of the new emperor to Rome, where he spent the rest of his life as a pensioner in the emperor's house, immersed in the peaceful occupation of writing history, till in the year 101, if the usual view is correct, he died. In the following chapters all this must be elaborated and discussed in detail, and an attempt must be made to elucidate the story of so strange a career. We must also essay the task of solving the enigma presented by the equivocal conduct of this extraordinary man, and of lifting a corner of the veil that hides the true nature of his personality. Was he a patriot who strove throughout to save and assist his misguided but beloved countrymen? Or was he a self-seeking, ambitious, unscrupulous, mendacious, sadistic, time-serving turncoat? It is probable that readers of his works have always passed contradictory judgments on his character; it has certainly been the case in the last few years. On the one hand we have the Regius Professor of Modern History in the University of Oxford defending him as 'a consistent member of the Jewish peace-party . . . (who) remained loyal to Jewry'. On the other we find the Reader in Jewish Studies in the same university denouncing him as 'the traitor of Jerusalem . . . the prototype of a quisling'. Two members of his own race dub him 'a renegade Jew' and 'a shameless opportunist'; while a Canadian writer finds him guilty of 'cowardice, duplicity, treason, arrogance, deviousness, horrifying brutality and foul deception'.

It will further be necessary to examine the four works which have come down to us from Josephus' pen. To summarize their contents, essential as that is, will not be enough; for they present great problems as regards their purpose, their subject-matter, and the form of their expression. We must also attempt to evaluate them as history and as literature. Of the major contribution which two out of the four make to our knowledge of the Jewish portion of the Roman world in the two centuries that preceded the author's death there can be only one opinion. But are they as objectively true as we would wish them to be? Are they unreasonably biased? Do they contain merely such a sprinkling of errors of fact and of judgment as are to be expected in any lively history of a difficult and confused period, or was the author guilty of deliberate prevarication? If so, is it within our power to separate the true from the false, to distinguish sober statement from gross exaggeration? Above all, is it possible to detect subtle misrepresentation of act or motive? And was the author at times moved by enmity and spite, or by the desire to justify himself? In reading the literature of days gone by we must beware of credulity, but we must beware also of scepticism and cynicism. Did not Herodotus and Marco Polo suffer injustice enough?

Finally we must set ourselves a task that is perhaps more important than any other—that of giving a true and intelligible picture of the two worlds that meet in our author's pages, of life in the two countries in which he lived and fought and wrote, and which combined to make his life the strange thing that it was, and his works the precious inheritance that has come down to us—a 'possession for all time' as truly as was the work to which its author first applied that famous phrase. We must consider too the mighty forces, material, intellectual, and spiritual, whose mutual impact brought about those events which Josephus so vividly describes. This task I have here put last; but it is the one that shall be tackled first.

PART ONE

Before the Conflict

CHAPTER I

The Might of Rome

AMONG THE GREEKS, LONG BEFORE THE TIME OF JOSEPHUS, THERE were some who had satisfied themselves that the Homeric conception of the world as a round, flat mass encircled by the River Oceanus did not represent the true facts of geography; but the Romans, less intelligent and not given to speculation, for the most part treated such questionings with contempt. The world was a circle of lands—*orbis terrarum*—bounded, at least on the west, by Oceanus, a term embracing the North Sea, the English Channel, the Bay of Biscay, and the Atlantic Ocean. Within that circle was a great sea—a salt water lake, landlocked but for a narrow strait at the western extremity—the sea which we, aptly enough, know as the Mediterranean, but the Romans more simply as Our Sea—*Nostrum mare*. The name was arrogant, but accurate; for from the time of Claudius every inch of the immense coastline was in Roman hands. If the world was a circle of lands, the Empire of Rome was a loop of lands within that circle, separated from the regions without by well-defined and for the most part natural boundaries—rivers, seas, mountain ranges, and barren deserts. Within those boundaries the inhabitants were in varying degrees civilized and to a large extent Romanized: without every race was 'barbarian', largely unknown, and, so long as they kept quiet, of no account in the eyes of the proud peoples on the right side of the line. For the most part they did keep quiet, the one notable exception being the Parthians, whose mounted bowmen had destroyed the legions of Crassus, and were to menace the Empire for centuries to come. How far it was from the limits of that Empire to the northern, eastern, and southern sectors of the circumference of the circle—of that the Romans had no idea. But of the lands within their own boundaries they had very full knowledge, and with every land they were in full

25

communication. For though the Greeks were indulging in a mathematical fantasy when they proclaimed that Delphi was the navel of the world, the Romans might with full justification have boasted that the City on the Seven Hills was the centre of their own dominions—the centre of government, the centre of civilization, and within a very few miles of the geographical centre of the Empire.

What an Empire it was! So vast in extent, so immeasurable in its enduring influence! From north to south it stretched over two thousand miles, from west to east nearly three thousand; and it had a population estimated at eighty million. I have described it as a loop. That loop, bent round the Great Sea, comprised in modern terms Spain, Portugal, France, the Lowlands and Britain; Switzerland, South Germany, Austria, Hungary, and the whole of the Balkans with much of Roumania; Turkey, Syria, the Lebanon, Jordan, and Israel; Egypt and the whole of the North African coastal strip as far as Morocco. Such was the extent: the enduring influence need not be laboured here; for our subject is the World of Josephus, and though he no doubt believed as implicitly as Horace had done that Rome was indeed the Eternal City, he can have had no conception of the multifarious ways in which she was destined to mould the civilization, not only of her own possessions but of the entire world. But the vastness of the Empire made a profound impression on his mind, and he realized that the tiny community which after a long and painful struggle to master Italy had brought such immense areas, such diverse peoples, such proud kingdoms under her sway, was unique in history and entitled to his fullest devotion. So marvellously and so relentlessly had she overcome all her enemies in the past that he was certain that no nation would ever in the future face her in battle and survive. He has been bitterly blamed, and with good reason, for preferring victory with the overwhelming might of Rome to defeat with the heroic gallantry of Jewry. His heart may not have been in the right place, but there was nothing wrong with his head: he knew that if the Jews fought the Romans, the Jews would be destroyed. He has left us a very full account of what he thought on that subject. It will be found in the long speech which in *The Jewish War* (pages 144-150 in the Penguin translation) he puts, very unconvincingly, into the mouth of King Agrippa the Second, his friend and companion during his long years in Rome. The oration is too lengthy to quote here, but a brief summary will make his argument clear.

The Jews, said Agrippa, should not protest at the insolence of Roman governors and provoke them: they should patiently submit to them and humbly flatter them. Could they face the whole might of the Empire when far greater nations had been forced to submit? The Athenians, though they had routed the huge army of Xerxes, had become slaves of Rome. The Spartans and Macedonians, for all their former glory, had gone the same way. Roman arms had conquered the world, and even the Euphrates and the Danube, the Libyan Desert and the Atlantic Ocean, were powerless to confine them. Like the Greeks and the Macedonians, all the peoples of Asia Minor paid tribute; and from Thrace to Spain and Britain the fiercest nations were kept quiet by tiny Roman forces. Had the Jews forgotten the fate of Carthage, or the subjection of Egypt? A third of the whole world had been brought under the Roman heel: if the Jews went to war they would bring upon themselves total destruction.

In spite of his adhesion to Rome, Josephus remained a Jew, and as a Jew he was convinced that every victory came from God. It was God who had enabled the Jews to defeat their enemies in the past, and to survive the onslaughts of the terrible Sennacherib; it was God who had enabled the Romans to conquer the world, and would enable them to annihilate the Jews; for God had deserted Palestine and migrated to Italy, and the Emperor Vespasian was none other than the world ruler foretold in Hebrew prophecy. Enjoying thus the divine favour Rome would continue to triumph. But however much the eyes of Josephus might be dazzled by the glory of Vespasian and his son, the still more wonderful Titus; however much the present triumphs of Rome might assure him of her future dominance; he must inevitably have often directed his thoughts to the stages by which Rome had become mistress of the world. For the people among whom this immigrant from Jerusalem chose to spend the last thirty years of his life were constantly preoccupied with the past. Indeed to many, brought up in the belief, not in a Messianic future but in a golden age long ago, the true greatness of Rome lay in the past, and the deeds of ancient heroes were glorified by schoolmasters and artists, by orators and poets. Romulus, Marcellus, the Scipios, the Catos—their praises were never exhausted. It is evident that Josephus not only had accurate information about the organization of the Empire under Nero and his Flavian successors, but was well acquainted with the achievements of their predecessors.

It had taken Rome more than eight hundred years to reach her then stature. She was to live on through four centuries more, and that other seat of Empire founded by Constantine in the East was to boast herself Roman for a thousand years after that. How different from the Empire of Macedon, which reached its final immensity in ten years of one man's lifetime, and perished with him! The stages of Rome's growth are familiar to all—the little town under its seven kings; the republic of consuls and pro-consuls, of senate and people, which at first slowly, and later at an ever increasing rate overran Italy and pushed out in one direction after another till the boundaries of empire were far removed from the mother-city; finally the Empire which acknowledged one man as its lord, *princeps, imperator,* and *dominus,* Caesar and Augustus. Equally familiar are the causes that brought about the two transitions—in the first case the notorious tyranny of Tarquin the Proud, in the second the galloping deterioration, both political and moral, that transformed the character of the Republic in the last hundred years of its existence, and went far to justify the extreme pessimism of Horace, who regarded every generation of Romans as inferior to its predecessor. Politically the outstanding fact was the inability of the Senate, after so many years of strong and wise administration, to control the provincial governors, now no longer limited to one year of power, and from the time of Marius backed by professional armies which acknowledged no allegiance save to their own commanders. Hence came the swift succession of calamitous civil wars, resulting in the establishment of increasingly powerful autocracies. 'I have seen Cinna wielding excessive power, Sulla lording it as dictator, and only yesterday

Caesar reigning as king,' lamented Cicero. But Caesar had been murdered, and then had come a far worse autocrat, in Cicero's eyes a veritable monster, Mark Antony, and two more civil wars, which, when Antony too was dead, were to leave the great nephew of Julius, Gaius Julius Caesar Octavianus Augustus, supreme in Rome and lord of the civilized world.

In the case of Augustus it was not, as it had hitherto been, prowess as a commander in the field that raised one man to the pinnacle of power; it was true statesmanship, sound judgment in the choice of subordinates, a genius for organization, and above all supreme tact, unparalleled in any Roman leader before or after, which enabled him to do what his great predecessor had so conspicuously failed to do—to concentrate all power in his own hands, while allowing consuls and praetors, senators and knights, to feel that all the privileges of their historic past were still securely theirs. And so solid were the foundations laid by this gifted, if unattractive, political innovator, that though the principate was destined to suffer innumerable shocks, and to be drastically reconstructed by both Diocletian and Constantine, there could never be any serious suggestion of restoring republican government in any form. It is not surprising that bitterly hostile as the Romans remained to the very name of kingship they acquiesced without hesitation in the principle of hereditary monarchy, and though Tiberius might be a morose, suspicious, dissembling misanthrope, Caligula a lunatic or little better, Claudius an undignified and timorous creature, and Nero a compound of all the vices and all the vanities known to men, these four were nevertheless accepted as monarchs because they were members of the Julian house. Unfortunately Augustus left no direct heir. It was the tragedy of the imperial epoch of Roman history that of the long line of emperors the great majority were incapable of producing heirs: of the first fifteen only one had a son to succeed him. That one was the patron and idol of Josephus, the sturdy, earthy countryman Vespasian.

In no way did Augustus display his characteristic tact more conspicuously than in the arrangements that he made for the government of Rome's overseas possessions. Where there was a competent native prince of undoubted loyalty, such as Herod the

Great, he was allowed to remain on his throne as a 'client king'; but in general the provinces were divided into two classes, those governed by *legati* appointed directly by the Emperor, and those governed by proconsuls responsible to the Senate but chosen in accordance with his known wishes. All the really important provinces, where internal instability or enemies across the border necessitated garrisons of considerable size, belonged to the former class. An instance is Syria, which was administered from Antioch and which included Palestine, making it the first sphere of Roman rule with which Josephus was acquainted. A *legatus* backed by strong military forces was always necessary in that turbulent region. On the other hand, Cyprus could safely be entrusted to a proconsul, such as that Sergius Paulus who was so impressed by Barnabas and Paul on their first missionary journey.

When Josephus, through the mouth of Agrippa, stated that great nations were held down by tiny Roman forces, he was telling the truth. But those forces, together with others stationed in Italy, amounted in all to a very formidable body of men, who in equipment, training, fitness, tactical skill, and above all discipline, surpassed anything ever seen in the ancient world. From the dawn of Rome's history her armies, conscript, professional, or mercenary, had had a magnificent record of success. It was to those armies that her survival and phenomenal expansion had been due. We have seen how impressed Josephus was by the power of Rome; he fully realized that this power depended on the character of her armies, and on that character he dwells with constant admiration, again and again pausing or digressing to describe this feature or that of the Roman military system. The many descriptions scattered through the short *The Jewish War* alone combine to give us a very detailed account of that system, and make a valuable contribution to our knowledge of the subject. They were certainly written *con amore*. And it was not only in words that our author showed the admiration that he felt; for when he was in charge of Galilee and for a short time dreamed of offering armed resistance to the threatened Roman invasion, he endeavoured to lick his raw levies into shape by following what he knew of Roman training methods.

To defend her ten thousand miles of frontier and to hold in check rebellious tribes within that frontier Rome employed some thirty legions and at least as many non-legionary auxiliaries. The legion, which in Josephus' time had its own contingents of cavalry and artillery, numbered about five thousand men, all of them Roman citizens. Non-citizens served as auxiliaries; but as an honourable discharge carried with it the privilege of hereditary citizenship, the many sons who adopted their fathers' profession served in the legions themselves. Thus it came about that both legionaries and auxiliaries were of foreign and mixed origin, and were all long-service professionals and mercenaries; for those who were Romans by race were no longer willing to serve, and conscription was a thing of the past. We must beware of thinking that the centurions and soldiers whom we meet in the pages of the New Testament were Romans in Macaulay's sense or even Shakespeare's, or that the armies which Josephus fought at Jotapata and later assisted at Jerusalem had been recruited on the banks of the Tiber. That he observed those armies with a keen and understanding eye is obvious from the fullness and accuracy of his descriptions, which cover arms and equipment, organization and training, the disposition of the various elements in the order of march, and the construction of the siege-towers, battering-rams, stone-throwers, and catapults, which reduced such fortresses as Jotapata, Gamala, Masada, and Jerusalem herself. The only error I have been able to detect, apart from some questionable numbers, is the curious mis-statement that the infantryman wore his sword on his left side, though, as every schoolboy knows, it was the peculiar habit of the Roman legionary to wear it on his right. This was probably a thoughtless slip. Nowhere does the writer show more clearly his awed admiration for the Roman soldier than in the description of the pay parade, when Titus drew up his troops in all their pomp and dazzling splendour outside the walls of Jerusalem in the later stages of the siege, for the deliberate purpose of destroying the morale of the starving population, who from every point of vantage watched the overpowering spectacle with despairing eyes.

As Caesar (the name was assumed by every emperor, no matter

what his lineage might be) was commander-in-chief of all the armed forces of the Empire, so each *legatus* was commander of the forces allotted to his province. But his duties were not purely military: he was also the head of the judiciary and of the civil administration. For the Empire could not have survived had defence been the sole preoccupation of Caesar's representatives abroad. Nor could the governors have performed their administrative duties without the assistance of skilled advisers, executives, and officials of every grade. The proconsul of republican days had made do with what he called his cohort—a gang of hangers-on chosen from among his friends. But in those days few cared anything about good government: the governor was there to feather his own nest by exploiting the unfortunate natives, Verres being the most notorious example, while young spendthrifts like Catullus went in search of the pickings. But under the Empire such conduct could not be tolerated: it was cruel to the provincials and detrimental to the interests of Rome herself. Under Augustus and even under Nero the conquered peoples could be as prosperous and happy as in republican times they had been pauperized and wretched. This was made possible both by the watch kept by Augustus over his viceroys—a permissible term, since outside Italy he himself was regarded as a king—and by the establishment of a Civil Service. In his time this was small, tentative, and undifferentiated. But it was rapidly expanded and elaborated, with a regular system of qualification and promotion, and for this development great credit must go to Vespasian, who saw that in no other way could honest and efficient administration be secured. Thus Josephus, so closely associated with him in both Palestine and Rome, was familiar with a bureaucratic structure embracing every kind of official from store-keeper to career diplomat.

For the satisfactory administration of the outlying provinces, such as the one in which Josephus spent the first half of his life, one other thing was necessary—an efficient system of communications, whereby army officers and civilian officials, military reinforcements and supplies, reports, petitions, and rescripts, could be conveyed safely and swiftly between the provinces and the central authority. Many parts of the Empire could be and often were reached by sea. But apart from the recurrent dangers of piracy and shipwreck this method of travel and transport, at all times extremely slow, was difficult in winter and for weeks at a time might be quite impossible, since the square sail amidships— a primitive device which the Romans had not the wit to modify —compelled the master of the vessel to wait until the wind was astern. Readers will hardly need to be reminded of the many months required for the conveyance of St Paul from Caesarea to Puteoli—a memorable voyage of which his companion and physician has left us such a lucid and entrancing record. It followed that all urgent journeys must be accomplished overland, and this necessitated the provision of firm, direct roads, suitable both for fast vehicles and for heavy traffic. Such roads the Roman engineers were able to provide, and their success in this immense undertaking has astonished the world ever since.

Along these roads there must have been inns and hostelries for the refreshment of man and beast: we should welcome more information about them. There must also have been methods by which travellers from distant parts could pay for what they required. In the absence of paper money it is difficult to see how this was managed. Did the traveller carry quantities of gold and silver coins? and were these acceptable in all parts of the Empire? or was there some ancient equivalent of travellers' cheques? I wonder how many readers of the Acts of the Apostles have paused to wonder how Paul and his companions overcame these difficulties in journeys that lasted months and years and covered thousands of miles. The fact that later, when he had been transported to Rome, he could live for two years in a rented house of his own suggests that means were available for transferring private wealth from one country to another, a belief confirmed by Josephus' ability to enjoy, when ten years later he arrived in the Imperial City, the revenues of the estates which his grateful patrons had assigned to him in distant Palestine.

One difficulty which faces the modern traveller did not exist in Roman times—the difficulty of conversing with men of different speech. There was a common language then, a language understood in every country east of Italy and in many regions west. That language was not Latin but Greek, the language of the university and the market-place, of literature, commerce, and everyday correspondence. It was the second language of the Galilaean apostles, the language which they wrote and in which they taught in every land; it was the first language of Paul the Roman citizen, who was ready to preach in it from Palestine to Spain. It was the language in which were written all the works of Josephus except the lost first draft of *The Jewish War*. It was in common use even in Rome herself, whose citizens, deeply versed in Hellenic and Hellenistic literature, employed it freely both in private letters and in daily conversation. *Pace* Shakespeare, was in Greek that great Caesar, the only writer of Latin prose who was actually a Roman, gently reproached his faithless friend Brutus as the last dagger was driven home?

It is evident therefore that the Roman Empire which Josephus esteemed so highly was a most efficient and well oiled machine. But what did it accomplish in terms of human happiness? What was life worth for the common folk of those diverse nations that once had been free but now were *pacati*—subject, and acquiescent in their subjection? As has already been pointed out, there had been a great improvement since republican times. Then provinces had existed for the military and economic advantage of Rome, and in the eyes of many Romans—for Romans were by nature far more grasping than the proverbial Jew—for the rapid enrichment of the governor and his cronies; but now thought was given also to the welfare of the provincials. Then Roman rule had been infamous; but now it was deservedly famous, and *pax Romana* was a splendid thing. In the words of Dr Charlesworth, 'all the lands that border the Mediterranean Sea and many regions lying beyond it were enjoying under one government the benefits of peace, law and order, and prosperity'. That government was in general benignant, and though the provincials were denied autonomy they enjoyed many privileges. Local prejudices were respected, loyal cults were tolerated, and though Roman law was imposed it was modified in deference to local custom. In general the governors were well chosen, though thanks in part to petticoat influence, if the anachronism may be excused, some bad mistakes were made in the case of Josephus' home province of Syria; and fear of Caesar's wrath was a strong deterrent to the abuse of vice-regal authority. If there was such abuse, the people could protest to the governor, and if satisfaction was refused could complain to the all-powerful authority in Rome. In general, therefore, the provinces were contented, though we must again point to the exception, Syria, in one part of which, Palestine, rebellion was likely to flare up at any moment. But since this was mainly due to the peculiar character of the Jewish people, so difficult for Romans to comprehend, it is quite possible that the governors and pro-curators who so conspicuously failed there might, if sent to other regions, have provoked no trouble at all.

No doubt there were many things that subject populations, even if they did not prefer self-government to good government, would have desired to have different. It will suffice to mention two notable injustices. The first was the distinction between citizens and non-citizens in the eyes of the law. The citizen who offended could still, as in the days of Verres and Milo, escape punishment by voluntary exile, which in most cases involved no loss of property or comfort: the non-citizen was liable to severe and often horrible punishments. As we see in the case of St Paul, the citizen was by law exempt from corporal punishment, let alone torture; and he, and only he, had the right of appeal to the Emperor himself.

The second injustice lay in the disproportionate financial burdens laid upon the provincials, who bore not only the expense of maintaining their own local economy, but in addition almost the entire cost of the central administration. Rome had for cen-turies battened on the victims of her military supremacy. As long ago as 168 B.C., after the conquest of Macedonia, the one direct tax laid on Roman citizens had been abolished. This was the *tributum* imposed from time to time for military purposes, a sort of forced loan to be repaid when circumstances permitted, very like our own Post-war Credits. From then on the only fiscal burdens which the Romans had to carry were a Purchase Tax of one-half per cent, a Legacy Duty of five per cent, and Harbour

Dues averaging perhaps half that percentage. Lucky Romans! It is enough to make an Englishman's mouth water. But the provincial's lot was very different. He had to contribute both in money and in kind. The *tributum* that he paid was not an occasional loan but an annual impost, levied sometimes on his land and sometimes on his poll. This was at first collected—or extorted —by a *publicanus*, the wealthy counterpart of the detested 'publican' of Josephus' native land; for before the institution of a Civil Service the Roman method was to farm out the taxes by auction, a system which laid itself open to glaring abuses. In imperial times the *procurator* gradually took over the work of the tax-collector. He was a financial official appointed by the Emperor and not answerable to the governor, a fact which made it difficult to call him to account. It was still possible to demand so much money that the less wealthy fell into the clutches of unscrupulous Roman money-lenders. This occasionally led to insurrections, notably the revolt of Boadicea with its ghastly consequences, a revolt traceable to the greed of the virtuous moralist Seneca, who like the 'noble' Brutus before him was an avaricious usurer.

How had Rome acquired the empire of which, for better, for worse, she was the undisputed mistress? Most of it had come under her control in the time of senatorial rule. The circumstances had continually varied, and the motives of her conquests had been mixed. Sometimes economic considerations had been uppermost, at others military necessities; for she was engaged in an everlasting struggle to obtain defensible frontiers. In the golden age of Augustus imperialism was as rampant as in the England of the nineties, and in the prevailing view the bigger the Empire the better. Horace exulted in the defeat of Egypt and announced the coming conquest of Mesopotamia, while the greatest of the court poets, Virgil, believed that Rome's divine mission was to rule the peoples beneath her sway, to spare the submissive and war down the proud. A Latin version of *Land of Hope and Glory* would have gone down very well at Rome.

But for the acquisition of particular territories there had been particular reasons. Sicily was needed in order to keep the Carthaginians out. So was the south of Spain, and that could not be held against warlike neighbours unless the whole Iberian Peninsula was reduced to submission. Gaul was conquered at a cost of two million lives to satisfy the military and political ambitions of one man, and to enable him to pay off his enormous debts. Britain, it appears, was occupied to add military prestige to the shaky reputation of Claudius. But what of the East, of Asia Minor and Syria? We can only sketch the story, which began with the defeat of Carthage. Rome was determined to suppress trouble-makers, especially foreign potentates who endeavoured to enlarge their dominations; for what was sauce for the goose was certainly not sauce for the gander. First of those potentates was the King of Syria, Antiochus the Great, whose conquests ranged from the borders of India to the western extremity of Asia Minor. His army was destroyed by Domitius Ahenobarbus at Magnesia and he evacuated Asia Minor. It was only a matter of time before the Romans would fill the vacuum. Their intervention was invited when the Kingdom of Pergamum was bequeathed to them by Attalus. This led to the formation of the province of 'Asia' at the western end of the great peninsula. It was attacks on this province by a second potentate, Mithridates of Pontus, that compelled the Romans to fight three full-scale wars, ending in the defeat of that monarch by Pompeius Magnus. Henceforth Asia Minor was Roman, thoroughly pacified, and reorganized, thanks to Pompey's remarkable foresight and efficiency, on a basis that was to endure for generations.

But Pompey had not been content to free Asia Minor from Mithridates. He had turned aside to invade Syria, which he took out of the hands of the quarrelling Seleucid princes, the last successors of Antiochus, and turned into a Roman Province. Thus was installed at Antioch the first of the line of *legati* which was to include, fifty or sixty years later, that Quirinius in whose time there was issued from the palace of Augustus the decree ordaining a world-wide registration or census. While he was in Syria Pompey was called on to settle a dispute between rival claimants to the throne of the Jewish kings—a dispute which led to his besieging and capturing Jerusalem. The Romans had earlier signed a treaty with Judas Maccabaeus, but this was the first time a Roman army had fought in Palestine. Of that more anon. The Romans had established a new province as the eastern bastion of their empire, and the headquarters of its governor not only had been the capital of mighty kings, the successors of Alexander the Great, but was one of the most splendid cities in the world, 'the crown of the East', now, as Josephus tells us, 'by virtue of its size and prosperity undoubtedly the third city of the Roman Empire', but doomed, alas, to be reduced to ashes six centuries after Pompey's visit. Pompey did not live to see how turbulent a province he had added to the Empire, how many headaches it would give to its governors and to their masters in Rome, what rivers of blood—Jewish, Samaritan, Syrian, and Roman—would flow from the clash of these irreconcilable peoples, what tragic material that clash would furnish for the pen of the Romanized Jew, Josephus.

Of the history of Romano-Jewish relations from the Maccabaean treaty to the catastrophic war to the death that ended two hundred and thirty years later Latin writers have left us no continuous record, only piecemeal information. For a detailed and methodical account we depend on Josephus, who in his *Jewish War* prefixed to his full story of the war itself an outline of earlier events, from the sufferings of the Jews at the hands of Antiochus Epiphanes to the fatal provocation they received from Albinus and Gessius Florus; years later in the last nine books of his *Antiquities* he covered the same ground again, correcting various errors in the earlier account and writing now at three times the length. Most of his pages are devoted to internal affairs or to Jewish relations with neighbouring communities; but every contact with the Romans is carefully recorded. Beginning with Judas' 'bold step of allying himself with Rome' he gives us the full text of the treaty, which was maintained by Judas' successors. Next he tells us how the appeal to Pompey to arbitrate between Hyrcanus and

Aristobulus led to the first capture of Jerusalem—that much beleaguered city—by Roman armies. He then describes the settlement of Palestinian affairs by Pompey, the doings of Scaurus the legate of Syria and his successor Gabinius, and the disgraceful conduct and disastrous end of Marcus Crassus, followed so soon after by the defeat and death of Pompey himself. The third member of the so-called triumvirate, Julius Caesar, now makes his appearance as senior partner in a fruitful alliance with Antipater, the father of Herod the Great. Interested in Roman history for its own sake as well as in the relations of each individual with the Jews, Josephus next relates 'the action of Cassius and Brutus, who treacherously murdered Caesar when he had ruled the Empire for only three years, seven months'; the defeat of the conspirators at Philippi; the frequent contacts and unbroken friendship between Herod and Antony; the support given by the legate Sossius to Herod in his successful siege of Jerusalem; the overthrow of Antony by Octavian at Actium; and the satisfaction rendered to Octavian by the compromised Herod, who later obtained from him—Augustus now—the condemnation of his own son Antipater. With the death of Herod came another problem for the Emperor to settle—the rival claims of Archelaus and Antipas. Varus, Sabinus, Coponius, Pilate, Petronius—each has his place in the story of Jerusalem and Judaea, while at Rome Augustus was succeeded by Tiberius, and Tiberius by Caligula.

And there we reach the year of Josephus' birth. We have good reason to be thankful that he took so much trouble to inform himself of events that occurred before he was born, and did not content himself with describing the extraordinary happenings of his own lifetime. But he was intensely concerned both with Rome and with his own country, and it was right and proper that he should set down a full record of the encounters, both friendly and savagely hostile, between the two. Of Rome itself we shall have something to say when we reach the point in our story where Josephus made that city his home and became a writer; it is time now to turn our attention to that little country where he spent his childhood and youth and became a man of action.

A Strange Land

IN THE PRECEDING CHAPTER WE MORE THAN ONCE HAD OCCASION to refer to Palestine as the birthplace and early home of Josephus, and to mention the fact that it was part of Syria, so that Syria was the first Roman province of which he had personal knowledge. This inclusive use of the name Syria belongs only to the period of Roman domination: the inhabitants of Palestine in an earlier age would have protested vehemently had anyone spoken of them as Syrians; for as readers whose memory of the historical books of the Old Testament has not worn too thin will no doubt remember, the kings of Israel were constantly at war with the kings of Syria, and their subjects rarely met except in battle. But this is not the only case where the Roman masters overrode ,national prejudice and used the name of one nation to include its incompatible neighbour: a far more glaring instance was the inclusion of Samaria in Judaea; for whereas the opposition of Syria and Israel belongs mainly to a period before Romulus set up the first wall round the infant Rome, the virulent hostility between Judaea and Samaria was never stronger than in New Testament and Josephan times. That pungent sentence 'Jews have no dealings with Samaritans[1] will spring to every mind: that to the Romans their hated neighbours should be 'Judaei' like themselves must have been a very bitter pill for the proud Jews to swallow.

Palestine then, in the first century of our era, was a part of Syria. But how big a part? It is customary to insert at the end of our bibles two or three maps showing Palestine (or the Holy Land, as we sometimes call it) at different periods of history. In actual fact we need a whole series of maps; for in the centuries before Christ the boundaries were constantly changing, and even in the Roman period they were not permanently fixed. But fluctuating

[1] John iv. 9.

boundaries apart, what right have we to speak of a country called Palestine or the Holy Land? It would surprise many people to learn that from the first to the last page of the Bible, that library of books so largely concerned with the country in question, the name 'Palestine' does not occur, save in a few passages in the Authorized Version of the Old Testament, where in every case the Revisers of 1885 correctly substituted 'Philistia'. The two names were in origin the same; but it is most surprising that we should ever have learnt to call the land of God's chosen people by the name of their hated enemies, the uncircumcised Philistines! The confusion probably was the work of the Greeks. Did they not call the Persians Medes, just as later the Romans were to call the Parthians Persians and the Ethiopians Indians? The Romans, indeed, were so vague as to the location of Palestine—a word which they rarely employed—that to Ovid the River Euphrates was *Aqua Palaestina* 'the Waters of Palestine'. Though in the fourth century Eusebius wrote a work entitled *Martyrs of Palestine*, and in his *Story of the Church* employed the name freely, there seems to be no evidence that either the early Christians or the Jews themselves called the land that meant so much to them both by either of the names which we ourselves employ. *The Jewish War* is almost wholly concerned with Palestine; but the name 'Palestine' does not occur in its pages.

If then it was not usual to call the country Palestine, by what name was it called? The surprising answer is that it was called by no name at all. Before the country was conquered by Joshua's warriors it might perhaps be referred to as Canaan; then we meet the name Israel, or more commonly Israel and Judah; for from the time of Rehoboam, if not earlier, there was not one nation and one country, but two rival peoples, often at war, and two tiny countries. The division lasted till both peoples were removed to Mesopotamia: when a small remnant of Judah returned their hostility to their northern neighbours was resumed, to last without a break until in the time of Josephus calamity befell them all. There was indeed no period when what we call Palestine was inhabited by a united people, conscious that they were citizens of a single country. Hence we have the strange phenomenon of a land without a name; for if in the early years of the Christian era it was not yet called Palestine it was no longer called Israel, a name which in the language of the New Testament denotes not a place but a people.

In spite of what has been stated in the foregoing paragraphs, it will be convenient to think of Judaea and Samaria, Galilee and Peraea as making up a single country, and in speaking of that country to use the accepted name. What kind of country was it? Descriptions usually begin with the statement that at least in size Palestine is similar to Wales. As regards the length from north to south, measured in the case of Palestine between the traditional Old Testament limits of Dan and Beersheba, the figure for both countries is almost exactly the same—a hundred and fifty miles. The breadth from west to east—about a hundred miles—is perhaps a trifle greater in the case of Wales. Furthermore the countries agree in having a long coastline on the west; but there, apart from the fact that both have mountains and lakes, the resemblance ends. Wales sticks right out from its bigger neighbour on the east and has a coastline at each end: Palestine is an enclave in the mainland, and its one coastline is flush with those of its neighbours to north and south, Phoenicia and Philistia. Wales has an irregular coastline with many sharp and jagged promontories, Palestine a smooth coastline broken only by the projecting end of the ridge of hills called Mount Carmel. Wales has a number of offshore islands, Palestine none at all. But, as we shall see, Palestine has many features which are to be found neither in Wales nor in any other land. Let us look first at those features, the features that still meet the eye of the pilgrim or traveller, and then see how Josephus describes the country as he saw it nineteen centuries ago.

The most clearly marked boundary of Palestine is the simple line of the coast, sandy, and broken by the mouths of numerous streams but no river of any importance. The absence of cliffs and estuaries meant that in early days there were no natural harbours, a fact which made coastal voyaging very dangerous, and would effectively have prevented the Jews from launching out into the Great Sea and seeking political or economic contacts with the West even if they had not had a natural distaste for seafaring. The port of Ezion-Geber, from which Solomon, a thousand years before Josephus' time, had sent forth his navy to seek the gold of Ophir, was more than a hundred miles beyond the southern boundary of Palestine as later generations knew it; and both that navy and the ships of Tarshish which came every three years bringing ivory, apes, and peacocks, were manned by the shipmen of Hiram, King of Tyre. On the east there was no clear line of demarcation: on that side lay the great Arabian Desert, which effectively cut off Palestine, and Egypt too, from direct communication with Mesopotamia, forcing all travellers to proceed by the immensely long route that ran through the Fertile Crescent. To the south also lay a desert region, though along the coastal strip a road from the ancient cities of Philistia gave easy access to Egypt. To the north-west lay Phoenicia, to the north Abilene and Syria, the latter in the Hebrew, exclusive, connotation of the name. Here too nature had provided no natural boundary, and the maps in Bible atlases will be found to differ considerably.

Within these boundaries, such as they are, the most striking feature revealed by a quick glance at the map is the line of the River Jordan—a line which, if we disregard the innumerable wiggles, runs straight from north to south, starting well beyond the Syrian border and ending in the largest of three lakes, and in its course separating Peraea on the one side from Galilee, Samaria, and Judaea on the other. But this is not the only thing that is parallel to the sides of our map; for the country is made up of four strips running lengthwise, which we must consider separately.

Let us start with the Coastal Plain, which is narrow at its northern end, but after it passes the barrier of Carmel grows steadily wider. Here in the Plain of Sharon, where the modern visitor finds luxurious orange-groves, there was formerly a waste of marsh and forest. But the southern section consisted of good agricultural land, admirably suited to the growing of cereal crops and the cultivation of those two necessities of the ancient world, the olive and the grape. Still further south was the Philistine Plain backed by limestone hills, over which the inhabitants of the lofty plateau surrounding Jerusalem looked out towards the sea.

Second of the four strips is the zone of the Western Highlands.

Immediately beyond the northern limit of the Holy Land rose the towering ridge of Hermon, the White Mountain, so called because it is formed of limestone and chalk; perhaps also because its highest peak soars to a height of ten thousand feet and is capped with snow even in summer. South of this ridge lies Upper Galilee, a lofty plateau which at its highest point rises three thousand feet above the sea, and looks down in an easterly direction to the northernmost of the three lakes, known in Old Testament times as the Waters of Merom. Between the second lake, the Sea of Galilee or of Tiberias, which is intermediate both in position and in size, and Mount Carmel, which shelters the modern port of Haifa, is Lower Galilee, so called not from being lower down the map, but from the much lower altitude of its irregular plateau, which contributed to its excellent fertility. In Lower Galilee were the many little towns which were visited by our Lord, but of which only three are named in the Gospels— Nazareth, Cana, and Nain. Here too were places that figure in *The Jewish War*—Gabara, Jotapata, Sepphoris, and Mount Tabor. Between the plateau and the long ridge running south-east from the headland of Carmel lay the lush Plain of Esdraelon, but south of the ridge rose the heights of Samaria, two thousand feet above sea level, with others further south a thousand feet higher still. Then came a broad valley cutting right across from behind Joppa to the region of Jericho. Across this valley could be seen the northern slopes of the Judaean hills, on which stood Jerusalem, Bethlehem, and the ancient city of Hebron. South of Hebron the land sloped down to Beersheba and the wild and largely barren area known as the Negeb, where we reach the end of our second strip.

Parallel with these Western Highlands, or Central Range, but on the other side of Jordan, runs the yet higher Eastern Plateau, broken by the deep fissures through which the four chief tributaries pour their waters into the main stream. This strip of land had in Old Testament times been divided into the fertile plain of Bashan in the north, famed for the strength of its bulls and the appetite of its kine; the highlands of Gilead, the country of grapes, of balm, and of physicians; the steppes of Moab and

Ammon, the ever-dangerous enemies of Israel and Judah; and the towering, inhospitable heights of Edom. In the writings of Josephus the first three regions are included under the names Decapolis and Peraea, while Edom has been replaced by a larger area called by the same name in a Hellenized form, Idumaea.

Now let us go back to the last and most remarkable of the four strips, the Rift Valley, a tiny tract of land that is without parallel in the world. It forms a diminutive part of the Great Rift which extends northward in the direction of Antioch through Caele-Syria, the valley—deep, yet nearly as far above sea level as the summit of Snowdon—which separates Lebanon from Anti-Lebanon and Mount Hermon, and southward through the Arabah and the Gulf of Aqaba into the Red Sea, and from there to the distant mountains of Ethiopia. Of that rift we shall have more to say later: for the present let us confine ourselves to the valley that divides Palestine from end to end, the valley down which flows the River Jordan, symbol of the barrier which separates earth from heaven.

This famous river is formed by the confluence of four streams, two of which spring from the lower slopes of Mount Hermon, the other two from between Lebanon and Anti-Lebanon still further north, where the ground is some two thousand feet above the level of the Mediterranean. The stream thus formed descends rapidly till it flows into the shallow Waters of Merom (known to the modern world as Lake Huleh) seven hundred feet below, whence in the short distance of ten miles it rushes headlong down to the Sea of Galilee, no longer above sea level but six hundred and eighty-two feet below. This lake, whose clear blue waters are still as well stocked with fish as they were in the days of Peter and Andrew, James and John, is a picture of beauty under the Mediterranean sun, but as those same disciples knew, subject to sudden and terrifying storms. The shores rise steeply save to the north-west, where on the Plain of Gennesareth stood Capernaum, Christ's 'own city', and Magdala, home of the most devoted of the women who ministered to Him. Capernaum comes into Josephus' story also, but he is more concerned with Tarichaeae, which is generally identified with Magdala, and with Tiberias further south. Since this was the most important place on that coast, and the capital city of Galilee, it is surprising to find it mentioned only once in the New Testament. But its foundations were not laid until the year in which the Baptist and the One whose coming he heralded began their ministry: it is more surprising to find no mention of Sepphoris, eighteen miles to the west; for while Jesus worked as a carpenter (or if Unamuno is right, as a builder) Sepphoris was the capital, and it was only an hour's good walk from His home at Nazareth.

Emerging from the southern end of the lake the river no longer cascades down as it did before; nevertheless it does not arrive at the north end of the third and last lake until in covering a distance, as the crow flies, of only sixty miles it has dropped another six hundred and ten feet. For the surface of the Dead Sea —Asphaltitis, as Josephus aptly calls it—is twelve hundred and ninety-two feet below the level of the Mediterranean. As it meanders along those sixty miles it absorbs the waters of many little streams flowing into it from the west, and of a few larger tributaries on the other side, of which the curving Jabbok is the most important. The lower reaches are difficult to cross, since the river bed sinks far below the surface of the ground as the swollen stream zigzags through dense, steaming jungle between the dismal, barren slopes of the awesome valley.

For many thousands of years—no one knows how many— all this water has been pouring into the Dead Sea, and none has flowed out. Yet the level has not risen, for the burning heat of the sun evaporates the water as fast as it flows in. The water of Jordan is fresh enough to be put in flasks and transported to our own country for the more effectual baptism of infant princes; but the water of the Dead Sea is salt—so salt that no fish can live in it; so salt that nothing can sink in it, and visitors can amuse themselves by floating on its surface. It is surely the strangest lake in the world, so buoyant, and so far below sea level. The Caspian is only ninety-seven feet lower than the Black Sea, and the Fayyum is no more than a shallow depression in the plain. The situation of the Salt Sea is all the more remarkable in that it is not a hollow in otherwise level ground: on either side rise steep slopes, and it is but a few miles to the Judaean hills whose tops are over three thousand feet *above* sea level, or to the peaks of Edom some two thousand feet higher still. In the precise language characteristic of St Luke, 'a certain man went down from Jerusalem to Jericho'. He did indeed: in his journey of fifteen miles he went down the best part of four thousand feet; and it was up that long and exhausting slope that the anxious parents of the boy Jesus had to retrace their weary steps when they found that He was missing from the caravan. On the slopes to east and west of the sea no crops can be grown, and in very few places was it possible to build towns. None of these is named in the Gospel story, but Josephus has a good deal to say about Machaerus, the fortress on the eastern crags in which the indignant Antipas imprisoned the wild prophet who had had the courage 'to speak the truth and boldly rebuke vice', and about Masada on the opposite side, where the heroic Jews put up such an amazing resistance to the invincible Roman besiegers. Further north are the famous caves of Qumran, and in the same neighbourhood dwelt, it seems, the monastic communities of Essenes, whose ascetic life and theological beliefs are described in one of the longest of the many digressions in *The Jewish War*. Beyond the western slopes in the direction of Jerusalem were miles of terrible country known as the Wilderness of Judaea, country more fit for wild beasts than for men, where Jesus Christ probably spent the forty days of stern preparation for His mission, and where perhaps his Nazarite forerunner had been in contact with the Essene 'philosophers', as Josephus calls them.

But of all the marvels that await the visitor to this profound and gaunt cavity in the earth, this physiographical monstrosity, this grim jest of Nature, none surely is more astounding than the fact that a man can stand near the point where the Jordan merges its waters in that bath of brine, feel the fiery sun scorching his head and shoulders, look around him at the tropical luxuriance of the fertile region about Jericho, then turn towards the north and slowly raise his eyes as he gazes up the long, long valley and at last, in the far distance, sees the summit of Hermon mantled in eternal snow.

Though this valley is long enough to divide Palestine from end to end, it forms, of course, only a tiny fraction of the Great Rift. That enormous cleft, the result of some gigantic upheaval of the earth's crust in prehistoric times, has at every period been subject to fresh disturbances, both seismic and volcanic. No doubt it was a sudden eruption, perhaps from a fissure in the ground, that overwhelmed the Cities of the Plain under a deluge of brimstone and fire, reducing them to dust and ashes. Josephus tells us that in his day there were still marks of the fire and the outlines of five cities to be seen south of the lake; but as he goes on to tell us that the fruits growing there look exactly like edible fruit, but when plucked dissolve into smoke and ashes, it is doubtful whether we should take his words 'the evidence of our eyes' to mean that he himself had visited this desolate spot. Nowadays it is thought that the remains of Sodom and Gomorrah lie hidden beneath the shallow waters at the southern end of the Lake, and an investigation by divers has been proposed.

As they looked back at the history of their people there was one fact of which the Israelites had no doubt at all—the fact that their deliverance from bondage and their acquisition of a permanent home had been miracles wrought by the hand of God: of the means by which He had done these things for them they were equally certain. These convictions they not only set down in their historical records: they expressed them in superb poetry by means of phrases as lucid as they were colourful. Thus Deborah sang:

> Lord, when thou wentest forth out of Seir,
> When thou marchedst out of the field of Edom,
> The earth trembled, the heavens also dropped,
> Yea, the clouds dropped water.
> The mountains flowed down at the presence of the Lord,
> Even yon Sinai at the presence of the Lord, the God of
> Israel.[1]

The unknown psalmist put it thus:

> When Israel came out of Egypt,
> The house of Jacob from among the strange people,

[1] Judges v. 4-5.

Judah was his sanctuary,
And Israel his dominion.
The sea saw that, and fled;
Jordan was driven back.
The mountains skipped like rams,
The little hills like young sheep.
What aileth thee, O thou sea, that thou fleddest?
Thou Jordan, that thou wast driven back?
Ye mountains, that ye skipped like rams?
Ye little hills, like young sheep?
Tremble, thou earth, at the presence of the Lord,
At the presence of the God of Jacob;
Who turned the hard rock into a standing water;
The flintstone into a springing well.[1]

The late Professor Garstang believed that similar 'acts of God' went far to explain most of the extraordinary events recorded in Exodus and the early chapters of Joshua. He suggested that most of the Plagues of Egypt were the result, direct or indirect, of a violent volcanic eruption; that a little later a seismic upheaval in the Red Sea produced a tidal wave in what is now the Gulf of Suez, overwhelming Pharaoh's chariots; and that such incidents in the story of the forty years' wanderings as those of water bursting from the rock and of the earth opening her mouth and swallowing up Korah, Dathan, and Abiram resulted from consequential disturbances. The close connection between these tremors and volcanic eruptions is of course clear enough in the biblical account. 'Mount Sinai was altogether on smoke, because the Lord descended on it in fire; and the smoke thereof ascended as the smoke of a furnace, and the whole mount quaked greatly.' When Joshua many years later led the hosts of Israel into the Promised Land, the earth had not yet resumed her tranquil immobility. Jordan had overflowed its banks, but it required only a minor tremor to enable the people to cross over in order to attack Jericho; for 'the waters which came down from above stood, and rose up in one heap, a great way off, at Adan, the city

[1] Psalm cxiv.

that is beside Zarethan'. This is a most precise statement, and it is fully confirmed by the fact that history has exactly repeated itself more than once, the last occasion being in our own time, in the earthquake of 1927, when the bed of Jordan was dry for nearly twenty-four hours, following the collapse of the high clay banks sixteen miles above Jericho—at El Damieh, opposite Zarthan! As for Jericho, Garstang had no doubt that a trifling movement of the earth would suffice to bring down her very badly constructed walls.

Recurrent earthquakes are a danger which in every period since it was first inhabited has hung over the inhabitants of Palestine. The collapse of Jordan's banks and the piling up of its waters might be harmless in 1927, and a providential boon when Joshua wished to cross the river more than three thousand years earlier. But some of the recorded earthquakes have been unmixed calamities. One such occurred in 31 B.C., causing a heavy loss of life and going far to demoralize the adherents of Herod the Great, who at the time was engaged in a life-and-death struggle with the Arabs for the mastery of Palestine. Of this disaster Josephus has left us two accounts, one in *The Jewish War* and the other in *Antiquities*. Here is the earlier account, in the translation of Dr. Robert Traill:

'While chastising his enemies, another calamity befel him, in the seventh year of his reign, and when the war of Actium was at its height. In the early part of the spring there occurred an earthquake, in which countless multitudes of cattle, and thirty thousand human beings, perished; but the soldiery, lying in the open air, were uninjured. Rumour in the meantime ever inclined to exaggerate misfortune, and representing Judaea as one scene of desolation, inspired the Arabians with increased confidence. Accordingly, thinking to possess themselves of a devastated country, they advanced into it by rapid marches, having first sacrificed the ambassadors who happened to have reached them from the Jews. Dismayed at this invasion, the nation was sinking, broken in heart by the magnitude of these successive calamities.'

Herod's method of dealing with this perilous situation was to call together all his followers, and to endeavour to rouse in them a spirit of resistance, by arguing that elation at the disaster which had fallen on the Jews would fill their enemies with an overweening confidence that would inevitably send them headlong to their ruin. 'Having in this strain reanimated his troops, observing their ardour, he sacrificed to God, and, this done, crossed the Jordan with his army.'

The account in *Antiquities* is in substance the same, though instead of saying that thirty thousand human beings perished Josephus now writes: 'About ten thousand men perished by the fall of houses'; and he puts a new and longer speech into the mouth of Herod.

A nation can survive eruptions and earthquakes if it has adequate resources in its minerals and its soil, its rivers and its lakes, and is blessed with a kindly climate and an adequate rainfall. How was it with Palestine? Did she deserve the title, so often bestowed upon her, of a land flowing with milk and honey? Compared with what they had endured in their desert wanderings the followers of Moses and Joshua might well think that she did, when their eyes were regaled with the samples of her produce brought back by the spies. We must beware of thinking that a country which now seems bare or yields little reward to the cultivator has always been the same. Fertility may decline for a variety of reasons; they include the desire of conquerors like Nebuchadnezzar to ruin a troublesome country, and the actual military necessities of such commanders as Titus, who, as Josephus tells us, used up all the trees for miles round Jerusalem in his efforts to replace wooden platforms and siege-weapons destroyed in desperate sorties by the fearless Jewish defenders. Certain it is that in both ancient and classical times Palestine was, at least in the days of peace, a pleasant country to live in, plentifully endowed by nature, and, in addition to possessing abundant supplies of fish, capable of raising excellent crops more than once in the year. In the south, it is true, there were barren regions to which I have already referred, the reason being that the 'former' and 'latter' rains were not evenly distributed; but there is ample evidence that in general the inhabitants had little to complain of. The evidence of Josephus himself which will shortly be quoted is convincing enough; and not even a Solomon or a Herod could have become so fabulously wealthy as both undoubtedly were, had the resources of their country been inadequate. Before Josephus is called to testify, let us take a look at the province of which throughout his life it formed part.

When Alexander died and his empire broke in pieces, it is not surprising that Seleucus Nicator, one of his successors the *Diadochi*, made Syria the centre of his own wide dominions, and in founding sixteen cities chose for his capital the greatest of them all, built on the Orontes and named after his father Antiochus. Those dominions and that famous city were to reach their greatest size a century later under Antiochus the Third, whose pretensions, as we have seen, were drastically curbed by the Romans. After him came less powerful kings whose control, even over their home country of Syria, became feeble, till at last Pompey arrived and Syria became a Roman province.

It was a rich plum that fell into the lap of Rome; the gateway to Egypt and Mesopotamia alike, and of the greatest economic value. As Dr. Charlesworth puts it: 'Antioch was an economic metropolis, the equal of Rome or Alexandria; while cities such as Damascus, Berytus (Beirut), Apamea, Byblus, Laodicea, Tyre and Sidon had trade connections that went back for centuries.' The cedars of Lebanon had been renowned for untold ages: now they were reserved for the use of Roman shipbuilders. Fruit of every kind was available for export, as were cereals and vegetables. Flax was grown and could be made into garments for Roman wearers; if linen was not good enough, Syria was the channel through which costly silks could be obtained from China. Glass, which was highly esteemed in Rome, not for use in windows but as a material from which vessels and ornaments could be fashioned —an art at which Syrian craftsmen excelled—was of the highest quality, thanks to the peculiar nature of the sand, which was to the glassmakers what the Derbyshire water is to the brewers of Burton on Trent. Josephus, who had a keen eye for anything that was curious, found space in his *The Jewish War* for a quite irrelevant digression in which he describes a hollow near Ptolemais, a seaside town of Galilee (or as we should say, Phoenicia) in which ordinary sand was mysteriously converted into crystal, to be replenished by nature as fast as it was emptied into the holds of a constant succession of visiting ships.

Now let us glance at the other information that he gives us about the products of his country, its fertility and its physical peculiarities, first briefly reminding ourselves of the areas into which it was divided in his time—Galilee, Samaria, and Judaea west of Jordan and its lakes, Peraea on the other side. As he includes at least the southern end of Phoenicia in Galilee, so he includes Decapolis, of which the greater part lay east of the river, in Peraea. Of each of the four areas, of Jordan, and of all three lakes, he has something to tell us in six digressions scattered through *The Jewish War*, supplemented by a few statements in *Apion Answered*.

After carefully stating the limits of the 'two Galilees, known as Upper and Lower', he goes on to speak of the abundant population as born fighters, who had invariably held out against the attacks of their powerful foreign neighbours, and as industrious farmers who had resolutely cultivated every inch of ground not occupied by valuable forests, raising abundant crops and herds. The fertility of the whole area, which was fruitful from end to end and the most productive in Palestine, was such that towns were numerous and villages innumerable. In the *Life* he gives the number of cities and villages as two hundred and four. This figure may very well be true; but when in the *War* he assures us that the smallest village had more than fifteen thousand inhabitants we may be excused if we suspect some exaggeration.

Peraea, though much larger than Galilee, was for the most part a stony desert unfit for cultivation. But in the few districts where the soil was workable a variety of crops was raised, and the three most valuable trees, the olive, vine, and palm, were successfully grown. Josephus makes no mention of the rainfall, but remarks that when the mountain torrents dry up water can be obtained from perennial springs.

Writing as a Jew, Josephus naturally excluded Samaria from Judaea, but he recognized that in their physical characteristics they were alike, 'hills and plains being interspersed through both;

the soil moreover being arable and extremely fertile, richly
wooded, and amply supplied with fruits, both wild and cultivated. Both are refreshed by frequent rains. The running water is
everywhere extremely sweet; and owing to an abundance of
good pasture, the cattle yield more milk than those in other
districts. And what affords the most unerring criterion of excellence and fertility—both districts teem with men.' Elsewhere he
quotes Hecataeus of Abdera, who in about 300 B.C. devoted an
entire book to the Jews, as saying that they occupied nearly a
million and a half acres of the best and most fertile soil. Of Judaea
itself he remarks that Jerusalem is so centrally placed as to merit
the name of 'the navel of the country'. In a later passage—by far
the longest of all his digressions—he gives a full description of
that renowned city and of its incomparable temple; but that we
must leave for a later chapter, as we must leave his descriptions of
Machaerus and Masada.

There was, of course, no need for *The Jewish War* to contain
descriptions of the Rift Valley, but fortunately the author was no
stickler for strict relevance. He found time to speculate on the
source of the Jordan. This he places at the Bowl, a pool fourteen
miles from Caesarea Philippi, from which it flows underground
to Paneum. From there it 'cuts through the still, marshy waters of
Lake Semechonitis'—the Waters of Merom—and fourteen miles
further south passes Bethsaida Julias and plunges into Lake
Gennesareth (Tiberias), from which it makes a long journey
through desert country, to finish up in the Dead Sea. Lake
Gennesareth impressed him greatly, with its sandy beaches, its
pure, clear water, superior to that of rivers and springs, and its
unique species of fish. Alongside were the nine square miles of the
wonderfully beautiful plain that bore the same name. There in the
rich soil and the temperate air every plant flourished—walnuts
that loved winter, palms that throve on heat, figs and olives that
wanted neither—natural enemies, which nature, as her crowning
achievement, had brought together in healthy rivalry, to bear
fruit all the year round.

In its course the Jordan flowed through the Great Plain, fourteen miles wide and flanked by uninhabitable slopes, burnt up in

summertime and knowing no rain. Near Jericho, however, there was a tiny but abundant spring, once poisonous till, Josephus tells us, it was purified by Elisha; this watered a plain eight and a half miles long so effectively that it produced a variety of rich palms and other trees, and quantities of honey and precious balsam, 'so that it would be no exaggeration to call the place divine—a place where the rarest and loveliest things are found in such abundance'.

The Dead Sea or Asphaltitis, which Josephus, so prone to exaggerate figures, believed to be much greater than it actually is —sixty-seven miles by seventeen, instead of forty-three by nine —was bitter and sterile. The heaviest things thrown into it soon reappeared on the surface, a fact verified by Vespasian, that gentle Roman, who in the interests of scientific discovery 'ordered several persons who were unable to swim to be plunged in to the bottom with their hands tied behind them. The result was that all floated to the surface, as if impelled upwards by the agency of air', as Traill rather quaintly translates the passage. Josephus was also impressed by the changing hues of the water; and he gives us a not very convincing description of the methods by which floating lumps of black asphalt resembling headless bulls were brought to shore, to be used both for the caulking of ships and for medicinal purposes.

It is evident, is it not, that Josephus so far from taking his country for granted and from letting familiarity breed contempt, regarded it with the same wonder, admiration, and awe as fill the pilgrims from lands as different as our own, and that he was only too anxious for his readers, both Greek and Roman, to share those emotions.

CHAPTER 3

A Peculiar People

IF PALESTINE WAS A REMARKABLE LAND, THE MEN WHO LIVED IN IT were no less remarkable. Possessed of a highly individual character, and of a homogeneity and a tenacious self-assurance that has enabled them to maintain their national identity through centuries and millennia, they differed markedly from the surrounding peoples—not only the Romans and the Greeks, respectively responsible for the government and the culture of the Mediterranean regions, and very remote from themselves in race and origin, but also from their Semitic neighbours in Syria, Mesopotamia, and Arabia, with whom they might have been expected to have much in common. They were, in fact, a peculiar people, and that in two senses. They were peculiar in that they differed so greatly from other peoples that they seemed incomprehensible to them; and they were peculiar in another sense, a sense in which they habitually applied the description to themselves as a title of honour. The word 'peculiar' means 'belonging exclusively to one person'; and they fully believed that they belonged to God as no other people belonging to Him. They were the people whom God had purchased, as Moses sang when they had escaped from the tyranny of Pharaoh; they were an holy people unto the Lord their God. The Lord their God had chosen them to be a peculiar people unto himself, as forty years later the great leader three times reminded them. 'Praise ye the Lord,' cried the exultant psalmist;

> Praise ye the Lord; for the Lord is good:
> Sing praises unto his name; for it is pleasant.
> For the Lord hath chosen Jacob unto himself,
> And Israel for his peculiar treasure.[1]

[1] Psalm cxxxv. 3-4.

So large a place did this conviction hold in the mind of every Jew, so ingrained was the habit of thinking and speaking in terms such as these, that more than a thousand years after Moses was laid in his unknown grave the leading apostles of Christ, knowing that the vineyard of God had been given to other husbandmen, applied the same language and the same ideas to the Church that knew no barriers of race or colour. Thus Paul to the Ephesians: 'He chose us before the foundation of the world, that we should be holy.'[1] And to Titus, his bishop in Crete: 'Christ gave himself for us that he might purify unto himself a peculiar people.'[2] And Peter to his motley flock scattered over vast areas of Asia Minor: 'Ye are an elect race, a holy nation, a peculiar people.'[3]

Such a departure from the hitherto unquestioned belief that Israel, and Israel alone, was the people of God would, of course, have seemed blasphemy to an unconverted Jew. Josephus was unconverted, and he accepted to the full the orthodox conviction. It is no doubt true that as the Christians believed that in rejecting Christ the Jews had forfeited their privileges as the people of God, so Josephus would have his readers believe that in rebelling against Rome his countrymen had finally and for all time offended the Deity, and driven Him as it were into the camp of their enemies. But there can be no doubt that he believed that up to those fatal years in the sixties they had continued to be the peculiar people of God: indeed it was the crowning tragedy and most dreadful consequence of their rebellion that by their own folly and wickedness they had thrown away their age-long unique position as a holy nation, God's own inheritance. In spite of their calamitous fall from grace, which in his earliest work, *The Jewish War*, he denounces with such merciless vehemence and such scathing contempt, pride in their religious and moral superiority—which he treats as a thing of the present, not of the past—fills the pages of his much later work, *Apion Answered*.

What was this people, which regarded itself as peculiar and holy? Historians and archaeologists have propounded a variety of

[1] Ephesians i. 4.   [2] Titus ii. 14.
[3] 1 Peter ii. 9.

opinions concerning the origins of the Jews; and modern critics have expressed very grave doubts, and sometimes complete scepticism, as to the accuracy of the biblical record. It may be retorted that this record is the best, perhaps the only, historical source available to us; but what matters when we are considering the World of Josephus, and in particular the world of his thought, the mental environment that conditioned his whole outlook and was the ground of all his opinions, is the beliefs that he inherited and fully accepted about his own people. Those beliefs were enshrined in the sacred writings of that people, and in considering what they were it makes no difference to us whether they are capable of withstanding the assaults of present-day critics. It will be worth while to sketch those beliefs in simple outline.

Hebrews; Israelites; Jews—we must beware of treating these names as interchangeable. The word 'Hebrew' (which most archaeologists identify with 'Habiru', a racial name found in non-biblical sources) does not appear often in the Old Testament, for the good reason that it included others besides the people of God. The promise made to Abraham was to be fulfilled only in the descendants of his younger son Isaac; but the descendants of the elder, Ishmael, were Hebrews too. Moreover, the word was not applicable to Abraham's descendants alone; for this city-bred Bedouin chief is himself referred to as 'Abraham the Hebrew', a phrase which could only be used if there were other Hebrews already. But when we come to the word 'Israelites', we have a name that denoted the people of God and covered no one else. For of Isaac's two sons Esau was rejected and Jacob accepted; and Jacob, renamed Israel, was the recipient of the divine promise 'A nation and a company of nations shall be of thee, and kings shall come out of thy loins.'[1] It was his descendants, the Israelites, who were to be the chosen people.

Who, then, were the Jews? They were the descendants of Judah, one of Jacob's children. For Jacob's four wives bore him twelve sons, and each was father of a family. The twelve families rapidly multiplied in Egypt, and became the 'company of nations', the

[1] Genesis xxxv. 11.

twelve tribes of Israel. The twelve were joint inheritors of the promises made to Abraham, Isaac, and Jacob, and together constituted the people of God. To us the important name is that of the Jews, and with good reason; for of all the tribes Judah grew to be the most influential, the most gifted, and the most aware of itself; it produced David, the most famous of the kings that came out of Israel's loins, and the only monarch to found an enduring line; it alone survived the onslaughts of the Assyrian conquerors; of it alone a remnant returned from captivity by the waters of Babylon; and from it, as the prophets foretold, sprang the Christ, the Son of David.

If this account bears any resemblance to the truth, the Jews might well claim to be an ancient people; for the first recipient of the promises, 'our father Abraham', if he existed at all—and modern archaeology has played havoc with the objections of nineteenth-century scoffers—came out of Ur of the Chaldees nearly four thousand years ago. It is not surprising that, in the eyes of the Jews who long centuries later smarted under the rule of Caesar's procurators, the Romans should have seemed an upstart race with a history much inferior to their own. The Greek people too were comparatively modern and, as Josephus points out, the earliest great event recorded in Greek literature, the Trojan War, took place when Jewish history had already reached an advanced stage. That any Greek should dare to suggest that the Jews were not an ancient people, or that their laws and wisdom did not antedate by centuries that of Lycurgus and Solon, appeared to Josephus nothing short of astounding, as he makes clear in the work to which we have referred as *Apion Answered*, but which should rather be known as *The Antiquity of the Jews*, since that, together with the reliability of the Jewish Scriptures which far exceeded that of the mendacious Greek records, is the subject of the book. The question of how Josephus' works were and should be entitled will be discussed in a later chapter.

Towering high above the heads of all other Jewish heroes, of prophets, priests and kings, even of David himself, stood Moses. As an infant he had been saved from the murderous hands of Pharaoh's minions by the ingenuity of his mother and the womanly compassion of the monarch's daughter, to be brought up at the court as her own son, and heir to the throne of Egypt. If Josephus' information was correct, he took command of the royal armies, led them against the Ethiopians, defeated them soundly, and married the love-sick daughter of their king. This story, as readers of Exodus and Acts are aware, is not to be found in our bibles; but Josephus was always ready to incorporate in his narrative a good story drawn from another source. Here he disregards the biblical account of the threat to Moses from one of his quarrelling countrymen, and attributes his flight to Midian to Egyptian envy of his military successes. All sources agreed that in Midian God was revealed to him in the Burning Bush; that conscious of a divine mission he returned to Egypt, and when the new king refused to let the people go, called down ten plagues on him and on his unhappy subjects; and that he was enabled by God to lead the rabble of Israelitish slaves through the Red Sea, to mould them into a nation during forty years' wandering in the desert, and finally to conduct them to the land of Moab, where from the summit of Pisgah could be seen the whole of the Promised Land which the new and disciplined generation of Israel were ready to invade and conquer.

But it was not as a prince, a statesman, or a military commander that Moses was most highly esteemed: it was as a lawgiver—as the greatest of all lawgivers. How much of the Law that fills so many pages of the five 'books of Moses' was in fact proclaimed and set down by him we must leave to the scholars to decide, if they can. There can be no doubt that at least some chapters of Exodus, chapters that closely resemble the Code of Hammurabi but are an immense improvement on it, are very ancient indeed; and the assumption that underlay so much destructive criticism in the last century—that Moses could not write—is of course too absurd to be taken seriously. What matters to us at the moment is the fact that till modern times the Mosaic authorship was not questioned; that it was taken for granted by those who heard Jesus himself declare that one jot or tittle should in no wise pass away from the Law; and that the author of *Antiquities* and *Apion Answered* had no doubt whatever on the subject. Assured that Moses had given the Law to his own people and to the world, and reverencing the Law from the bottom of his heart, it was inevitable that he should hold Moses himself in the highest honour, and that the pen of such a ready writer should set down the eloquent tributes that adorn his writings, tributes at which it will be worth our while to glance.

Apollonius Molo, a Carian who had taught rhetoric to Cicero and Caesar, 'partly from ignorance but chiefly from hostility has made comments neither just nor true about our lawgiver Moses and about his laws, slandering the man as an impostor and fraud, and alleging that the laws instructed us in vice, never in virtue.' Josephus retorted: 'We have laws perfectly designed to encourage true religion, social justice, and international good will.' Nations which had accepted the rule of law were entitled to be called civilized; laws must be introduced by a lawgiver; and 'our lawgiver was far earlier than those named in the records of any other country'. Why, until recently the Greeks had not even known the word 'law'. Moses had taught an entire people about the nature and will of God; but Pythagoras, Plato, and the rest had no message except for the select few. Moreover, the legislators of Greece had taken no steps to ensure that their laws, even if understood, should be put into effect; but Moses had made certain that his laws should be taught, memorized, accepted, and carried out. He 'made the Law the standard and canon, that living under it as father and master we might do no wrong either wilfully or through ignorance. . . . It is not often that a law is broken: it is not possible for the punishment to be avoided by making excuses.'

Josephus concludes his spirited defence of the Mosaic Law and his refutation of its traducers with an eloquent peroration which deserves to be quoted in full:

'Our lawgiver has been reviled as beneath contempt; but to his excellence witness was paid long ago by God, and has since been paid by time. Our laws need no lengthy defence: no one who looked at them could fail to see that they taught not irreligion but religion at its highest; for they induce men not to hate each other but to share the good things of life; they are the enemies of wrong, the champions of right; they drive out idleness and prodigality by teaching the virtues of self-reliance and hard work; they prohibit wars of aggression, but stimulate heroism in defence of the laws themselves; their ears are shut to all excuses; and they have no truck with studied words, but at all times take their stand on deeds. And so I should not hesitate to say that the world has us to thank for many of the most precious things. For what is more precious than religion that stands unshakeable? what more right than obedience to the laws? and what is of greater benefit than to be on good terms with other men, in adversity bound together and in prosperity free from arrogance and quarrelling; in war to treat death with contempt, in peace to apply oneself to handicraft or agriculture; to be convinced that every thing in every corner of the universe is under the eye and governance of God? Had these principles been either put in writing by others first, or up-held by them with greater constancy, we should as loyal disciples have owed them gratitude; but if it is evident that we adhere to those principles more faithfully than any, and if I have shown that it was we who first discovered them, then let the Apions and Molos and all who delight in lies and abuse be shown up for what they are.' (My translation.)

A noble tribute, and not without justification, however much the writer may have been swayed by patriotic fervour, rhetorical exuberance, and the desire to trounce his opponents. It may not have been literally true that the Law was known to every Jew, 'accepted, memorized, and carried out.' Does not St John, who had an extraordinary gift for understanding the thoughts of his Master's opponents and recording their very words, tell us how the Pharisees said with contempt that the multitude who knew not the Law were accursed?[1] Nevertheless, that the Law was beyond measure superior to the code of any other nation in the ancient world can hardly be questioned; that those who lived under it revered it and were ready to die for it is a fact of history; that it was esteemed even by those who saw the dangers of legal-istic religion and believed that the law of liberty had superseded it, is manifest when we remember that the fiercest critic of the Law, the religious genius who taught that the power of sin was

[1] John vii. 49.

the Law, declared also that the same Law had been our tutor to bring us to Christ.[1]

If Moses was pre-eminently a lawgiver, he was also the first of the prophets—of that long line of historians and prognosticators, preachers and poets, that continued for a thousand years and seems to have had no parallel in any other country. They fall into two groups, those who spoke and acted but of whose writings, if any, we have no certain knowledge, and those who set down their inspired thoughts, mostly in verse, and left behind them works of greatly varying length, some of which seem to many people today to be the most illuminating sections of the Old Testament; for with the possible exception of the Psalms they contain the loftiest thoughts of the Jewish people, and the clearest expression of their developing religious understanding. Those writings are very different from the Law; there is nothing legalistic or ceremonial about them; they breathe an altogether freer spirit. As every Sunday School pupil knows, a prophet was not primarily a foreteller, but a forthteller: he spoke in the name of God—'Thus saith the Lord'—and proclaimed a message that was mainly concerned with the conduct of his hearers in the present, though it did at times reach far into the future. We may add that the distinction between the two classes of prophet was by no means absolute: the makers and reprovers of kings, such as Samuel, Nathan, Gad, Elijah, and Elisha, must surely have conveyed to the 'Sons of the prophets' the information on which were based those wonderful, vivid stories which, as Sir Flinders Petrie insists, could only come from absolutely honest eyewitnesses. On the other hand Isaiah, the greatest of the writing prophets, was as ready to use his tongue and to advise, comfort, and scold his powerful sovereign as Nathan and Elijah had been.

Many of the prophets were rejected in their own lifetime, persecuted by kings, bitterly opposed by priests and nobles, and disregarded by those whom they wished to save. It was an enduring characteristic of the Jews to venerate the prophets of an earlier age and to hound those of their own. 'Ye build the sepulchres of the prophets,' said our Lord, 'and garnish the tombs of the

[1] Galatians iii. 24, R.V.

righteous, and say, if we had been in the days of our fathers, we should not have been partakers with them in the blood of the prophets. Wherefore ye witness to yourselves that ye are sons of them that slew the prophets.'[1] However bitter might be their hostility to the Baptist and to the Nazarene ('Art thou also of Galilee?' said the Pharisees, careless of historical truth, to Nicodemus; 'Search, and see that out of Galilee ariseth no prophet.'[2]), of the inspiration of the ancient prophets from Moses to Malachi they had no doubt at all. Everyone accepted it; everyone was prepared to quote the prophets' words as settling an argument without any question. Our Lord himself, who constantly quoted the Sacred Writings, three times routed the devil with passages from Deuteronomy, and drew more support from Isaiah than from any other book.

What made the prophets, and the psalmists too, so exciting to a generation smarting under the yoke of Rome and longing to recover the glories of the Davidic kingdom, was their repeated declaration that a deliverer should come. Hints, vague but unmistakable, could be found in the promises to Eve and to the patriarchs. A clearer message came from Moses when he said to the people in the desert: 'The Lord thy God will raise up unto thee a prophet from the midst of thee, of thy brethren, like unto me.'[3] The later prophets, notably Isaiah and Jeremiah, promised an Anointed One, a Messiah or Christ, a King of the house of David; and the Jews looked for such a one to deliver them from foreign domination. He would come to save his people: that he would come to save them, not from the Romans but from their own sins, was a thought that never crossed their minds. Nor did they, as did the Christians on the authority of Christ himself, pay any heed to that other picture presented in the later chapters of Isaiah (chapters written, as is generally thought, though Kissane denies it, not by Hezekiah's adviser but by a later seer, 'the great prophet of the Exile'). This was the picture of a Suffering Servant, led as a lamb to the slaughter. So it came about that very few saw in Jesus the fulfilment of prophecy and the satisfaction of their patriotic ideas. What happened on Palm Sunday shows that those who believed

[1] Matthew xxiii. 29-30.   [2] John vii. 52.   [3] Deuteronomy xviii. 15.

in Him expected Him to proclaim himself King and to triumph over the Romans: what happened five days later shows how bitterly disappointed they were by His failure to do so. That even the chosen apostles clung to the current crude interpretation of prophecy is clear from the question put by them to their Master just before His final departure from them: 'Lord, dost thou at this time restore the kingdom to Israel?'[1] That one Jew could interpret prophecy in a very strange way indeed we have seen already: the Messiah, in Josephus' eyes, was none other than the destroyer of the Jewish people, Vespasian the Emperor—to everyone who spoke Greek, Vespasian the King.

During the period covered by the prophets, disaster befell the tribes of Israel. Ten of them, forming the Northern Kingdom, succumbed to the assaults of Shalmaneser and Sargon; the capital, Samaria, was destroyed; and the population was transported to Mesopotamia, never to return. The brutal conquerors then turned their attention to the little Southern Kingdom; 'the Assyrian came down like the wolf on the fold', and as Jews, Greeks, and Baby-lonians in their several ways recorded, 'the might of the Gentile, unsmote by the sword, Melted like snow in the glance of the Lord.' Jerusalem escaped, but not for long: four generations after the rout of Sennacherib the Assyrian a new potentate, Nebuchad-nezzar the Babylonian, destroyed the city and removed most of the people to Babylon, the rest later fleeing into Egypt. Thus began the Captivity from which, when Babylon in her turn had fallen to Cyrus the Persian, a remnant was to return. That remnant, under the influence of Ezra and Nehemiah, determined that Israel should never again be guilty of the sins to which they attributed their calamities. Polytheism and idolatry were stamped out, and to guard against contamination through contact with the other races in partial occupation of the country the Jews became rigidly exclusive. They still had prophets but they had no king. God was their King, and they were His people. In other lands there was monarchy, oligarchy, plutocracy, democracy: in Judah alone there was theocracy. The word is thought to have been invented by Josephus, who towards the end of his reply to Apion

[1] Acts i. 6.

offered a vigorous defence of this system of government. He was not thinking particularly of the period following the Return: theocracy had been established by Moses; it was his crowning achievement and had held sway ever since.

'Moses succeeded in making the whole nation dependent on himself, and having won their unquestioning obedience he did not turn this in any way to his own advantage. At the very time when those at the head of affairs are wont to assume despotic powers and to accustom the masses to live subject to no law at all, he, though his authority was so great, chose the opposite course: he felt that he must make religion his guide and organize all the affairs of the nation on the basis of law. . . . There are endless differences of detail between the customs and laws of mankind in general. To put it very briefly: some have bestowed on monarchies, some on oligarchies, some on whole citizen bodies, authority to govern. Our own lawgiver had no use for any of these methods: if it is not straining language too far, we may say that the government which he established was a theocracy, since it was to God that he assigned the power to rule. . . . What kind of rule could be more holy than this? What more fitting honour could be paid to God? Why, the whole nation is fashioned for religion; a special responsibility is entrusted to the priests; and all government is carried on in the manner of some sacred rite! Practices which other nations call mysteries and sacred rites, but are unable to keep up for more than a few days, *we* keep up with joy and unshakeable determination throughout our lives.'

Our own generation judges conduct by three different standards. There is the standard of religion: is an action in accordance with the will of God? is it righteous or sinful? There is the standard of ethics: does an action conform to the moral code? is it right or wrong, good or bad, praiseworthy or blameworthy? There is the standard of legality: is the action permitted or forbidden by the State? The third is the standard by which most people judge: if lechery is not a crime, then it is not sinful or wrong; if divorce is not punished in courts of law, then religious objections do not count, even with those who profess loyalty to Him who forbade it. But for the Jew there was only one criterion —conformity with the Law of God, revealed through Moses. To make 'the commandments and statutes and judgments' of God the standard to which men must conform was psychologically sound, and in the case of the average fallible human being the strongest inducement to right conduct.

The belief that the key to everything in life was religion, and that religion gave men power to face death nobly, can readily be seen in the literature of the period between the Return from Babylon and the arrival of the Romans in Palestine. To this period belongs that remarkable book, Ecclesiastes, with its impressive final message: 'Let us hear the conclusion of the whole matter; fear God, and keep his commandments: for this is the whole duty of man. For God shall bring every work into judgment, with every hidden thing, whether it be good or whether it be evil.'[1] To that period belongs too the First Book of Maccabees, which describes the heroic struggle of Mattathias and his sons against the sacrilegious king, Antiochus Epiphanes, the desecrator of the Temple. Their struggle was inspired by devotion to God, and by the conviction that anything was worth while rather than allow His Name to be insulted, His Laws to be broken. Is it to be wondered at that the author of *Apion Answered* twice retold this inspiring story, in *The Jewish War* and in *Antiquities*?

It was not religion in general that meant so much to the Jews; it was their own particular religion, so different from those of all their neighbours. 'Hear, O Israel: the Lord our God is one Lord.'[2] They had no use for the religion of Persia with its dualistic conception of transcendent authority, with its belief in the everlasting rivalry between Ormuzd and Ahriman; still less for the ten thousand deities of the Babylonians. They were convinced that the Ruler of the universe was also the source of all morality: 'Shall not the Judge of all the earth do right?'[3] God was righteous, and His priests must be clothed with righteousness. What must they have thought of the Greeks and Romans, who in spite of all the protests of enlightened philosophers worshipped a host of gods

[1] Ecclesiastes xii. 13-14.   [2] Deuteronomy vi. 4.   [3] Genesis xviii. 25.

and goddesses dissociated from morality and practising all human vices on a superhuman scale, served by priests no better than their neighbours and appointed—perhaps like Julius Caesar to the supreme pontificate—for political reasons or through bribery? Josephus, a priest himself and familiar alike with Jewish theology and with Graeco-Roman mythology, makes some pungent comments in his retort to 'the Lysimachuses and Molos and other writers of the same type, fraudulent sophists, misleaders of the young'. Moses had expressly forbidden any scornful criticism of other people's religion; but as comparisons had already been drawn by the critics of Judaism, it was impossible to remain silent.

'Which of the renowned philosophers of Greece has not condemned their most famous poets and their most trusted law-givers for sowing from the start such ideas about the gods in the minds of the public? They make them out to be as numerous as they themselves fancy, children of each other and produced in all kinds of ways. They assign these to different habitats and ways of life like species of animals, some under ground, some in the sea, and the eldest batch chained in Tartarus. Over those who have been given a place in heaven they have set a so-called "Father"— in reality a despotic tyrant. In consequence his wife, his brother, and his daughter (whom he produced from his own head!) conspired against him—to arrest him, if you please, and lock him up, just as he himself had done to his own father. These stories richly deserve the scorn poured upon them by the more intelligent Greeks, who go on to ridicule the notion that some of the gods are boys in their teens, others old men with beards; that some are appointed to trades, one god being a smith, one goddess a weaver, and a third deity a soldier who fights with human beings, while others play the lyre or amuse themselves with bows and arrows; and again that they range themselves in opposing factions and quarrel about human beings, till they not only come to blows with each other but even get wounded by mere men and send up howls of distress. But the most revolting thing of all is surely the attribution of illicit unions and promiscuity to pretty well all the deities, male and female alike. Why, the noblest of the lot, divinity number one, the Father himself, seduces women, and when they become pregnant allows them to be imprisoned or drowned without lifting a finger to help them!' (My translation.)

A just condemnation, surely, though the man who pronounced it had too keen an eye for the main chance to allow his contempt for the religion of his masters to estrange him from those with whom he had found so comfortable a niche. But it is easy to understand why the Jews, blest with an enlightenment denied to their pagan contemporaries, felt themselves to be a peculiar, separate, and holy people. They were the people of the Law, and all other nations were outside the Law. Did not Peter denounce his fellow-Jews because they had crucified and slain Jesus of Nazareth 'by the hand of lawless men'[1]—that is to say, the Romans? The Romans lawless! This conviction that they were separate made them hold aloof from other races, unwilling to intermarry with them, and regarding it as shocking even to eat under a Gentile roof, as Peter did on one famous occasion. This aloofness naturally alienated the Gentile world. Diodorus remarked that the Jews, alone of all peoples, utterly refused to have dealings with any other people and regarded all men as enemies. In that strange Hebrew work in which God is never mentioned, the Book of Esther, we read that Haman said to King Ahasuerus: 'There is a certain people scattered abroad and dispersed in all the provinces of thy kingdom; and their laws are diverse from those of every people; neither keep they the king's laws: therefore it is not for the king's profit to suffer them. If it please the king, let it be written that they be destroyed.'[2]

This separation was not one between races; it was between those who acknowledged Jehovah as the only God and those who did not; between those who gave their allegiance to the Law of Moses and those who rejected it. If these conditions were fulfilled a man of any race might be accepted—even Candace's eunuch from Ethiopia.[3] Did not the strait-laced Pharisees compass sea and land to make one proselyte?[4] Galilaeans and Edomites were Jews by religion but not by race. The builder of the great Temple

---

[1] Acts ii. 23, R.V.   [2] Esther iii. 8-9.
[3] Acts viii. 27.   [4] Matthew xxiii. 15.

whose desecration filled our Lord with such indignation was not a Jew. The one essential was the acceptance of circumcision, a rite practised in many lands but of such peculiar religious importance to the Jews that they contemptuously referred to other races as 'the uncircumcised'. Here let Josephus speak, through the prim mouth of William Whiston. 'Hyrcanus also took Dora and Marissa, cities of Idumea, and subdued all the Idumaeans; and permitted them to stay in that country, if they would circumcise their genitals, and make use of the laws of the Jews: and they were so desirous of living in the country of their forefathers, that they submitted to the use of circumcision, and the rest of the Jewish ways of living; at which time therefore this befell them, that they were hereafter none other than Jews.' But if the Jews were proud of being circumcised, that very thing made them contemptible in the eyes of the Romans, and became a provocation to anti-Semitism. *Vin tu curtis Judaeis oppedere?* wrote Horace in one of his less poetical moments. Ben Jonson would have translated the question literally, but for more delicate ears we may paraphrase it as 'Shall we go and cock snooks at mutilated Jews?'

Second only to circumcision in importance among Jewish customs was the Sabbath. The origin of this observance is wrapped in mystery, for Delitzch's theory that it was borrowed from the Babylonians has been subjected to severe criticism. It is familiar to us all because it is laid down in detail and with all possible emphasis in one of the Ten Commandments, a code which in its present or perhaps some simpler form almost certainly goes back to the time of Moses. Most probably a week of seven days was established to accord with each successive quarter of the lunar cycle. The one thing that is beyond dispute is that by the beginning of our era the Sabbath had secured a tight hold on the Jewish people, so that neglect of the observance was a very serious offence. Originally it was perhaps no more than a simple day of rest and worship, but the Scribes were given to lading men with burdens grievous to be borne, and they succeeded in dividing the work that must not be performed on the Sabbath into forty categories save one, each of these being further subdivided. But whether burden or privilege, the Jews clung to their Sabbath with ferocious tenacity, compelling their Roman masters, even though they considered the Sabbath to be as comical as circumcision, to exempt them, and them alone, from service in the army. Had they been willing to serve they would no doubt have fought as valiantly as they have done on many fields. For Jews have always been doughty fighters. In our own time they have distinguished themselves on the battlefields of two world wars, and more recently, in the Sinai Desert; in ancient times they displayed the utmost heroism in their struggles against the hosts of Antiochus, later against the more disciplined armies of Pompey, and last of all against the overwhelming forces of Vespasian and Titus. How gallantly they fought can be read in page after page of the two chief works of Josephus. But not even the desire for victory or the necessity of survival could make these devoted men forget their duty to the Sabbath. Should they fight on the day of rest? At first they answered No; later they were compelled to compromise. This chapter will be brought to a fitting end if we listen to two passages from *Antiquities*; and once more Whiston shall be the author's interpreter.

This from the story of the Maccabaean revolt:

'The king's forces fought against them on the Sabbath day, and they burnt them as they were in the caves, without resistance, and without so much as stopping up the entrances of the caves. And they avoided to defend themselves on that day, because they were not willing to break in upon the honour they owed the Sabbath, even in such distresses; for our law requires that we rest upon that day. There were about a thousand, with their wives and children who were smothered and died in these caves: but many of those who escaped joined themselves to Mattathias, and appointed him to be their ruler, who taught them to fight even on the Sabbath day; and told them that unless they would do so, they would become their own enemies . . . and that nothing could then hinder them but that they must all perish without fighting. This speech persuaded them; and this rule continues among us to this day, that if there be a necessity, we may fight on Sabbath days.'

And this from the story of Pompey's assault on Jerusalem a century later:

'A bank was raised, day by day, with a great deal of labour, while the Romans cut down materials for it from the places round about; and when this bank was sufficiently raised, he brought his mechanical engines and battering-rams from Tyre, and placing them on the bank, he battered the Temple with the stones that were thrown against it; and had it not been our practice, from the days of our forefathers, to rest on the seventh day this bank could never have been perfected, by reason of the opposition the Jews would have made; for though our law gives us leave then to defend ourselves against those that begin to fight with us and assault us, yet does it not permit us to meddle with our enemies while they do anything else.'

What *could* the Romans make of such a people as this?

CHAPTER 4

The Imprint of the Herods

THE PHARISEES IN THEIR OVERWEENING PRIDE DID NOT SCRUPLE TO boast that they had 'never yet been in bondage to any man';[1] but in sober truth they had rarely been anything else. Slaves in Egypt; oppressed by one tyrant after another in the period of the Judges; tributary to Assyria; carried away captive to Babylon; at the mercy of the Persians; dominated, when the handful that returned had settled down, by the successors of Alexander in Egypt and Syria; and finally incorporated in the Empire of Rome; they had had little experience of national independence. The rule of Rome continued for centuries, but there was a period that lasted about eighty years and ended soon after Josephus was born, during which the Roman government controlled Palestine, or large areas of it, not directly but through client kings, all members of one great family. That family was the family of the Herods; and it is the purpose of this chapter to give some idea of what the Herods were like, what they did to Palestine, and what sort of country they left to the generation whose terrible struggle with Rome Josephus witnessed, took part in, and made famous for ever.

Students of Roman history know how complicated is the genealogy of the Julio-Claudian dynasty. That of the Herods is far more complicated, baffling in its complexity, and made the more difficult to disentangle both by the constant recurrence of the same names and by the multiple relationships between members of the same huge family. It was possible to have a succession of wives or, like Herod the Great, to have several at once and ten in all. Marriages regularly took place between members of different generations and within the prohibited degrees, and the stock suffered from persistent in-breeding. Fortunately, in this book it will only be necessary to refer to a few members of the family,

[1] John viii. 33.

and if two are called Antipater, two Agrippa, and four or five
Herod, I trust that the reader will be able to keep them distinct in
his mind. The first of the family to become king was the man
whom we all call Herod the Great; but before we discuss that
extraordinary person we must go back a little.

Before the Captivity the Jewish kings had all been descendants
of David; unlike its northern neighbour Israel, where assassination
was habitual and dynasty succeeded dynasty, Judah stuck to one
line throughout. That line ended with Zedekiah, whose eyes
Nebuchadnezzar put out before binding him with fetters and
carrying him to Babylon. David's descendants were never again
to occupy the throne: for four hundred years and more after the
Return under Zerubbabel the Jews managed without a king; then
in 105 B.C. a member of the Hasmonaean family, Aristobulus,
assumed the crown. The last of his successors, another Aristobulus,
was twice conveyed as a prisoner to Rome, and with him that
line of kings came to an end. From henceforth there might be
kings of the Jews, but there were to be no more Jewish kings.

South of Judaea lay Idumaea—in former times called Edom—
the country which Hyrcanus, in the same high-handed way in
which the Duke of Venice was in a later age to decree that
Shylock must 'presently become a Christian', had compelled to
adopt the Jewish religion. A later Hyrcanus, brother and rival of
the second Aristobulus, had an Idumaean friend called Antipater,
'who was very rich, and in his nature an active and seditious
man'. His father, whose name is variously given as Antipater or
Herod, had been made king of Idumaea by the father of the two
rivals, and he himself was anxious to secure his own hold on the
kingdom by friendship with Hyrcanus in Jerusalem and with
Aretas, king of Arabia, in the rose-red city of Petra. He was soon
to find himself in the good books of the Romans also; for when
Pompey's general, Scaurus, during an incursion into Arabia, was
unable to feed his troops, Antipater first supplied him with corn
from Judaea, and then, as ambassador of Scaurus, persuaded
Aretas to bribe Scaurus (how ready the Romans were to receive
bribes!) to leave his country alone.

When Pompey had been defeated at Pharsalus and murdered

off Alexandria, it behoved Antipater to make himself useful to
Pompey's conqueror, the invincible Julius, who had followed him
to Alexandria, and after succumbing to the charm of Cleopatra
had found himself in a desperate military situation. Mithridates of
Pergamus attempted to march to his assistance, but could not get
beyond Askelon. This was Antipater's opportunity: he went to
Mithridates' assistance, bringing Jews, Arabs, and Syrians to
reinforce him. Together they marched to Pelusium, and it was
Antipater whose assault on the fortifications enabled Mithridates
to capture that key city. Next he exerted his diplomacy, and
induced the Egyptians who were blocking the advance not only
to withdraw their opposition but to supply money and provisions.
A pitched battle against Caesar's Egyptian enemies followed, in
which Antipater first defeated his own opponents and then
rescued the struggling Mithridates from his. Finally, though
wounded, he captured the enemy camp. No wonder Caesar was
delighted with him: he made him a Roman citizen, exempted
him from all taxation, and appointed him procurator of
Judaea. Antipater escorted Caesar out of Syria and returned to
Jerusalem.

Many years before he had married a woman of his own race
who had borne him four sons—Phasael, Herod, Joseph, and
Pheroras—and one daughter—Salome. This Herod, one of the
ten who appear in Josephus' pages, was to become the great and
notorious monarch. The others too were all to play important
parts in the story. Antipater lost no time in making use of his two
eldest sons. He was a born organizer, and knowing that Hyrcanus
was a feeble creature he took upon himself the general oversight
of all Palestinian affairs, and after rebuilding the walls demolished
by Pompey installed Phasael as governor of Jerusalem, and gave
the more gifted Herod, still only twenty-five years old, the more
difficult task of enforcing order in Galilee. This task he carried out
with such vigour that Phasael was encouraged to be equally active
in the capital city, and their father reaped his reward, 'such respect
as is due to kings, and such honours as he might partake of if he
were an absolute lord of the country'. Antipater continued to
show respect to his nominal overlord, Hyrcanus; but some of the

leading Jews were bitterly jealous, and resolved to strike at him through his second son. They persuaded Hyrcanus to summon Herod to stand his trial for putting a bandit to death without the permission of the Sanhedrin. Herod's reaction was typical of the man. He arrived in Jerusalem with a bodyguard; then, finding that the danger was real, he slipped away to Damascus, bribed the Roman governor of Syria, Sextus Caesar, to give him an army, and marched on Jerusalem; but his more prudent father calmed his fury and persuaded him to retire.

Alas! murder was in the air. Sextus Caesar was assassinated by Caecilius Bassus. The forces of his kinsman Julius took the field against Bassus, assisted by the ever-loyal Antipater; but at this very time Julius himself fell, pierced by the daggers of his most trusted friends. Having brought down Caesar only to raise up Antony the treacherous assassins fled from Rome. Cassius arrived in Syria and demanded vast sums of money from the unfortunate Jews. Antipater and Herod were too wise to oppose him; those who did were treated with appalling, and typically Roman, brutality. Cassius and his fellow-conspirators were destined to die not many months later; but Antipater's turn came first. In the year 46 one Malichus, 'who was ill-disposed to him', but had been treated with great consideration, bribed the butler of Hyrcanus to poison him. 'Thus died Antipater, a man that had distinguished himself for piety and justice, and love to his country.' Our author's tribute was surely deserved.

If Josephus was impressed by the qualities of Antipater, he was much more deeply impressed by the daemonic energy of his most famous son. Herod's accession to power, his tremendous achievements, and his appalling tragedy, though they had little relevance to the avowed subject of *The Jewish War*, occupy very many pages of that book. In the later work, the *Antiquities*, though he does not seem to have gathered much new information, Josephus tells the whole story a second time at more than twice the length. Into the details of that story we need not enter here; many of them had very little direct effect upon the world of Josephus, and those who wish to know them can read the whole story in either of the two works named above—the shorter, earlier account is the more readable; or they may turn with pleasure and profit to the excellent books of Stewart Perowne. It will be sufficient for our purposes to sketch the career of this most vital king, and to consider what his reign contributed to the production of the Palestine Josephus knew.

When Antipater died Herod was only thirty, but though young in years he was old in experience; and experience, united with limitless energy, with unusual skill both as soldier and as statesman, and with complete freedom from any moral scruple or sense of pity, made a formidable combination. His father had seen that even though the army of Crassus had been destroyed by the Parthians the might of Rome was invincible, and that his surest hope lay in being on good terms with whatever Roman leader was for the time being in the ascendant. Herod had learnt that lesson, and all his success was due to his applying it throughout his life. He had already made Sextus Caesar his friend and carried out with enthusiasm the behests of Cassius. When Cassius was defeated at Philippi, with characteristic realism he promptly transferred his allegiance to the victorious Antony, who many years earlier had been the guest of Antipater. Herod had been engaged in bitter fighting with his Hasmonaean rivals; and now deputations, one of them a thousand strong, were sent to accuse him before Antony, who had fallen victim to Cleopatra's enticements and was on his way to Egypt. The tongues of the accusers spoke eloquently enough; but the gold of the accused spoke more eloquently still. Herod and Phasael were appointed tetrarchs to administer all Judaea, and many of the delegates never got back alive.

But disaster lay ahead. The Parthians swooped upon Syria, and Pacorus, the king's son, in return for a bribe of a million pounds and five hundred women, undertook to set Antigonus, the last Hasmonaean claimant, on the Jewish throne. The Parthian prince advanced southwards along the coastal route and entered Jerusalem, where Herod and Phasael were engaged in a bitter struggle with the supporters of Antigonus. Phasael was kidnapped by trickery, and escaped torture only by suicide. Herod slipped out of the city and made a dash for the fortress of Masada, whence he set off to seek help in Petra. Meanwhile the Parthians looted

Jerusalem and set up Antigonus as king. From Petra Herod received no encouragement; so he went on to Pelusium, and from there to Alexandria, where turning a deaf ear to the blandishments of the insatiable Cleopatra he took ship, though it was the middle of winter, for Rome. Arriving there after a stormy voyage he went straight to his powerful patron. Antony, 'recalling Antipater's hospitality and filled with admiration for the heroic character before him, decided on the spot that the man he had once made tetrarch should now be king of the Jews'. Lest the reader should credit Antony with none but altruistic motives, Josephus in telling the story the second time adds the remark: 'Herod offered him money to make him king.' Like Aeneas after his flight from Troy, Herod was never at a loss for appropriate gifts, which in his approaches to Antony were on a vast scale. Antony had a political motive too: Rome could never tolerate a Jewish king who owed his throne to their most dreaded enemies, the Parthians. The Senate unanimously approved his action, and escorted by the consuls and all the magistrates, Herod proceeded through the streets, walking between Antony and Octavian, joint rulers of the Roman world.

He now set sail for Palestine, raised an army, and marched against Antigonus. There were Roman forces in the country, sent to tackle the Parthian menace. Antigonus had bribed both their commander, Ventidius, and his contemptible subordinates, Silo and Machaeras. Herod however capped his bribes with bigger ones, and though the campaign which he was compelled to fight up and down the country was extremely difficult, he waged it with such extraordinary vigour that he was even able to bring aid to Antony, then engaged in attacking Samosata, a fortress near the Euphrates. It was an opportunity to place Antony under an obligation, and Herod seized it with both hands. He finished the siege, killed masses of the enemy, and captured quantities of booty. Antony showed his gratitude by heaping honours upon him.

But Herod had left trouble in his rear. His brother Joseph, whom he had put in complete charge, took a rash step which led to his utter defeat and death. Many parts of Palestine and Idumaea went over to Antigonus. When Herod heard the news he raced back to Galilee, where he was joined by two Roman legions put at his disposal by Sossius, Antony's new governor of Syria. He advanced rapidly, attacking and ruthlessly destroying all who stood in his way, and though delayed by a phenomenal storm soon arrived outside Jerusalem. It was three years since he had been proclaimed king in Rome; it was now 37 B.C. and Herod was thirty-six. He was joined by large additional Roman forces, commanded by Sossius himself. The siege was begun, conducted with relentless fury, and bitterly resisted. Herod chose this extraordinary moment to go off to Samaria, there to celebrate his second marriage. But it was a prudent thing to do; for the wife he had already, Doris, was of humble birth, but this one, Mariamme, was the granddaughter of Hyrcanus, high priest and king; she was a Hasmonaean and a princess. The siege lasted some five months: when the soldiers at last broke in they carried out an indiscriminate massacre, and were with the utmost difficulty restrained from looting. To satisfy them, and to keep up his payments to Antony, Herod had to part with all his personal treasures; on top of this he soon had to avert the hostility of Antony's mistress, the Egyptian queen, with an annual subsidy of two hundred thousand pounds. But at least his rival was gone. Antigonus had flung himself at the feet of Sossius, who contemptuously renamed him Antigone and handed him over to Antony, to die 'as such a coward deserved—by the axe'.

Throughout his career Herod's fortunes were bound up with those of Rome. It was Rome that had bestowed on him the name of king, and it was Rome that had enabled him to achieve the reality of kingship. In return he rendered Rome great services. But he who depended on Rome must needs walk warily; for the potentate of one day might be overwhelmed the next, and obeisance might have to be made to a new master. While Herod was still governor of Galilee the great Julius had been stabbed to death, and Herod had put himself in the hands of Cassius. Two years later Cassius had been swept away and Herod acknowledged the authority of Antony, to whom he committed himself entirely. Six years after Herod's entry into Jerusalem Antony too was gone.

He had yielded himelf body and soul to the last of Ptolemy's line, the woman to whose charms one Roman after another had fallen; the shadow of the vigorous, effective man he had once been, he had offered but feeble resistance to his younger rival, and his defeat at Actium had been followed by the flight of both the jaded lovers. Herod was in great danger: he was gravely compromised, for he had throughout been Antony's man, and in the final struggle he had got ready to take the field with him. And now Antony was no more, and Gaius Julius Caesar Octavianus, soon to become Augustus, was the sole and unchallengeable master of the Roman Empire. A lesser man than Herod would have grovelled before the vanquisher of Antony; but not Herod. 'The king determined to come to grips with his danger, and sailing to Rhodes where Caesar was at the time, sought an audience without his crown, in the dress and with the appearance of a commoner, but with the haughtiness of a king. He kept back nothing and spoke as man to man.' His speech was short, tactful, and dignified. Caesar accepted his explanation, confirmed him in his kingship, and set the crown once more on his head. Shortly afterwards he became so convinced of the worth of Herod's friendship that he greatly enlarged his kingdom. 'But what in Herod's esteem was of still greater value, he was loved by Caesar next to Agrippa, and by Agrippa next to Caesar.' As Agrippa was the chief minister of Augustus, this was a very happy state of affairs.

Herod was now at the height of his power, and his reign was to last another twenty years. Wealth poured into his coffers, and he spent it lavishly. His generosity, Josephus tells us, was superb, and largely devoted to works of piety. Temples and palaces, cities and fortresses, theatres and hippodromes rose all over the country. The appearance of Palestine was transformed, beautified, modernized, and to a large extent hellenized. The sights that met the eyes of Jesus, and later on the eyes of Josephus, were largely Herod's work. It would be hard to name anyone who has left behind him monuments in stone so numerous and so magnificent. Most famous are his great buildings in Jerusalem—his palace and towers, the fortress of Antonia, and the Temple, unique in the world. These it will perhaps be best to describe, as does Josephus, when we approach the story of their destruction. For the present let us look at some of the other structures with which this man of vision filled his little country.

To secure his kingdom against attack from enemies without, and his own life against conspiracies by enemies within, he built a number of fortresses at strategic points. Most important of these were the buildings in Jerusalem mentioned in the previous paragraph, all of which were highly defensible. The others were so cleverly sited, so elaborately fortified, and so lavishly provisioned, that anyone would have believed them impregnable, especially Machaerus and Masada, of which there are detailed descriptions in *The Jewish War*. Within the fortresses, two of which were called Herodeion after the king, were royal palaces. Of course they were not impregnable. In the great war with Rome every one of them fell, from the north of Galilee to the south of Judaea. History has shown, time and again, that no fortress is impregnable. In all the centuries has any people other than the Spartans ever seen that if wars are to be won they must be won in the field, and that the only walls that can give protection are walls built of human bricks?

Herod was fond of commemorating his kinsfolk and friends by building cities which he named after them. In memory of his brother Phasael he built both a tower in Jerusalem and the city of Phasaelis in the Jordan Valley. To his mother, Cypros, he dedicated a fortress with the same name to guard Jericho. Near Joppa he chose a site 'in the loveliest plain in his kingdom with an abundance of rivers and trees', and there, as a tribute to his father, he founded the city of Antipatris; for 'if ever a man was full of family affection, that man was Herod'. All the persons mentioned so far have been Idumaeans; the name of no Jew was enshrined in Herod's forts and cities; but whether his subjects liked it or not, he was bent on honouring (or flattering) his Roman friends and patrons, as were his sons after him. It must have been grievously wounding to God's devoted worshippers to see the name Agrippa engraved over the gate of His Holy Temple, though they may not have minded when the coastal town that had hitherto borne the Greek name Anthedon was rebuilt and renamed

82   THE WORLD OF JOSEPHUS

Agrippeion. Herod's most ambitious schemes, it goes without saying, were carried out to the glory of the Emperor himself. The ancient city of Samaria, in which King Ahab had built his ivory house, had been destroyed by Sargon, its successor by John Hyrcanus. Herod now built a new city 'with magnificent walls over two miles long' to provide homes for six thousand colonists. His motive, according to Josephus' earlier account, was 'his lavish generosity'; according to his later account he wanted 'a fortress for himself against all the people, to keep the country in awe. . . . He was always inventing somewhat further for his own security, and encompassing the whole nation with guards.' As usual he gave the city a new name, Sebaste; for Sebastos was the Greek equivalent of Augustus. He might of course have called it Augusta; but the language of Herod was Greek, not Latin. It is interesting to note that though the district of Samaria and the Samaritan people figure prominently in the New Testament, the capital city is never mentioned by name.

This new city had the most august of names; but a much greater achievement was the transforming of a decayed coastal town, Strato's Tower, into the great limestone city of Caesarea, where Herod built a splendid palace and established the seat of his government. Strato's Tower had had no harbour; there was not one haven of refuge in a rocky coastal strip fifty miles long, so that mariners were in constant danger. Herod was determined that Caesarea should have a harbour, and a harbour of exceptional size, protected by a mole two hundred feet wide built on a foundation of tremendous blocks of stone and supporting a row of towers, one of which was called after the Emperor's stepson Drusus. As the water was twenty fathoms deep the difficulties must have been stupendous: here as elsewhere it is evident that great engineering skill, unlimited labour, and immense financial resources were at Herod's disposal. At this port St Paul disembarked from his second missionary journey; at this port he embarked for Rome.

That Herod had no scruples about treading on Jewish corns is clear from the way in which he furnished his new city. All images were an abomination to the Sons of the Law: they were expressly forbidden by the Second Commandment. But Herod set up a colossal statue of Augustus and another of Rome—idolatry indeed. Here also, as in Jerusalem, he built a theatre and an amphitheatre, an affront to the Jews, who were unaccustomed to the sight of men running, leaping, and wrestling naked in the Greek fashion, and had no stomach for such disgusting spectacles as delighted the Romans—combats to the death between armed gladiators, between different species of wild beasts, and between beasts and unarmed men. Worst of all, he built a magnificent temple for the worship of the Emperor. The man who was building the great temple for God in Jerusalem showed the hollowness of his Jewish faith by doing the same for Augustus in Caesarea; and not in Caesarea only, for he had erected a vast shrine in Sebaste, and another at Paneion; and as Josephus tells us admiringly, 'when he had filled his own country with temples these tributes overflowed into his province, and in city after city he erected a Kaisareion.' If he did not display his paganism by building one in Jerusalem itself, he did at least put up a golden eagle—an object of Roman worship—over the Great Gate of the Temple, provoking a riot which he suppressed with revolting cruelty, burning the chief offenders alive.

How did Herod afford all this building? How did a man who began his reign with empty coffers and was compelled to find huge sums in order to placate Antony and Cleopatra, to be followed by lavish expenditure on presents and entertainments for Antony's conqueror, find means to finance this orgy of construction, which was by no means confined to his own dominions? Whence came the capital the proceeds of which were to provide entertainments and prizes, 'perpetual feasts and merry meetings', year after year at one festival or another? We may well ask. Some assistance, it is true, was forthcoming from the centre of power. For the sports celebrated every five years at Caesarea in honour of Augustus that monarch's wife sent Herod equipment worth five hundred talents.[1] Another source of wealth was the tomb of

[1] The value of a talent was estimated a century ago at about £250, equivalent today to £1,000 or more. If Josephus' figure is correct, the equipment was worth at least £500,000.

David. Herod was told that his predecessor Hyrcanus had removed from it silver worth three million pounds; so he entered
the tomb in strict secrecy to try his own luck. He found that all
the silver was gone, but there was abundance of gold and other
precious things, and he took the lot.

But for the most part he relied on the contributions of his unfortunate subjects to pay for all his ambitious schemes: the
'generosity of his soul' was that of a man who denies himself
nothing and nobly gives away the money of other people.
Josephus, who prided himself upon the impartiality of his judgment, is very frank about this. Herod, he tells us, was quite overcome by his passionate ambition for honour; so he was munificent
wherever there was any hope of future memorial or present
reputation. As his expenses were beyond his means he was
compelled to ill-treat his subjects. 'What he thought the most
excellent present he could make another, he discovered an
inclination to have the same presented to himself.' When Herod
was dead, a Jewish embassy to Rome told the Emperor just what
they thought of their late master. He had assumed the irresponsible
authority of a tyrant, and had used that authority to destroy the
Jews. A great many had perished; but the survivors were far more
unfortunate, as they stood in constant danger of being deprived
of their property. He never left off adorning those cities that were
inhabited by foreigners, with the result that Jewish cities were
ruined. When he took the kingdom it was in an extremely
flourishing condition; but he had reduced the nation to abject
poverty. Besides the taxes laid on every citizen he required them
to make liberal presents to himself, to his domestics and friends,
and to such of his slaves as were privileged to collect his taxes:
there was no way to secure freedom from violence except by
paying gold or silver for it. There can be little doubt that Herod
was bitterly hated by his subjects, and that the financial burden
laid on their shoulders was a major cause of that hatred.

However the money was raised, it was certainly spent to some
purpose. Herod boasted that he was more Greek than Jew, and
the Greeks, who more than any other race were lovers of beauty,
let no such scruples as restrained the Jews inhibit their work of

artistic creation. It was nothing to Herod that the Jews objected to the representation of human features, or of divinity in human guise. He built cities and temples everywhere, and both the architecture and the adornments were Greek. We are apt to think of Palestine as a Jewish country, Semitic through and through, and very like the land which pilgrims visit today. We forget the destruction wrought by the Romans; we forget the changes brought about by centuries of Arab occupation. We perhaps have never realized that the chief aim of Herod was to hellenize his kingdom, and that he did it with immense thoroughness. Caesarea and Sebaste were Greek; so was the new city of Jericho, and so was Jerusalem itself. The very Temple, so far from resembling those of Solomon and Zerubbabel, was a triumph of Greek art, with its magnificent porticoes and Corinthian columns. The theatres, amphitheatres, and hippodromes; the public baths; the sports and entertainments; all these were Greek or Graeco-Roman. Herod transformed the appearance of Palestine and to a large extent transformed the outlook of its inhabitants. Thanks to Herod, Jesus Christ, and Josephus after Him, Jews by birth and Jews by upbringing, saw Greek architecture all around them and encountered Greek culture on every hand.

Hellenization did not begin with Herod, though he enormously increased its scope and speed. From the time of Alexander there seem to have been plenty of Greek books in the country, and a population able to read and enjoy them. Much of that population was Gentile and with many Greek was the first language; but the Jews themselves were familiar with Greek—the Hellenistic or common Greek—and it was the language of official life and of polite society. It is hardly possible that the conversation between Pilate and his innocent prisoner was conducted in any other language. The case was surely the same when nearly forty years later Josephus had his momentous interview with Vespasian. Not only was Greek generally understood: it affected also the Jewish vernacular—which, *pace* the Authorized Version and the New English Bible, was not Hebrew but Aramaic—to such an extent that over one word in five of the current vocabulary was of Greek origin, and a Greek word was used even for the most Jewish of institutions, the synagogue. Many customs also were hellenized, especially those connected with meals. The guests reclined at table and dipped their hands in the dish, while the dilution and circulation of the wine were controlled by 'the ruler of the feast'. Such practices did not offend our Lord, nor even Simon the Pharisee. Nor was any objection raised to the Greek musical instruments that accompanied worship in the Temple.

If hellenization did not begin with Herod, it did not end with him either; for his sons were as eager as he to win lasting renown by leaving behind them great monuments in stone. On his death his kingdom was divided and shared between his surviving sons, Archelaus becoming ethnarch of Judaea, Antipas tetrarch of Galilee and Peraea, and Philip tetrarch of Ituraea and Trachonitis. Archelaus lasted only nine years: he ruled so badly that in A.D. 6 Augustus banished him to Gaul. Antipas hung on for forty-two years, until in 39 he was driven by his wife Herodias to apply to Caligula for the title of king, and for his pains was packed off to Spain. Philip, a sensible and temperate ruler, as Josephus assures us, showed himself more circumspect and retained his throne to the last. These two had time for the grandiose building-projects so dear to Herodian hearts. Antipas rebuilt his capital Sepphoris. Then he fortified a town in Peraea and renamed it Julias after Julia (Livia), the Emperor's consort. Finally he chose an ideal site on the shore of the Sea of Galilee and built a splendid new capital, furnished with palatial baths fed by hot springs, and named it Tiberias in honour of the new Emperor. All these cities were of course Greek. His brother managed to commemorate both the Emperor and himself by building Caesarea Philippi; and by converting the village of Bethsaida into the city of Julias he ingratiated himself with the most powerful woman in the world. This cultivation of the imperial consort was a shrewd practice, which was to be followed by Josephus too.

Of Herod's unhappy domestic life little need be said. It fills many pages of Josephus, and has been dramatized and romanticized by modern writers. It was in truth neither tragic nor romantic: it lacked the dignity that tragedy requires; and poly-gamy, suspicion, jealousy, and multiple murder are not romantic but revolting. He divorced a faithful wife in order to marry a princess. Then while professing a passionate devotion to her he executed her grandfather, the weak but harmless Hyrcanus, on a trumped-up charge, and after appointing her brother Jonathan high priest at the tender age of sixteen resented the sympathetic tears of the Temple congregation and arranged for him to be drowned in a swimming bath. Is it to be wondered at that Mariamme hated him? Her own turn was not long in coming: Josephus gives us two irreconcilable accounts of what happened, but it is plain that her reproaches so infuriated her terrible spouse that though she had borne him five children he ordered her instant execution, executing at the same time his sister's husband. The next victim was his wife's mother. That was far from being the end. He allowed his firstborn, Antipater, to rouse his suspic-ions against Mariamme's two sons, Alexander and Aristobulus, with the result that after several changes of mind Herod convened a court to try them *in absentia*, and a little while later sent them to Sebaste to be strangled.

The way was now clear for Antipater to succeed his father, but that cup was never to reach his lip. Herod at last realized that the dead youths—for they were little more—had been the innocent victims of their elder brother's machinations, and he determined to destroy this son too. He delayed a decision for a long time; then at last, when, in the grip of a horrible malady which was soon to prove fatal, he was vainly seeking relief from his agonizing pains, he sent his bodyguard to kill Antipater. So ended the tale of his domestic murders. But Herod's appetite for blood was insatiable. Knowing that the Jews would greet his death with wild rejoicings he endeavoured to ensure that tears should be shed in plenty. He collected the leading men of every village in Judaea and locked them up in the hippodrome at Jericho, giving orders that his death should be the signal for the soldiers to massacre them all, and so fill the whole of Judaea with grief. Would such a monster have hesitated to slaughter a few babies at Bethlehem rather than allow an infant King to live?

What was the impact of this sordid story on the Palestine that
Josephus knew? On so speculative a matter a brief answer must
suffice. We cannot say what sort of monarchs the murdered sons
would have proved. Herod had intended them to be his heirs, and
had already given them the title of king. Alexander and Aristobulus had been carefully trained in Rome, and seem to have been
promising and popular young men. It may be that, had one of
them become ruler of Judaea instead of the tactless, brutal, and
incompetent Archelaus, that unhappy country might never have
become the prey of Roman procurators. If Pontius Pilate had never
occupied the palace of Caesarea, had never from his vantage-
point in the Tower of Antonia attempted to keep order among the
turbulent Jews and to satisfy their clamorous demands with a
contemptuous and cynical judgment, there might never have
been a Golgotha. And if there had been no Gessius Florus to
plunder the country and provoke its inhabitants beyond endurance, the Jews might never have risen in revolt, Josephus might
never have made his infamous surrender, Palestine might never
have been laid waste, and the pilgrim might still have seen the
grim fortress of Antonia, the gorgeous palace of Herod, and the
three colossal towers standing erect before him; he might still
have gasped at the majesty of the Temple, its gilded pinnacles
gleaming in the dazzling light of the sun.

CHAPTER 5

A People Divided

THE PEOPLES OF PALESTINE—WE MUST NOT USE THE
singular—were separated by a variety of barriers, geographical,
governmental, racial, religious, political, and social. Let us take a
look at conditions in the third and fourth decades of our era, or
perhaps in the twelve years beginning in A.D. 26—a short period,
but long enough to include the ministry and deaths of John the
Baptist and Jesus Christ, the governorship of Pontius Pilate, and
the birth of Josephus. At the start of the third chapter of his gospel,
St Luke makes a valiant attempt to fix the date of John's public
appearance as precisely as the clumsy chronological methods of his
day allowed. He informs us that 'in the fifteenth year of the
principate of Tiberius Caesar, when Pontius Pilate was in charge
of Judaea, when Herod was tetrarch of Galilee, his brother Philip
tetrarch of the districts of Ituraea and Trachonitis, and Lysanias
tetrarch of Abilene, and when the high priesthood was shared by
Annas and Caiaphas, the word of God came to John the son of
Zacharias in the wilderness.' Here in miniature is a picture of the
divided state of Palestine. The domains that only thirty years
before had made up the kingdom of Herod the Great, and fourteen
years later were to be reunited under his grandson Agrippa the
First, were now divided into four. One part was ruled by a Roman
procurator, the other three by tetrarchs. Of these tetrarchs two
were sons of Herod the Idumaean, one (Antipas) by Malthace, a
Samaritan woman, the other (Philip) by Cleopatra of Jerusalem,
whoever she may have been. The third tetrarch was a Syrian of
Greek or Macedonian origin. The sole Jewish authority was the
high priest, and there too there was division; for, as Luke so
explicitly states, Annas and Caiaphas were both high priest at the
same time—one, it is evident, in the eyes of the Romans, the other
in the eyes of the Jews. A Roman governor had deposed Annas

and appointed his son-in-law. But according to the Law of the
Jews a high priest remained high priest till he died, and they
refused to recognize Caiaphas. Hence the devilish procedure
followed at the trial of Jesus, who was sent first to Annas and then
to his official successor in order that both Jews and Romans might
be satisfied.

Let us take a closer look at the four regions.

The Jews of the Diaspora or Dispersion were scattered over the
whole eastern half of the Roman Empire, and groups, large or
small, were to be found in nearly all the townships of Syria. But
the number of Jews in Abilene was probably insignificant, and as
the tetrarchy of Lysanias plays no part in the story of Josephus'
own lifetime we may leave it now without more ado. With the
tetrarchy of Philip the case is different. It was a much larger area,
projecting far to the east of the others and comprising, in addition
to Ituraea and Trachonitis, Gaulanitis, Auranitis, and Batanaea.
All these names appear in our author's pages, together with those of
fortresses—Gamala, Gadara, and Hippos—captured by Vespasian
during the great revolt, and of places with interesting geographical
features, such as the rival sources of the River Jordan. It is plain
that at least the western strip was Jewish enough to be involved
in what happened on the other side of the great valley, in Galilee;
though in the region as a whole Jews formed only a small part of
the population, Philip's subjects being to a large extent Arabs,
Idumaeans, Syrians, and Greeks. The region was entirely hellenistic in sympathy, and it is worthy of note that though Antipas,
who had no authority in Judaea, is known to have visited Jerusalem for the feasts, there is no record of his brother doing the
same. That there were Jews in the western strip appears also from
the fact that our Lord, who was not sent but unto the lost sheep
of the house of Israel, more than once visited the eastern shores of
the Galilaean Lake, and was in the neighbourhood of Philip's
capital when He put to His disciples the momentous question:
'Who say ye that I am?'[1]

Far more important, both in Jewish history and in world
history, were the other two regions. The territory of Antipas

[1] Matthew xvi.15.

consisted of two districts, Galilee and Peraea, which not only lay on opposite sides of the Jordan but had no direct contact with each other, being separated at the nearest point by a strip of land ten miles wide, over which the tetrarch seems to have had no authority. The population of Galilee was mixed, and it is impossible to say with certainty whether Jews or Gentiles predominated. Many who were Jews by religion were Gentiles by race; for the Jewish religion had been forced upon an earlier generation of this mixed people. It will be recalled that one of the apostles, who came from Bethsaida of Galilee, was able to converse with his Master's Greek visitors, and bore a Greek name himself. Many others, especially those brought in by the Herods to fill their cities, remained pagan. This heterogeneous population was, as we saw in an earlier chapter, despised by the people of Judaea, and that contempt was increased by the fact that the Galilaeans spoke a dialect of their own, as Peter discovered to his cost when his speech betrayed him. In Greek the same word is used for both Jews and Judaeans, and careful readers will observe that it was the habit of Josephus, as of St John, to apply the word normally to the inhabitants of Judaea, and to refer to those who lived in the northern region as Galilaeans. It is doubtful, as I have said, whether Jews or Gentiles were the more numerous in Galilee: in Antipas' other dominion, Peraea, we may be sure that Gentiles constituted the majority. In that dominion there was one place of importance, the terrible fortress of Machaerus, where Salome delighted her step-father with her dancing and secured for her revengeful mother the head of John the Baptist. We shall come to Machaerus again in Josephus' pages, when we reach the last chapters of *The Jewish War*.

Far eclipsing in importance and renown the other three regions, Judaea was at this time governed by a Roman procurator, whose term of office was subject only to the judgment or whim of Caesar. There had been a succession of governors since the expulsion of Archelaus, Pilate being the fifth. That this man held office for ten years, far longer than most, may seem surprising in view of his egregious tactlessness and continual misgovernment, but Tiberius who appointed him was not in favour of frequent change. He knew that this led to inefficiency, and he knew also that since a new governor brought with him a new army of helpers whose main purpose was to make a fortune quickly, 'a change of rulers meant another swarm of bloodsucking flies', as Furneaux translates a memorable comment of Tacitus. Had Pilate behaved better he might still have been ruling in Caesarea when Josephus was born.

We saw earlier that Roman Judaea embraced both Judaea proper and its northern neighbour, Samaria—a strange pair of yoke-fellows. Hostility between them was mutual and bitter, so bitter that travellers between Judaea and Galilee avoided the little country that lay between them so embarrassingly, preferring to cross the Jordan twice and follow the longer route through Peraea. When an inoffensive person ventured to pass through Samaria he was apt to be cold-shouldered and refused lodging, and as we know from the case of Jesus Christ, the reactions of his Jewish or Galilaean friends might be violent. This antipathy was of long standing. The kingdom of David had split in two on the accession of his grandson Rehoboam, and from that time till the end of the Northern Kingdom Israel and Judah had been repeatedly at war. The new settlers introduced by the Assyrians to replace the captured Israelites were of mixed race and worshipped heathen gods; alien to the Jews at that period they were hated much more bitterly three centuries later, when under the influence of Nehemiah the remnant that had returned, already struggling for survival, had become rigidly exclusive. 'The Samaritans,' writes Josephus, 'being evil and enviously disposed to the Jews, wrought them many mischiefs.' Race and politics combined with religion to prevent any amicable approach; for though the Samaritans worshipped the same God they recognized no sacred books except the Pentateuch, and being excluded from the Temple at Jerusalem had dared to erect one of their own on Mount Gerizim, provoking furious indignation in Jewish bosoms.

Here was division indeed! The people of Judaea, contemptuous of the Galilaeans, and forced into double-harness with the Samaritans! Our Lord, of course, had no use for any racial animosities. He more than once chose to journey through Samaria. He talked kindly to a Samaritan woman; He healed a Samaritan leper and praised him at the expense of his Jewish companions; and in His famous parable He went out of His way to rap the knuckles of the learned man who did not know who was his neighbour. His disciples, commissioned to be His witnesses 'both in Jerusalem and in all Judaea and Samaria',[1] carried out His command with splendid enthusiasm and complete impartiality. It was very different with the unconverted Jews: Josephus tells us of horrible things that happened in his lifetime as a result of the hatred that continued unabated. One violent incident resulted in both sides appealing to Claudius, who took drastic action against both the leading Samaritans and the Roman officers who had failed to enforce order.

Of all the regions Judaea was the most Jewish in race, religion, and national consciousness. But even here there were cities and areas where Jews were in a minority. The most important of the cities was of course Caesarea, the capital, where the Jewish colony numbered not much more than twenty thousand. The city, says Josephus, was full of Syrians, both soldiers and civilians; and 'Syrian' is the word which he applies also to an enclave in the south-west, the district that had once been Philistia and still included the ancient cities of the uncircumcised, Ashdod, Ashkelon, and Gaza, along with Anthedon or Agrippeion.

Gentile cities, as we have seen, were dotted all over Palestine; but special attention must be drawn to one of the strangest features in the political geography of this patchwork of a country. Probably under the terms of Pompey's settlement the right of self-government had been given to a number of scattered cities, all Greek and all very prosperous, most of them being situated on the main roads leading into Palestine from the north and east. The number, though later increased, was originally ten: hence the name Decapolis. These cities, stretching from Damascus in the north to Philadelphia (Amman) in the south, were independent alike of each other and of the tetrarchs. They formed a kind of confederacy, combining to make highways, aqueducts, and commercial agreements for their mutual benefit; and the name was

[1] Acts i. 8.

sometimes used to denote not the cities but a considerable stretch of country lying between Philip's tetrarchy and Peraea, and thrusting west of Jordan to drive a wedge between Galilee and Samaria. Within that wedge was the ancient city of Beth-Shan, where after the defeat of Israel on Mount Gilboa the headless bodies of Saul and Jonathan had been displayed by the Philistines. The city was now known as Scythopolis, and is believed to have been the capital of Decapolis, though separated by the river from all the rest. In each of these cities there was a Jewish colony, but they were essentially Gentile, and so hated by the Jews that when the war broke out they destroyed as many of them as they could. But in peacetime they must have passed through some of them frequently. The Galilaean who wished to attend the Passover in Jerusalem was bound to go by way of these or other Greek cities. If he ventured to go through Samaria, he must either choose the hill route and pass through Sebaste itself, or descend to the valley and pass through Scythopolis (or Tiberias), Phasaelis, and Jericho. If he preferred to travel on the other side of Jordan he must go through Pella and then Jericho. Such contacts could not be avoided.

From these external divisions let us turn to others, more subtle but not less damaging. There were, says Josephus, three 'philosophies' or systems of thought, taught by three 'sects'. These he traces back to the time of Jonathan the Maccabee, over two centuries before his own time. He had a personal interest in all three, since he had been associated with each of them in turn, as we shall see when we come to consider his life; and they seem to have been something of a bee in his bonnet, buzzing repeatedly and at unsuitable moments; for having discussed them at considerable length in one of the many irrelevant digressions in *The Jewish War*, he returns to the subject half a dozen times in *Antiquities*, twice confessing that he has dealt with them fully in his earlier work. He gives most space to the Essenes; but his preference was for the Pharisees, who, as he says, were held to be the most authoritative exponents of the Law and counted as the leading sect; or, as he puts it elsewhere, a sect more pious than the rest and stricter in the interpretation of the Law. We do not, however, rely on Josephus alone for our knowledge: his account of them, as F. W. Farrar pointed out long ago, can by no means be exclusively trusted. 'No doubt many good and faithful men, like Nicodemus and Joseph of Arimathaea, existed in their body, but Jewish writers themselves admit, and the Talmud amply and in many passages confirms, the terrible charges brought against them by our Lord in His Great Denunciation.'

The Essenes, who since their recent identification with the community at Qumran have roused a great deal of interest, do not appear in the pages of the New Testament. This is hardly surprising: for the most part they kept themselves to themselves, whether in their secluded settlement near the Dead Sea or in the small groups scattered elsewhere; and their tenets were such that they were unlikely either to show hostility to Jesus and attempt to trap Him with cunningly devised questions, or by objectionable practices to invite criticism from Him. Of the two better-known sects the New Testament writers have given us a much more vivid picture than do Josephus' scattered references: there is nothing in his writings to compare with what St Luke tells us in the twenty-third chapter of Acts: 'When Paul realized that one half of the Sanhedrin were Sadducees, the other half Pharisees, he called out: "Gentlemen, I am a Pharisee, as my ancestors were before me. The hope and resurrection of the dead are what I am being tried for." This declaration started a bitter set-to between Pharisees and Sadducees, and the assembly was sharply divided. For the Sadducees say there is no resurrection, and no angel or spirit; while the Pharisees believe in both. Complete uproar followed . . . so the Roman commander, alarmed lest Paul should be torn in two between them, ordered his battalion to jump in and rescue him from their clutches.'[1]

However, in examining the world of Josephus we must fix our thoughts on these sects as they appeared to him, and as he has described them in much less vigorous language. As we should expect, he lays considerable stress on the differences between them. The Essenes were unique in their monastic habits. They lived in a celibate community, subject to a very severe discipline,

[1] Acts xxiii. 6-10.

employing no servants and possessing no private property. They were strict Sabbatarians—so strict that they would not even empty their bowels on the Sabbath day. They performed many ablutions, recited many prayers, and presumed to offer their own sacrifices, with the result that they were excluded from the services in the Temple. They laid great stress on morality, and like Jesus himself taught that devotion to absolute truthfulness which makes any oath superfluous. In *The Jewish War* we are told that they had large colonies everywhere, but in *Antiquities* their total numbers are given as only four thousand.

The other two sects were much more in the public eye, and lived far more normal lives; but they agreed on little else. The Pharisees, whom Josephus describes as abstemious, conscientious, and courteous, but also as proud and cunning, were much admired for their 'consistent moral conduct' and exerted great influence over the public at large: the Sadducees, who apparently were not interested in morality and even asserted that God did not see sin, appealed only to the rich and made very few converts, but 'these were of the greatest dignity.' The Pharisees were friendly to one another and endeavoured to be on good terms with the generality of people, whereas the Sadducees were disagreeable even to each other, and as harsh to their fellow-countrymen as they might be to foreigners. The Pharisees accepted as the word of God all three sections of the Hebrew Scriptures—the Law, the Prophets, and the Writings: the Sadducees paid little heed to the last two (being concerned with ceremonial rather than with spiritual enlightenment): the Law was enough for them, and they rejected the Tradition of the Elders, which the Pharisees obeyed with meticulous care.

On two of the great questions that have exercised the minds of men from time immemorial all three schools held different opinions—the freedom of the will, and survival after death.

The Essenes were uncompromising fatalists; fate governed all things, and nothing could befall men that was not determined by it. This fate was not a blind or impersonal force; for all things were best ascribed to God. It is evident that they did not see the impossibility of reconciling such metaphysical principles with the fact of individual responsibility, acceptance of which was involved in their vehement condemnation of moral lapses and their insistence on both retributive and reformatory punishment. The Sadducees went to the opposite extreme. They flatly denied the existence of fate: every man was free to choose between good and evil and must decide his own course for himself. In this they were in complete accord with Moses and with commonsense: we all know that we can and must choose for ourselves, and deserve condemnation if we choose wrongly. But Sadducaic commonsense was accompanied by spiritual blindness: in their deistic conception of God there was no place either for divine assistance in human choice, or for divine knowledge and disapproval of human mischoosing. The Pharisees solved the perplexing problem with a philosophically unsatisfactory compromise. We are told in the *War* that they ascribed everything to fate or to God: the decision whether or not to do right rested primarily with men, yet in every action fate took some part. In *Antiquities* this is put in a still more unsatisfactory form: some actions but not all were the work of fate, and some of them were in our own power, and were liable to fate but not caused by fate.

On the subject of survival the Sadducees took an equally negative view, which bore a marked resemblance to that of Epicurus. For them, as Paul said, there was no resurrection and no hope: death was the end; the soul perished with the body; and there was no beyond, no place of rest and joy or of torment and misery, no Judgment, no separation of sheep from goats. Neither in life nor in death were there any divine sanctions. The Pharisees on the other hand, conforming to more normal Greek thought, were satisfied that souls had an immortal vigour in them, and that under the earth there would be rewards or punishments, according as men had lived virtuously or viciously in this world. The second type of men would be confined in prison for all time; the first type would be free to return to life. The Essenes, as Josephus clearly saw, also derived their doctrine from the Greeks, and readers will be reminded of the two descriptions of the next world given by the Platonic Socrates. Let Dr. Traill again render for us the words of Josephus:

'The opinion obtains among them, that bodies indeed are corruptible, and the matter of them not permanent; but that souls continue exempt from death for ever: and that, emanating from the most subtle ether, they are enfolded in bodies, as prisons, to which they are drawn by some natural spell. But when loosed from the bonds of the flesh, as if released from a long captivity, they rejoice and are borne upward. In this opinion harmonizing with the sons of Greece, they maintain that virtuous souls have their habitation beyond the ocean, in a region oppressed neither with rains, nor snows, nor heats; but which the ever-gentle zephyr refreshes, breathing from the wave: while to the bad they allot a gloomy and tempestuous cavern, full of never-ending punishments.'

It may surprise the average reader of the Gospels to learn that the warring sects derived some of their most important beliefs, not from their own scriptures, but from the pagan literature of Greece.

To the three great schools of thought Josephus adds a fourth, of which the founder was a rabbi, Judas, whom he sometimes calls the Gaulonite, sometimes, like St Luke in the Acts, the Galilaean. In general his followers shared the beliefs of the Pharisees; but they were devoted to liberty, and determined to serve no ruler but God. Rather than call any man their master they would fearlessly face death, and expected their kinsfolk and friends to do the same. This reversion to theocracy was to Josephus a 'mad distemper', which drove the Jews wild under the provocation of Gessius Florus and led to the great revolt. For that and all its terrible consequences our author sets the blame squarely on the shoulders of these two men, Florus and Judas.

And here we pass from religion and philosophy to political and social discontent. The trouble started in A.D. 6 when, after the expulsion of Archelaus, Caesar's legate in Antioch, Sulpicius Quirinius, was straightening things up—that Quirinius who had been in office years before when Augustus had ordered a census or registration of all his subjects. This, in the words of the Revised Version, 'was the first enrolment made when Quirinius was governor of Syria'.[1] Quirinius now instituted a second, which

[1] Luke ii. 2.

involved paying taxes to the Romans. There was no Herod the Great this time to keep order with an iron hand, and Judas, declaring that it would be cowardice to pay such taxes, instigated a short-lived revolt which cost him his life. But his philosophy lived on. He had founded the Zealots, zealous for Israel and for Israel's God, who were to keep up a continuous agitation against Roman rule until, just sixty years later, their zeal brought about the disastrous and final explosion.

If, in the Zealots, political objectives could not be disentangled from religious principles, the same cannot be said of the Herodians, who seem to have been a political party pure and simple, motivated by the desire, shared by few of their fellow-Jews, that the rule of the Herods should continue. They knew that the Herods were not Jews by race, and that their Jewish religious convictions were barely skin-deep; but they probably considered that half a loaf was better than no bread, and an Idumaean-Samaritan monarch preferable to a pagan Roman official. Whether the party had been constituted in the reign of the first Herod we cannot say: we find no mention of Herodians in Josephus' writings, and the only contemporary allusions to them that have come down to us are the statements of St Matthew and St Mark that on two occasions they combined with the Pharisees in an effort to destroy Jesus, whose opinion of Antipas, of which He made no secret, must have been highly offensive to them. What we know of them from later sources will be mentioned a little further on.

What political ideas can we find in the three main sects? The Essenes seem to have shown no interest in politics of any kind. It is true that in the war they suffered terribly at the hands of the Romans, 'who racked and twisted, burnt and broke them, subjecting them to every torture yet invented'; but the reason was not their political attitude but their religious intransigence. With the other sects it was different. The Pharisees, whose name is thought to mean 'the Separated' and who despised all races and religions other than their own, were bound to chafe under Herodian rule and to object strongly to being dominated by pagans from Europe. They would not co-operate with the

Romans, and many of them refused to take the oath of allegiance. The fact that they were prepared to ally themselves with the Herodians only serves to show the intensity of their bitterness against the revolutionary Prophet who had taken them so severely to task. We do not find them collaborating with the Sadducees; and small wonder. For the Sadducees were the Establishment, the closed circle of aristocratic families, the select few, the party of wealth. They had always been ready to compromise with the occupying power, and they knew very well on which side their bread was buttered; it paid them handsomely to keep in with their Roman masters. They had no use for those who provoked the procurators, under whom they retained their rights and privileges. Of course Roman interference with priestly appointments might be rather annoying at times; but after all, if Annas was deposed from the high priesthood it was no doubt a nasty knock for Annas, but it was very pleasant for Caiaphas; and as we have already seen, there were ways and means of getting round that particular little difficulty. Religious scruples? They did not worry the Sadducees, who were the rationalists of the nation, content with the externals of religion, and happy to continue the lucrative business of the Temple ceremonial, but with nothing of the mystic about them: they were as worldly and unspiritual as the bishops of eighteenth-century England.

If the Sadducees did not greatly desire deliverance from a foreign yoke, they did not expect it either. Reference was made in an earlier chapter to the Messianic hope that pervaded the nation and distinguished the Jews from every other race. That hope took several forms, but in general it was the hope of a Davidic king who would overcome the nation's enemies by military force. How ever-present was that hope, how imminent the expected deliverance seemed to the Jews, was shown not only by the cries that went up on that emotion-filled Palm Sunday, but by the readiness of the Galilaean crowd on a much earlier occasion, when their hunger had been satisfied by a miracle they had not deemed possible, to seize the Son of David and make Him king then and there. The same thing was shown also by the constant succession of pretenders who presented themselves to the people as Messiahs throughout our Lord's life and the early years of Josephus—thousands of them, if his witness is to be believed—and who invariably succeeded in collecting a band of credulous followers. Herein we find another division in the Jewish people. The Sadducees differed from the rest in rejecting these hopes, not only because they found the foreign yoke easy to bear, but because the notion of a divine deliverer was based on the promises of Isaiah, Jeremiah, and the other prophets, and on the apocalyptic visions of Daniel; and the Sadducees paid little regard to any of the sacred writings other than the ceremonial enactments of Moses. The cult of the promised deliverer must have been most distasteful to the Sadducees. Apart from them there may perhaps have been one group that did not share the popular expectation; for there are statements in two or three writers that the Herodians thought the Messiah had come already—in the form of Herod! In view of Josephus' identification of the deliverer with Vespasian these statements may well be true.

One of the most potent causes of disunity in a nation, and one of the most detestable, is snobbery. This may take many forms: there is snobbery of ancestry, of position, of wealth, of intellect. The form to which the Jews were specially prone was religious snobbery. Jesus Christ, in a masterly character-study, portrayed for us the man who because he fasted twice a week and gave away a tenth of all his gains felt himself entitled to thank God that he was not as other men were.[1] The Pharisee's dislike of the publican was partly political: the publican served the Romans. It was partly selfish: the publican lightened his pocket. But it was also largely religious: he was filled with contempt for the man who paid no heed to the niceties of conventional religion. And why was the multitude that knew not the Law deemed to be accursed? For the selfsame religious reason; and for another and more surprising reason which also was religious. The accursed multitude was the Am ha-Arez, a term which denoted first the labourers on the land, and then the ignorant poor of country and town alike. They were despised first because they were ignorant; and since this meant ignorant of the Law the snobbery was not so much

[1] Luke xviii. 9-14.

intellectual as religious. But they were despised also because they were poor, and this was religious snobbery rather than social; for it sprang from the belief that the poor must be specially wicked people who for their wickedness were being specially punished by God. Hence poverty called not for pity but for contempt. One of the most sensational things that Jesus Christ did was to repudiate both this contempt and the mistaken doctrine of which it was the fruit. But that we must leave for another chapter.

CHAPTER 6

A New Religion

JUST TEN YEARS BEFORE THE BIRTH OF JOSEPHUS A NEW religious movement was born in Palestine, a movement which in the short period of three years was to win the support of large sections of the population, to challenge the public teaching, the personal conduct, and the private morals of the established leaders and professional instructors of the people, and to enrage and terrify the supreme rulers of Galilee and Judaea. In the next two generations, that is to say in the lifetime of Josephus, it was to spread over the known world and to make its way even into the household of Caesar. A little later it was to cast the entire Roman Empire into a new mould; and ultimately it was to prove the most powerful and all-pervading force the world had ever known. That this movement made so little impression on Josephus, who was in Palestine for years after it had begun to extend its activities from Jerusalem to all parts of the country and was daily gathering momentum and gaining new members, and who was in Rome when that city was displacing Jerusalem as centre of the movement's operations, may puzzle students of the period. But we must remember that there were innumerable subverters of established ways, prophets or pseudo-prophets, would-be kings, and claimants to the title of Messiah. It is not surprising that when a genuine prophet arose and pointed to the true Messiah, and then both were executed and appeared to be finished with, a man in whom religion was not the supreme interest but only one side of an elastic but nationalistic and backward-looking *pietas*, and who was gifted with little or no spiritual insight, failed to realize who or what they were, and the real significance of what they had done. Nor is it difficult to see why these two are mentioned so rarely and so briefly in our author's works; for neither the Baptist nor his Successor had had any recognizable part in bringing about the events which it was the purpose of those works to record, nor could they assist the author in his endeavours to justify in *The Jewish War* the conduct of the Romans, or to prove in *Antiquities* the praiseworthiness of the Jews.

Josephus was not alone in feeling that little need be said about the Founder of Christianity or His inspired forerunner: allusions to them in contemporary Latin authors are scarce indeed. That is still less surprising; for it would have taken remarkable insight to enable a Roman to see the importance of a movement which must have seemed to those in the Imperial City to be no more than a particularly ridiculous aberration of the incomprehensible Jewish mentality. Such allusions to the movement as can be found in Josephus will be considered later in this chapter: the vexed question of their authenticity must be left for Appendix I.

Such mentions of the Baptist as are to be found in non-Scriptural sources, whether Greek or Latin, provide no reason to doubt the accuracy of the account of his life and character presented with such clarity and consistency in the four gospels. The picture is familiar to all. John's birth was remarkable, though there is no suggestion that it was miraculous. His father was one of the very numerous priests, and his mother likewise a descendant of Aaron. They were getting on in years and had remained childless—a state which the Jews regarded as a divine punishment and a disgrace—so long that they had given up hope of ever being otherwise. Hence the appropriateness of the name given to the child at his circumcision—John, 'God's Gift'. For reasons clearly stated by St Luke, the boy was from the start recognized as one destined to play a conspicuous part when the longed-for Messiah came to establish the new kingdom of Israel. Of his early years we are told nothing except that the child grew and waxed strong in the spirit. We have no justification for interpreting the next statement—that he was in the deserts until the day of his shewing unto Israel—as referring to this period of his life. It may refer only to the last few years of his preparation, when he was over thirty years old.

The desert in question was the stretch of desolate and terrifying country already described which descended steeply from the ridge east of Jerusalem to the shore of the Dead Sea. It was a region almost without human habitation: its denizens were the wild beasts of which St Mark makes mention. On the torrid lower slopes lived the monastic community whose documents were found in the Qumran caverns; and it has been suggested that John derived at least some of his ideas from them, whether or not they are to be identified with the Essenes. The suggestion is interesting, and in view of what our various sources have to tell us about these people it is certainly reasonable. We need hardly suppose that John spent years communing with his own soul!

When John began to preach, his convictions were clear enough. He was not the Messiah foretold by Isaiah and Jeremiah; he was not Elijah, whose return had been prophesied by Malachi; he was not the prophet of whom Moses had spoken. He was a voice crying in the wilderness, Make straight the way of the Lord. He knew that his mission was to prepare the people for the advent of One infinitely greater than himself, and that he must bring them to their senses with a jolt. He knew that though the professed standards of the Jews were high, they had in practice fallen woefully below them. He must revive their sense of sin and reawaken their sleeping consciences, shaking them out of their complacency. His method was simple, psychologically sound, and intensely practical. He must turn the people's minds from self-indulgence and pleasure to duty and service; so he kept the stern Nazirite vows and practised complete self-denial and austerity. He was a prophet and must appear like a prophet, especially the most famous of all prophets, Elijah. He was not himself Elijah, but he came in the spirit and power of Elijah, and must show Elijah's courage in rebuking every class from the lowest to the highest. First things must be put first. The Kingdom of Heaven was at hand, and in order to be ready for it everyone must repent, must show a change of heart, must turn his back on the past and make a fresh start. This repentance must be sanctified and reinforced by an outward and visible sign, a symbolical washing that meant an open renunciation of sin.

How well John understood the people who were moved by his

eloquence and asked him what they must do! He knew their besetting sins, and in his short, sharp replies he hit the nail on the head every time. To the genuine enquirer he gave a helpful answer; but when the Pharisees and the Sadducees came to him he knew that such answers would be of no use; these self-satisfied humbugs needed different treatment, and boldly denouncing them as the offspring of vipers he warned them of the wrath to come, of the axe laid to the root of the trees, and of the futility of relying on their descent from Abraham.[1] Such vehement rebukes must have been very difficult for these arrogant people to stomach.

But always in the forefront of his thoughts was the fact that he was but a forerunner: when his Successor appeared he must disappear.

How great was the influence of this lone figure, whose active life was to be terminated so quickly? We should infer from the references in Josephus, scant as they are, that it was very considerable; and the evangelists, who were much less prone to exaggerate than he was, are unanimous on the point. Luke speaks of the 'multitudes' who went out to be baptized by him: Matthew and Mark tell us that there went out to him Jerusalem, and all Judaea, and all the region round about Jordan. John records that the Jews in Jerusalem thought it necessary to send priests and Levites to find out who he claimed to be, while other emissaries sent by the Pharisees wished to know by what right he baptized. The greatest tribute to his importance was paid by Antipas, who when John denounced him for marrying Herodias, shut him up in prison, but dared not put him to death until he was trapped into it by the sinuous allurements of his step-daughter (whom Josephus names as Salome) and the blood-thirsty determination of her spiteful mother. John had had good reason for his denunciation; for Antipas was a professing Jew, and he had violated Jewish law by marrying a woman (his niece) when he already had a wife and she a husband, and that husband his own brother. John's courage cost him his life; but Antipas had not done with him. He lived in fear, and when he learnt of the miracles wrought by John's Successor he thought that the man whom he had beheaded had come back from the dead.[2]

[1] Matthew iii. 7-10.   [2] Mark vi. 14-29.

It may be added here that John's influence continued when both he and his slayer had gone from the scene. His work was remembered by the many converts whom he had made ready to come into the Kingdom so soon to be established on earth. And he had made disciples, some of whom went far from Palestine and formed groups which acknowledged his teaching and baptism. One such group, twelve strong, was found by Paul in Ephesus during his second missionary journey, and the fact that Apollos knew only the baptism of John implies the existence of a similar group in Alexandria.[1] The twelve at Ephesus were baptized into the name of Jesus and confirmed by Paul, and we may surmise that this happened in one place after another until, about a century later, the last group of John's disciples was brought into the Christian fold.

Jesus, a kinsman of John on His mother's side, and six months his junior, did not begin where John left off: He began where John had begun, and proclaimed the identical message: 'Repent ye, for the Kingdom of Heaven is at hand.'[2] But having thus acknowledged the authority of John and the continuity of their work He showed himself no imitator of His great predecessor. He followed a different path, used different methods, displayed a different character. If John was a new Elijah, Jesus bore some resemblance to Elisha, living with men, showing kindly thought for them, more concerned to help than to denounce (but filled with a tenderness towards little children which was very different from Elisha's attitude and indeed had never before been seen in Israel). He did not live alone but in the company of men, with devoted women ministering to His needs. He wore not camel's hair but the ordinary garments of the day—garments of good quality, as is plain from the story of the drawing of lots at the foot of the cross. He ate not locusts and wild honey but fish, bread, and whatever His hosts offered Him. Being no Nazirite he did not eschew wine and strong drink, but lent His presence to wedding feasts and saw to it that there was wine in plenty. He himself stressed the contrast between His life and John's, a contrast which, since their preaching had so much in common, did not prevent

[1] Acts xviii. 24–xix. 7.   [2] Matthew iii. 2 and iv. 17.

their arousing the same hostility: 'John came neither eating nor drinking, and they say, He hath a devil. The Son of Man came eating and drinking, and they say, Behold, a gluttonous man and a winebibber, a friend of publicans and sinners!'[1]

These differences between the two prophets were external. They would not in themselves account for the one increasing while the other decreased, for the disciples of the first transferring their loyalty to the Second, for Jesus making (and through His disciples baptizing) more disciples than John.[2] The personality of Jesus was different: He was the *friend* of publicans and sinners, He invited himself to the house of the repentant Zacchaeus,[3] He treated with the utmost gentleness (albeit with no condoning of sin) the shunned woman of the city and the adulteress caught in the act. And his manner of speaking was not, like John's, uniformly denunciatory: it was never fierce unless fierceness was called for; and He invited the heavy-laden to come to Him and find rest to their souls. What love He showed to Martha, Mary, and their brother![4] How well He knew how to address both His intimate friends and the curious crowds! He appealed to their hearts and to their imaginations; He quoted their proverbs; He drew lessons from sky and earth, from bird and beast, from tree and flower, from the work of the labourer in field or vineyard, from the little details of domestic life. He taught them to pray, giving them the only prayer that can be repeated endlessly without growing stale, and removing all difficulty from the concept of prayer by portraying God as an understanding, loving Father. He told them parables, those vivid, exciting, and touching stories which they could understand, but which contained much that the superficial listener could not grasp, but which rewarded so richly the sincere disciple who pondered the fullness of their message. The most unlikely hearers were deeply impressed. The officers sent to arrest Jesus returned to the chief priests and Pharisees and exclaimed 'Never man so spake!'[5] No wonder the common people heard Him gladly! No wonder the rigid conservatives and wooden-minded traditionalists were shocked

---

[1] Matthew xi. 18-19.   [2] John iv. 1-2.   [3] Luke xix. 5.
[4] Luke x. 38-42 and John xi. 1-44.   [5] John vii. 46.

by the unorthodoxy of His methods and jealous of His success!

Tenderness was not something entirely new: very gentle words had been spoken in Palestine centuries before, as those who have troubled to read the little book of Hosea will remember. But tenderness, sympathy, and a fellow-feeling for those in distress, were rare qualities, nearly as rare in Palestine as in Rome, where one of the most enlightened of Josephus' contemporaries, the philosopher Seneca, declared that only a fool would weep for the sorrows of other people. But here was One who reassured sinners and consorted with them; who not only caressed little children but solemnly warned His disciples that unless they themselves became like little children they could never enter His Kingdom; who never treated women as inferiors but gave them—and every generation of women since—a position they had hitherto been denied; who pitied the lonely widow and the bereaved parent; and who shrank from none but actually touched the diseased and the leprous, and laid His hand on the dead man's bier.

Perhaps nothing was more strikingly novel than His truly revolutionary attitude to the poor. It was not simply a matter of gentleness and sympathy: He repudiated altogether the accepted belief so prominent in book after book of the Old Testament, though vehemently challenged in Job, that, since God rewarded goodness and punished sin, prosperity and wretchedness were a sure indication of how men were regarded by Him; so that a rich man might automatically be adjudged good and a poor man bad. It was typical of Christ that He began His Sermon on the Level Place with the, to Jewish, ears, startling paradox, 'Blessed are ye poor . . . but woe unto you that are rich.'[1] At a later stage He astounded His apostles, so slow to grasp the tenour of His teaching, by the yet more startling declaration that it was easier for a camel to go through the eye of a needle (and He meant the eye of a needle) than for a rich man to enter the Kingdom of Heaven. Well might His puzzled disciples exclaim, 'Who then *can* be saved?';[2] for it had never crossed their minds that the rich were not highest in the estimation of their Maker.

All this would in any case have sufficed to win Christ a great

[1] Luke vi. 21 and 24.   [2] Matthew xix. 25

number of devoted followers and to convince thousands that a
new day had dawned. But there were two other factors that made
His impact greater still.

The first was His miracles. These have been a stumbling-block
to many in the last two or three generations. But to Christ's own
contemporaries and to Christians in most ages they were something of tremendous import. The number recorded in the gospels,
both synoptic and Johannine, is immense: they form a large part
of the narrative, and cannot possibly be removed from their
context without tearing the whole fabric to pieces. Attempts to
explain them away are unconvincing and in many cases ludicrous:
the evidence for them is overwhelming. Nor did miracles cease
when Christ himself departed from this world. As He had foretold, the apostles and other believers performed them in His
name, and as the very early writers quoted by Eusebius inform us,
they continued right into the second century of the Christian era.
As we shall see shortly, we have reason to believe that the facts
were known to Josephus. Not that the miracles of Jesus persuaded him to be a Christian. Christ had himself declared that
there were some whom nothing could convince: 'If they hear not
Moses and the prophets, neither will they be persuaded if one rise
from the dead.'[1]

But on many the effect of the miracles was very great. Mention
has already been made of the miracle that resulted in an attempt to
make Jesus king. John, as readers of the Revised Version know,
always calls them 'signs', because they opened people's eyes to
what lay behind them, and to the true nature of their author. Thus
the result of His first miracle at Cana was that 'His disciples
believed on him.'[2] So too Mark records that after the stilling of the
waters they asked each other 'Who then is this, that even the wind
and the sea obey him?';[3] and we read in the third gospel how
Peter, overwhelmed by the wonder of the great draught of fishes,
fell on his knees with the agonized but salutary cry: 'Depart from
me, for I am a sinful man, O Lord.'[4] It is not to be doubted that
very many were drawn irresistibly to Christ when they saw His
wonderful works. All must have seen that they were never done

[1] Luke xvi. 31.   [2] John ii. 11.   [3] Mark iv. 41.   [4] Luke v. 8.

as a demonstration of power: some must have seen in them proof
of a love they had never dreamt of.

The second factor was the recognition that the 'carpenter' of
Nazareth was not just an inspired teacher—there had been many
such—but something far greater. He was the Son of David, the
Christ of prophecy: some even hailed him as the Son of God. Such
appellations must have swelled the number of His supporters:
what could more appeal to a patriotic people than the belief that
here was the divinely appointed king who was to overcome their
enemies and restore their liberties? Of course, when this conception of His nature and purpose proved mistaken, when the
Roman governor treated His claims with amused contempt, and
to appease a clamorous mob inflicted on Him the punishment of a
common criminal, when all hope of deliverance from their
enemies and the inauguration of an age of glory had disappeared,
the disillusionment and revulsion of feeling must have been most
damaging to the Christian cause, and many adherents were no
doubt lost for ever. But those who had eyes to see realized that
there were other prophecies that had been fulfilled in Him.
Isaiah had spoken of a Suffering Servant, led as a lamb to the
slaughter, and the Baptist had hailed Jesus as the Lamb of God that
took away the sin of the world. At last they understood, and as we
may read in the early speeches recorded in the Acts (Revised
Version), the first Christians recognized Him as that Servant and
as that Lamb.[1]

What claims did Jesus make for himself? As we know, He
refused to let His enthusiastic supporters make Him king, and
later assured Pilate that His Kingdom was not of this world.[2] It is
therefore no surprise to find that though the title Son of David
was often applied to Him He never applied it to himself, no doubt
because of its political implications. Furthermore, He went out of
His way to deprecate its use by putting to His opponents the
spontaneous question: 'If David in the Spirit calleth him Lord,
how is he his son?'[3] This does not mean that He did not wish to
be regarded as the Messiah or Christ. He informed the many-

[1] Isaiah liii., John i. 29, Acts iii. 13 and viii. 32.
[2] John xviii. 36.   [3] Matthew xxii. 45.

husbanded Samaritan that He *was* the Messiah, and on very many occasions allowed himself to be called the Christ without protest. On one famous occasion Peter declared that He was the Christ, the Son of the living God, and received the highest commendation for so doing. Jesus from time to time applied each of these titles to himself, but He much preferred to speak of himself as the Son of Man. No error could be more glaring than to suppose that this was a sign of modesty or humility, or a way of emphasizing His humanity. The truth is the exact opposite; for He was claiming to be the One foretold by Daniel, and with much greater fullness in the book of Enoch—apocryphal perhaps, but often alluded to in the New Testament and once directly quoted. That One was the divine Judge who was some day to descend from heaven in majesty to hold the final assize. So far from saying that He was not the Messiah, Christ was declaring in season and out of season that He was something far greater and more terrible. If with that in mind we read again some of the sentences in which this title occurs, we shall find them take on a new meaning. 'Foxes have holes, but the Judge of all mankind has nowhere to lay his head'; 'You will not have gone through the cities of this little country before the Final Judge appears'; 'At a moment when you least expect it your Judge will confront you'; 'The divine Judge will take his seat on his glorious throne'.[1] It is not to be wondered at that, though Jesus continually called himself by this name, there was only one man who ever dared use it of Him, and he paid for that daring with his life.

That this was His favourite title for himself must have been known to everyone. It is clear also that although on a particular occasion Peter was told not to broadcast his knowledge of who Jesus was, the two titles which Peter had applied to Him were not kept secret. When our Lord's death was followed by startling physical occurrences, the centurion (who was, of course, not a Roman but probably a Samaritan) exclaimed 'Truly this was the Son of God', meaning 'He undoubtedly was what he claimed to be.'[2] If we go back a page or two in Matthew's account we find a

[1] Matthew viii. 20, x. 23, xxiv. 44 and xix. 28.
[2] Matthew xxvii. 43 and 54.

vivid picture of our Lord as He stood before the president of the Sanhedrin. Here the three great titles are brought together. Two of them—the two used by Peter in his great confession, the two which John declared to be the great essentials of Christian belief by which we may have life in His name—were known to Caiaphas already. The third, deliberately employed by the Prisoner and its implications made explicit, had an electrifying effect on the court. 'The high priest said to him: "I order you in the name of the living God to tell us whether you are the Christ, the Son of God." Jesus replied: "It is as you say; but I tell you this—very soon you will see the Son of Man invested with all the majesty of God, and coming on the clouds." Then the high priest tore his robe and said: "That is a blasphemous utterance! Why should we bother with any more witnesses? You have heard the blasphemy: give your verdict." They replied: "He deserves the death sentence."' Jesus had refused to defend himself, but in the presence of that murderous throng He unflinchingly proclaimed what He was, and in effect told Caiaphas: 'You judge me now, but soon I shall judge you, and from my judgment there will be no appeal.' They understood Him well enough, as some four years later they were to understand the first of His martyrs when he told them that the One whom they had betrayed and murdered was the Son of Man, revealed to him now in all the glory of God. The result was the same. Once they had torn their robes and crucified Jesus: now they stopped their ears and stoned Stephen.[1]

What happened in the interval between the crucifixion of Jesus and the birth of Josephus to the disciples who retained their faith in the claims of their Master is so well known that we need to do no more at this point than refresh our memories. When the One of whom they had expected so much was laid in His grave, their hopes were buried with Him. When two days later they were amazed to find the tomb empty, and saw Him, then and many times more in the weeks that followed, alive and triumphant, they were filled with joyous expectancy, and waited as they were bidden till at Pentecost the promise which John had made at the very beginning and Jesus had confirmed with almost the last

[1] Matthew xxvi. 63-66 and Acts vii. 56-59.

words spoken before His ascension was fulfilled, and they were baptized with the Holy Ghost and with fire. The effect was tremendous, and these timid men who in His moment of danger had one and all left their Master and fled, and whose leader had three times denied any acquaintance with Him, were filled with such extraordinary courage that they were ready to face all danger and torment, and to glory in the privilege of sharing His sufferings. They knew that He was indeed the Christ, the Suffering Servant of God, once led as a lamb to the slaughter but now exalted to the heavens. They delighted to call Him 'the Lord', giving Him the title which the universally read Greek version of the Scriptures had substituted for the sacred name Jehovah; and they openly addressed prayers to Him.

Their confidence and boldness were shown in the fearlessness with which in the presence of great crowds or powerful and hostile officials they proclaimed their faith in their risen Lord, the Prince of Life, and denounced those who had brought about His death. Listen to the last sentence of Peter's speech at Pentecost, with its pungent conclusion: 'So let all the people of Israel know for certain that God has made him both Lord and Christ—this Jesus—whom YOU CRUCIFIED!'[1] No wonder his hearers were 'pricked to the heart', and meekly accepted his demand that they should repent. Nor was Peter alone in his audacity. When Stephen the deacon was brought before the Sanhedrin and accused of threatening to destroy the Temple, his judges saw his face 'as it had been the face of an angel'. How strangely these words have been misunderstood! In what sentimental tones they are read aloud in church, as if this heroic man had the soft, feminine features which the word 'angel' conjures up in popular imagination! The biblical angel is a strong, masculine, and awe-inspiring emissary of God, ready to rebuke the doubting Zacharias, to smite the presumptuous Agrippa, or to annihilate the host of Sennacherib. That is what the astonished councillors saw in the face of the protomartyr, who proceeded to lay bare their age-old iniquities, and with words of fire to brand them as stiff-necked and uncircumcised in heart and ears, betrayers and murderers of

[1] Acts ii. 36.

The Righteous One, and breakers of the law ordained by angels.[1]

Such courage and such eloquence were quickly rewarded. The speech of Peter brought in some three thousand converts who were baptized that very day, and no doubt rapidly conveyed the message to their homes in many places far afield; for not all his hearers lived in Jerusalem or Judaea: some of them came from Arabia, Parthia, Media, Elam, and Mesopotamia; from Cappadocia, Pontus, Asia, Phrygia, and Pamphylia; from Egypt and Libya; from Crete; from Rome itself. In Jerusalem, where the opposition to Christ had been most bitter, and where those who had always denied the possibility of any resurrection were in power and feared that they would lose that power if their beliefs were proved false, the number of Christians increased rapidly, eloquence and courage being assisted by the ability of some at least of both the apostles and the deacons to heal the sick and impotent in the name of Jesus.

When Stephen died, his witness produced two most important results. The first was immediate: the church in Jerusalem was so violently persecuted that most of its members were dispersed, to make converts elsewhere. For the first time but not for the last it became evident that, as Tertulian says, *Semen est sanguis Christianorum.* Philip the Deacon went down to Sebaste, where his preaching and his 'signs' met with instant success, so that the two chief apostles were sent from Jerusalem to lay their hands on the numerous converts, and did not return till they had preached the good news in many Samaritan villages. From henceforth, as far as the Christians were concerned, the barrier between Judaea and Samaria was down for ever. Philip's next task was to give the message of salvation to Queen Candace's eunuch, who conveyed it to the distant land of Ethiopia where was established one of the oldest surviving churches of Christendom. Finally Philip went to Caesarea, where Jews were in a minority and, as Josephus tells us, at the mercy of the hostile Syrians.[2]

The second result of Stephen's witness was most unexpected and most far-reaching. A young man, a rigid Pharisee, who had watched the whole scene, was so impressed by the martyr's

[1] Acts vi. 15 and vii. 51-53.   [2] Acts viii.

demeanour that he found it desperately hard to kick against the goad, and in a vain effort to stifle his growing awareness that he was fighting a losing battle flung himself into a violent struggle to exterminate this swiftly-growing threat to Jewish orthodoxy. He devastated the Church, flinging men and women alike into prison. Then, perhaps thinking that his work there was complete, he set off to do the same thing in Damascus, which, though far outside Palestine, must presumably have been second only to Jerusalem as a centre of Christian activity. But as a result of what happened on that memorable journey, what he did in Damascus was not to assail the Church but to accept baptism in all humility and, regardless of the contempt and hatred that his change of front must bring upon him, to face the Jews in their synagogues and confound them by his forceful demonstrations that Jesus whom he had persecuted was the Christ, the Son of God. His acceptance of the Faith was complete, and he was soon by his energy and enterprise, his spiritual and practical wisdom, and his heroic endurance, to do more for the propagation of that Faith than any other man before or since. But that work belongs to a later period, extending through the first thirty years of Josephus' life. The scope of this chapter is limited to the ten years before Josephus was born; so for the present we will say no more about God's chosen vessel.[1]

What has Josephus to tell us about all this? Disappointingly little. For that some reasons have already been suggested, and other suggestions will be made at the end of the book, when we come to consider the origin and authenticity of certain passages dealing with persons who figure in the New Testament narrative. For the present we will content ourselves with seeing what is stated about them in his two historical works.

His accounts of Pontius Pilate, Caiaphas, Antipas, and Herodias do add to our knowledge of this unpleasant quartet. Pilate, whom Tiberius had appointed procurator 'with the deliberate intention of abolishing the Jewish customs', did what none of his predecessors had ever done: under cover of darkness he sent into Jerusalem the *signa* of his infantry, on which were effigies of the

[1] Acts ix. 1-22.

Emperor. Furious at this flouting of their Law an enormous crowd rushed off to Caesarea, seventy miles away, to beg Pilate to remove the idolatrous objects. On his refusal they lay for five days prone round his house. Then he called them into the Stadium to hear his answer, ordered the soldiers to surround them with drawn swords, and threatened to cut them to pieces unless they accepted the images. At this they prostrated themselves again, prepared to die rather than accept them, and the astonished Pilate gave in.

Later he gave fresh offence by drawing on the Temple treasure to pay for an aqueduct. When he visited Jerusalem he was shouted down, but on a prearranged signal soldiers disguised as civilians attacked the people with cudgels, and in the resulting panic many were trampled to death.

Finally he overreached himself. He sent a mixed force of horse and foot to attack a harmless concourse of Samaritans, killed some of them, and executed all the more distinguished prisoners. Whereupon the Samaritans complained to Vitellius, Pilate's superior in Antioch, who sent Marcellus to supersede him and packed him off to Rome to explain his conduct to the Emperor. When he arrived, Tiberius was dead and Caligula was on the throne. Various traditions relate that he was banished, that he committed suicide, that he was beheaded by Nero, and that he became a Christian: Josephus, unfortunately, sheds no light on his fate; but he tells us that when Vitellius expelled him from the country he at the same time took action against Caiaphas, depriving him of his high-priestly office.

Concerning Antipas Josephus gives a full account of one incident which, with its sequel, falls within the period we are now discussing. Antipas had two brothers called Philip. One was the mild-mannered tetrarch of Trachonitis, whose death is recorded by Josephus as having occurred in A.D. 34. The other was a private citizen, who lived at Rome with his wife Herodias, daughter of that Aristobulus who had been strangled by his father, Herod the King. When Antipas was on a visit to Rome and was Philip's guest, he persuaded the wife of his host and brother to marry him as soon as it could be arranged. But the tetrarch's own wife was not deceived: she was the daughter of the Arabian king Aretas, and by cajoling her husband into sending her to Machaerus on the border of his dominions she contrived to reach her father at Petra, and to inform him of the plot. He, enraged, sent an army which joined battle with the forces of Antipas and destroyed them. Antipas appealed to Tiberius, in whose favour he stood high, and Tiberius responded by ordering Vitellius to bring Aretas to Rome, dead or alive. Vitellius marched south with his legions; but while he lingered in Jerusalem he received news of the Emperor's death, and cancelled the expedition.

Josephus, who was always ready to attribute misfortunes to the vengeance of God and to name the offence which had called down retribution, interrupts this narrative to mention that the Jews, or some of them, were of the opinion that the destruction of Herod Antipas's army was the deserved punishment of his treatment of John, known as the Baptist, a good man who exhorted the Jews to practise virtue and piety and drew crowds to his baptism. Herod, who was of a suspicious temper, and feared that a man with such influence might provoke a rebellion, imprisoned John in his castle at Machaerus and there put him to death. There is no mention here of John's denunciation of Herod's morals, of the hatred of Herodias and the use she made of Salome, of the platter and the headsman's axe.

That is all that we are told about John in *Antiquities*, and those who study *The Jewish War* in Whiston's translation or Traill's will find no mention of him there. But readers who consult the Loeb edition or the translation in Penguin Classics will find a number of extra passages headed *The Slavonic Additions*. These will be discussed later, along with the passage quoted above. For the moment we need only take a quick glance at the two longish passages that refer to John; for so it seems, though he is not named in either. The first states that soon after the death of Herod (when John was in fact still a small child) a man of wild appearance, clad in animal's hair, called on the Jews to abandon their evil ways and be baptized in Jordan, and promised that a king would come to deliver them. Brought before Archelaus he claimed to be called by the Spirit of God, and defied his judges when threatened with torture. He was then allowed to resume his work on the other side of Jordan. The second passage tells a story (which could only be true if the Tetrarch Philip died years earlier than the date given in *Antiquities*) of how the same man correctly interpreted one of Philip's nightmares. Philip (here confused with Philip of Rome) died, and Antipas married his wife Herodias. Whereupon he was fiercely assailed for his breach of the Law by the same 'strange creature', who alone dared to face him, and told of his impending exile and death. Herod ordered him to be flogged, but the warnings were repeated until Herod had his tormentor killed. The passage adds that he had never touched bread or meat, wine or strong drink.

Far more important are the statements concerning our Lord. Here the case is the same as before: we find one passage in *Antiquities* in which He is named, and others among the *Slavonic Additions* in most of which He is not. According to the first of these, in the time of Pilate Jesus appeared, 'a very able man, if man is the right word; for he was a worker of miracles, a teacher of those who were glad to hear the truth, and he won over many Jews and many Gentiles. This man was Christ; and when at the prompting of our leading men Pilate had sentenced him to the cross, his original adherents remained faithful; for two days later they saw him alive again. . . . And the group called Christians after him is not extinct even now.'

The first of the five passages to be found among the *Slavonic Additions* is similar to the foregoing but very much longer. Starting with the same doubt as to the appropriateness of the word 'man', it goes on to mention marvellous cures, a new attitude to Sabbath observance, the rejection of popular demands that he should destroy the Romans and make himself king, the machinations of the high priest, an appearance before Pilate, which owing to the healing of the procurator's sick wife ended in an acquittal, the later acceptance by Pilate of a heavy bribe (an allegation almost certainly true), and crucifixion carried out with his permission by the Jews themselves. The second passage relates how the miracle-worker's followers convinced many that he was still alive, and worked such marvellous 'signs' that for a time even the procurators dared not touch them. Next we are told of a placard hung up outside the Sacred Precincts, announcing that Jesus, the king who never reigned, had been crucified for prophesying the destruction of the Temple. Then we have an account of the rending of the Veil that followed the crucifixion, and of the impossibility of explaining away the resurrection stories. Finally we are told that while some referred an old oracle about world-ruler to Herod, others to Vespasian, there were some who referred it to 'the crucified miracle-worker Jesus'.

These passages may or may not be from the pen of Josephus. Apart from them he has told us very little about any of the characters in the gospel drama, and has done almost nothing to confirm or refute the New Testament account. But how much space did he give to *all* the events that happened in Palestine during the ten momentous years to which this long chapter has been devoted? In the *War* one small page; in *Antiquities* six!

CHAPTER 7

Josephus Child and Man

WE HAVE NOW REACHED A BOUNDARY LINE. ON ONE SIDE LIES the immeasurable period stretching from Creation to the death of Tiberius, all of which Josephus was to cover in his immense historical survey, the *Antiquities*, drawing his information from every written source on which he could lay his hands. On the other lies the tiny period of sixty years or less that he was to record on the basis of his own memories and perhaps diaries, and to some extent the writings of others who had witnessed the same exciting and appalling events as he himself. We must in the course of this book survey his whole life against the background of contemporary history: in this chapter we shall confine our attention to the years of his nonage. For our knowledge of his life and character we depend wholly on his own writings; which is unfortunate, since in writing of himself he is anything but impartial, and is at all times defending himself against criticism. It was a general characteristic of Roman citizens to blow their own trumpet: witness the self-praise that Cicero, Horace, and even Paul bestowed upon themselves. And the most ardent admirer of Josephus would not claim that his *apologia* was objective. But as we have no other sources of information we must take his account as it stands.

In the preface to his earliest work he announces himself as Joseph son of Matthias, a Hebrew by race and a priest from Jerusalem. For the rest we must turn to what may have been his last work, the *Life*, or as we should say, *Autobiography*. In this he is so anxious to justify his conduct during the war that he devotes almost the whole of the work to a period of five years, and what he has to say of the first twenty-five years of his life occupies only two small pages. He was very proud of his ancestry; for in Jewish eyes a connection with the priesthood was evidence of an illustrious line, and his ancestors had belonged to the first and most famous of the twenty-four courses, and to the most distinguished of its subdivisions. On his mother's side he was of royal blood, as she was a Hasmonaean; and on his father's he could give all the names from his great-great-great-grandfather onwards. His father Matthias, though distinguished by his noble birth, was honoured still more for his high character, and was one of the best known men in Jerusalem. With such a pedigree, which could be verified from the public registers, he could snap his fingers at anyone who ran his family down.

He himself was born in the year of Caligula's accession and was brought up with an elder brother. He made rapid strides with his education, showing himself possessed of an exceptional memory and intelligence. At the age of about thirteen he won golden opinions by his devotion to book-learning, so that he was repeatedly called on to advise the chief priests and magistrates on legal points. When nearly sixteen he decided to see the various Jewish sects from the inside—the Pharisees, the Sadducees, and the Essenes—so that he might be in a position to choose the best. He subjected himself to discipline and strenuous exercises till he had passed through all three. But being still dissatisfied he became the enthusiastic disciple of an ascetic hermit named Bannus, with whom he spent three years. Then at the age of eighteen he returned to the City and adopted the Pharisaic way of life which, he tells his Greek and Roman readers, resembled the Stoic.

We have now arrived at the year 56, and must pause to consider what had been happening all this time in the world of Josephus. How much of what was going on attracted the attention of this clever schoolboy, this precocious exponent of the Law, this experimenter in religion and philosophy, this priestly Pharisee, we cannot tell; during his three years in the wilderness he may perhaps have lost touch with current affairs, but presumably he had spent the other fifteen or sixteen with his parents in Jerusalem. However, it would seem that when in *The Jewish War* he wrote his first account of these eighteen or nineteen years he had very little information at his disposal, for he got it all into eight small pages. If it be suggested that he was intentionally writing only a brief summary of events leading up to the critical years before the conflagration, and that nothing more was necessary to his purpose, the answer is that he had devoted eight times that number to the doings of King Herod, which were far less relevant to a work on the Jewish War. The simple explanation is that Josephus wrote with plenty of written material about Herod on his desk, and with very little about the sixty years that followed the accession of his sons. His later and longer work does add something to the information conveyed in those eight pages; but it is mostly about events outside Palestine, from Rome to Babylonia and Parthia, some fifty pages being taken up by the assassination of Caligula, told in minute detail. Josephus seems to have acquired few fresh data about events at home.

As we have already learnt from the *Life*, Josephus was born in the year of Caligula's accession. That monarch began his monstrous and mercifully brief reign on the 16th, or perhaps the 26th, of March, A.D. 37. Two other events of that year have also been mentioned—the arrival of Pontius Pilate in Rome some months after his expulsion by Vitellius, and the deposition of Caiaphas, whom the same governor turned out of office at the Passover Festival. A further event, which in the eyes of Josephus was very important, took place in Rome at almost the same time—the appointment of Agrippa to his first kingdom. Josephus took a keen interest both in this Agrippa, the grandson of Herod and brother of Herodias, and in his son Agrippa the Second, who was his personal friend. He was also keenly interested in all that happened at Rome, and evidently had plenty of written sources; for he was always glad to introduce scraps of Roman history, however irrelevant, into his shorter work, and much longer stretches into its much longer successor. Agrippa was a link between the two halves of Josephus' world, and he wrote about him at very great length, reporting *verbatim* many speeches that must have been delivered in private.

We must go back for a moment to the previous year. Agrippa, who seems to have been a most objectionable person, had for years lived at so extravagant a rate that he had been forced to depend on charity, to move from one place to another, and to borrow money right and left. Now he arrived at Capreae to pay court to the Emperor; and when Tiberius discovered that he was up to his eyes in debt and had absconded from Palestine for that reason, he turned him out. Nothing daunted, Agrippa borrowed from Peter to pay Paul; he went first to Antonia, mother of Claudius who was one day to mount the throne, and obtained from her the sum owing, then to a freedman who lent him three times that sum, and so enabled him both to repay Antonia and to purchase the friendship of Gaius Caligula, who was Tiberius' immediate heir. To cut a very long story very short, he then made the mistake of telling his new friend that he hoped Tiberius would soon leave the stage clear for him. This indiscreet remark was duly reported to the monarch, who clapped Agrippa in prison, and kept him rigorously confined till he himself made his final exit. Caligula did not forget the friend who had paid the penalty for flattering him: he released Agrippa and made him king over the lands which Philip had once ruled as tetrarch, and thither Agrippa, who was always happiest in Rome, repaired two years later.

His arrival had an unexpected result. He had been made king straightway; but his uncle Antipas, after ruling for forty-two years to the satisfaction of three emperors, was still only a tetrarch. This was too much for his consort. As Jezebel had once goaded Ahab, so this ambitious woman gave her cautious and easy-going husband no peace till he agreed to make the long journey to Rome and petition the Emperor to grant him the same title as his nephew. But Herodias had reckoned without Agrippa. It was nothing to him that she was his sister and Antipas his brother-in-law; so he too hurried off to Rome (or sent his freedman, if the second version of the story is correct), and charged the tetrarch with preparing to revolt against Rome. Caligula believed the story, and packed off husband and wife to Spain (or was it Gaul?). To crown the discomfiture of the banished pair, the property of Herodias and the dominions of her husband were alike made over to the man who had informed against them.

Caligula was already halfway through his short reign; but there was time enough left for him to cause an upheaval in Palestine.

Determined to be everywhere worshipped as a god, and completely blind to the danger of exacerbating such a stubborn people as the Jews, he ordered Vitellius' successor to march with an army to Jerusalem and set up a statue of himself in the Temple: if he encountered opposition he was to execute the objectors and enslave the rest of the people. Petronius set off from Antioch at the head of three legions and numerous allies, and marched rapidly to Ptolemais. The horrified Jews gathered in such formidable numbers to make their protest that he left the statue in the city and summoned the people with their leading men to a meeting at Tiberias. There he discussed the matter with them in the most reasonable way possible; and when arguments and threats proved equally unavailing he took the bold step of leading his forces back to Antioch and sending from there a letter in which he explained the situation to Caesar and urged him to cancel his instructions. Caligula replied with a threat to punish his audacious legate with death, but a month before the reply was delivered news reached Petronius that the tyrant had died by the hand of an assassin.

Agrippa, who less than four years before had been so closely associated with Caligula's accession, was already back in Rome, and he lost no time in putting the next emperor in his debt. He made himself the intermediary between the Senators, who had some hopes of recovering their ancient power, and Claudius, who was backed by the Praetorian Guard. He made several journeys between the two parties, till the question was settled by the Senate's own soldiers, who rushed off to join the winning side, followed by the panicking Senators themselves. Agrippa again reaped his reward: the grateful Claudius gave him Abilene, the region that had once belonged to Lysanias, with additional territory in the east and, most important of all, the countries that for thirty-five years had been governed by procurators, Judaea and Samaria. Agrippa's kingdom was now as big as his grandfather's had been, and wealth flowed into his treasury. He would have been no true Herod if he had not followed his grandfather's example and poured that wealth into grandiose building projects. 'He was', says Josephus, 'a great builder in many places, and he

paid a peculiar regard to the people of Berytus [Beirut], for he
erected a theatre for them, superior to many others of that sort,
both in sumptuousness and elegance, as also an amphitheatre,
built at vast expense; and besides these he built them baths and
porticoes, and spared for no costs in any of his edifices, to render
them both handsome and large. He also spent a great deal upon
their dedication, and exhibited shows upon them, and brought
thither musicians of all sorts, and such as made the most delightful
music of the greatest variety. He also showed his magnificence
upon the theatre, in his great number of gladiators; and there it
was that he exhibited the several antagonists, in order to please the
spectators; no fewer indeed than seven hundred men to fight with
seven hundred other men; and allotted all the malefactors he had
for this exercise, that both the malefactors might receive their
punishment, and that this operation of war might be a recreation
in peace. And thus were these criminals all destroyed at once.'
(Whiston.)

How truly Roman! How utterly un-Jewish! and how dearly
the strange Jew who wrote this account loved it all, or at least
hardened his heart against any feeling of disgust or pity.

At Jerusalem the King's passion for building found different
expression. He began the construction of new fortifications to
enclose an area as big as the existing city. His wall ran north from
the Temple Enclosure for half a mile, then west for a much greater
distance, and finally south till it joined the battlements of Herod's
palace. These fortifications were so huge that had they been
finished, Josephus tells us in the *War*, it would have been useless
for the Romans to attempt a siege, and the City could never have
been captured. It would in truth have been difficult to undermine
or batter down a wall built of bonded stones measuring thirty feet
by fifteen, rising, when later the Jews had hastily completed it, to
a height of over thirty-seven feet, and surmounted by ninety
great towers. But Agrippa was not permitted to finance and
supervise the later stages: before the wall reached its full height
his three years' reign came to an abrupt end. Or, as Josephus
tells us later in the same book (perhaps drawing on a different
authority, for his childhood memories would hardly avail

him), he had only laid the foundations when he halted the work through a sudden realization that if the Emperor saw those massive ramparts he would suspect that an insurrection was intended.

The end of Agrippa was indeed sudden. As in the *War* we are told merely that he died at Caesarea, it would seem that at the time of writing Josephus had no further information. In *Antiquities*, however, the story is told luridly and in full, and we may surmise that it was drawn from the same source as furnished the writer with so many details of Agrippa's tumultuous career. Josephus, of course, did not know that to ingratiate himself with the powerful Sadducaic oligarchy the King had executed St James and imprisoned St Peter. But he did know that he had been in Jerusalem for the Passover and had shown due interest in the Temple ceremonies. He also knew that he was equally at home in ceremonies consecrated to the worship of the Roman Emperor. Agrippa went to Caesarea to celebrate games in Caesar's honour, and at sunrise he entered the theatre clad from head to foot in silver, which shone so dazzlingly in the brilliant light that the spectators acclaimed him as a god. A more prudent man would have feared nemesis, but he accepted the 'impious flattery'. Then 'he saw an owl sitting on a rope over his head, and at once understood that it was a messenger of evil'. He was then seized with such violent pains in heart and bowels that he was hurriedly carried into the palace, and while the crowd prayed and lamented outside he lay for five days writhing in agony till at last he died, at the early age of fifty-three.

Now this story presents us with a difficult but fascinating problem. Readers who remember the equally vivid account furnished by St Luke in the twelfth chapter of Acts will see at once that, while there are significant differences between his account and Josephus's, the two are fundamentally in agreement and so remarkably alike that they can hardly be independent. Did Josephus copy from Luke? or Luke from Josephus? or did both draw on a common source? The first suggestion is unlikely, for nowhere else does Josephus show any sign of being acquainted with Luke's work. The second may safely be ruled out; for

Josephus did not publish *Antiquities* until the year 93, and Luke can hardly have written as late as that, even if he was still alive. The third seems probable; but whence arose the discrepancies between the two accounts? The problem is further complicated by the fact that Josephus' version is reproduced in Book 2 of Eusebius' *Ecclesiastical History* or *Story of the Church*, but with one important sentence in a form much more easily reconciled with Luke's version. As we have no grounds for accusing Eusebius of tampering with the text, we are left wondering whether his reading or the accepted one is correct; for our manuscripts of Eusebius are just as old as our manuscripts of Josephus, and the copy of *Antiquities* that lay on Eusebius' desk was at least six, and perhaps more than eight centuries earlier than the oldest that we possess. We must leave the problem at that: anyone who wishes to pursue it further will find it discussed in any standard edition of Eusebius.

The deceased monarch left three daughters and one son, called Agrippa like himself, who being only sixteen—nine or ten years older than Josephus—was judged too young to succeed his father and remained with his patron Claudius in Rome. The short-lived kingdom therefore reverted to Roman rule, and never again was there a King of the Jews. Claudius sent out Cuspius Fadus as procurator, not, like his predecessors, of Judaea and Samaria only, but of the whole Herodian territory. He had been in office for little more than a year when two events occurred, both of which serve to link *Antiquities* with Acts.

The first was the famine that caused such misery in Judaea. St Luke tells us that the Prophet Agabus foretold this, with the result that Barnabas and Paul were sent to convey to the presbyters in Jerusalem for the relief of distress within the Christian community there the generous contributions made by their brethren in Antioch.[1] Josephus tells us at immense length how the Jews in Jerusalem, some of whom were dying for want of food, were relieved by the arrival of a great quantity of corn and dried figs, presented by a woman who had recently adopted the Jewish religion. This was Helena, the Queen-Mother of Adiabene

[1] Acts xi. 27-30.

in the neighbourhood of ancient Nineveh. Her son Izates had also become a Jew and had insisted on being circumcised. Perhaps this conversion, besides bringing welcome relief to the starving people of Jerusalem, may have done something to clean up the Augean filth of royal morals in Adiabene. For Izates was the child of a union between Helena and her brother, and himself acknowledged the paternity of forty-eight children.

The second event was concerned with a rebel named Theudas. Luke tells us that at a meeting of the Sanhedrin held in the very early days of the Jerusalem church the Rabbi Gamaliel reminded his hearers that during, or before, the census of Quirinius, Theudas had risen, 'giving himself out to be somebody', and had collected about four hundred followers: he had been killed, and they had been dispersed.[1] Josephus tells us that while Fadus was procurator an impostor named Theudas persuaded a huge number of people to carry their goods and chattels to the Jordan, which being a prophet he would divide for them by a mere command. Many were taken in, but the cavalry of Fadus suddenly attacked them, killed or captured large numbers, and cut off Theudas' head. Now the census took place in A.D. 6 or 7, and Fadus did not arrive in Judaea till late in 44; so those scholars who regard Josephus as a historian and deny the title to Luke accuse the latter of inventing the speech of Gamaliel and putting an anachronism into his mouth. It will be noticed, however, that there is no great similarity between the two stories apart from the name Theudas, which was nearly as common as the habit of following self-trumpeting upstarts, and we cannot be certain that the two incidents are the same. Nor have we any independent evidence that Josephus, writing half a century—perhaps nearer a whole century—after the event, was correct in his attribution of it to the time of Fadus. The two accounts were brought together by Eusebius, who failed to perceive the discrepancy, and I would again refer readers who may be interested to the editions of that author's work.

After two years as procurator Fadus was succeeded by Tiberius Alexander, whose period of office was equally short: we shall

[1] Acts v. 33-36.

meet him again when he, a Jew, appears as the chief assistant of
Titus in his destruction of the Jews. He was faced with yet another
rising, led this time by the two sons of Judas, the Galilaean or
Gaulonite who has already appeared in our pages, and was
mentioned with indisputable accuracy in the speech of Gamaliel.
He disposed of them by the usual Roman method, crucifixion.
His retirement in the year 48 coincided with the death of Herod,
the brother of Agrippa and King of Chalcis, a small area in the
valley of the Orontes which separates Lebanon from Anti-
Lebanon. The younger Agrippa now appeared on the stage. Aged
twenty or twenty-one, he received the crown of Chalcis from
Claudius, who was as devoted to him as he had been to his father.
Agrippa was to fulfil a difficult role in the next twenty years,
always subservient to Rome but under an obligation to the
Jewish subjects of his late father.

The two procurators of Judaea, Fadus and Alexander, like the
legates of Syria, Vitellius, and Petronius, a few years previously,
knew how to handle the Jews without provoking them: they
left native customs severely alone and preserved the precarious
peace. But with Alexander's successor Cumanus trouble began,
and some of it at least Josephus, now eleven years old, must have
seen for himself. It was not all the fault of Cumanus, unless we
are to hold a commander responsible for every breach of discipline by his subordinates. The Jews had gathered in their tens of
thousands for the Passover ceremonies at Jerusalem. As always,
the garrison of Antonia mounted guard to keep order on that
always dangerous occasion. One soldier wrecked everything. 'He
pulled back his garment, and cowering down in an indecent
manner, turned his breech to the Jews, and spake such words as
you might expect upon such a posture.' Whiston's version is
quaint, but he missed Josephus' meaning altogether. St John
Thackeray understood him better, and translates: 'Raising his
robe, he stooped in an indecent attitude so as to turn his backside
to the Jews, and made a noise in keeping with his posture.' Had
not Horace's friend, some ninety years before, suggested that they
should amuse themselves by insulting the Jews in Rome in exactly
the same vulgar manner? The sequel was disastrous. The infuri-

ated crowd appealed to Cumanus to punish the offender, while the younger men pelted the rest of the soldiers with stones. The procurator sent for reinforcements, whose arrival caused an immediate panic. The Jews fled from the Temple, and in their frantic struggle to escape thirty thousand, we are told, were trampled or crushed to death.

Other calamities followed. On the highroad about eleven miles from Jerusalem a slave of Caesar was robbed of all his baggage by a gang of bandits. Cumanus held the people of the district responsible, and sent a force to arrest them all. In one village a soldier found a copy of the Law and tore it to pieces. Enraged beyond measure, the people ran in their thousands to Caesarea and so frightened Cumanus that he ordered the wretched man to be beheaded. For the time being the people were appeased. But trouble flared up again when the murder of a Galilaean as he passed through Samaria to attend the Feast brought swarms of Galilaeans to the spot, bent on avenging him. Their leaders appealed to Cumanus to intervene before it was too late, but the Samaritans had bribed him and he did not lift a finger to help. Furious crowds then poured out of Jerusalem, led by Eleazar, a bandit chief, and swooped upon Samaritan villages, bent on slaughter and plunder. Cumanus now took action, bringing in his infantry and arming the Samaritans. Many Jews were killed or captured: most of the rest were persuaded by the Jerusalem magistrates to disperse to their homes, but many turned to banditry and plundered right and left. Seeing the hopelessness of trying to get justice from Cumanus, both Samaritans and Jews sent ambassadors to Tyre, where the governor of Syria, Quadratus, happened to be at the time. Quadratus promised to take action in due course, and moving to Caesarea proceeded to crucify all Cumanus' Jewish prisoners, to behead eighteen other people, and to despatch to Rome not only the leading men from Jerusalem and Samaria, but Cumanus and his subordinate Celer as well. They all appeared before Claudius, and Agrippa, who was in Rome as usual, not only acted as advocate for the Jews but induced the Emperor's wife Agrippina to put pressure on him. The result was what might have been expected. Claudius found

the Samaritans guilty, executed their three chief men, banished
Cumanus, and sent Celer to Jerusalem for the Jews to torture,
drag round the City, and decapitate. Did Josephus, now a boy of
fourteen, watch this edifying spectacle?

A difficult situation faced Antonius Felix when in 52 he was
sent to clear up the mess left by Cumanus. He had once been a
slave, for he was brother to Pallas, the Emperor's freedman and
favourite, who secured for him the post and enabled him to
retain it for seven or eight years. He had reason to maintain good
relations with his northern neighbour, whose dominions Claudius
had greatly enlarged by the addition of the old tetrarchies of
Philip and Lysanias; for Drusilla, the lovely wife of Felix, was
Agrippa's sister. Like Antipas he had coaxed another man's wife
into forsaking her husband. The bonds between him and his
brother-in-law were strengthened when he gave the name of
Agrippa to Drusilla's child (who later perished in the eruption of
Vesuvius). We know from Roman sources that Felix was mean,
profligate, and cruel, and the bloodthirsty severity which he
exercised caused the Jews to send protests to Rome. These, however, went unheeded; for the influence of his powerful brother
was not diminished by the change which, two years after the
appointment of Felix, took place at the centre of power, where
Claudius, who in his final experiment in matrimony had in the
best Herodian fashion wedded his niece Agrippina, was poisoned
by that lady in order to secure the throne for his great-nephew,
stepson, and son-in-law, Nero.

For the time being Felix' drastic methods produced some
semblance of order in Palestine. He captured Eleazar, who had
begun his career of banditry twenty years before, and sent him
with a large section of his gang to Rome. Many others were
crucified, and villagers without number who had co-operated
with them were also punished. But no sooner was quiet restored
in the countryside than trouble broke out in the City. The streets
of Jerusalem were made unsafe, even in broad daylight, by men
whom Josephus calls by the Latin name *sicarii*. Carrying small
daggers concealed in their clothing these assassins mingled with
the festival crowds, and after stabbing their victims melted into

the throng of would-be avengers and escaped detection. Their first target was the high priest Jonathan, and similar murders became a daily occurrence, filling the citizens with terror and making them suspicious of their closest friends.

No less pernicious were the impostors and pseudo-prophets who, to bring about a revolution, led the City mob out into the desolate regions of Judaea, there to be cut to pieces by the soldiers of Felix. The climax of this upsurge of madness came when an Egyptian arrived who posed as a seer, and persuaded thirty thousand of his credulous victims to go by a roundabout route through the wild country and assemble on the Mount of Olives. There this would-be Joshua assured them that at his command the walls of the City would fall down, enabling him to enter in triumph with them as his bodyguard, and overwhelm the Roman garrison. But Felix, who knew all about it, did not wait for this to happen, but led out his cavalry and infantry and attacked the helpless mass, killing four hundred and capturing or scattering the rest. The Egyptian himself escaped and was never seen again.

The events recorded in these last three paragraphs are related in the *War* and *Antiquities* in varying terms but with very little difference in the substance. Perhaps Josephus was drawing not on written sources but on his memory of what he saw and heard at the time. For though this was the period of his studies under Bannus, we need not assume that he remained in the wilderness throughout the three years, or that he was ever out of touch with the City.

Before we conclude this chapter we must for the third time try to bring Josephus' account into relation with St Luke's.

Not long after the incidents recounted above, the Apostle of the Gentiles visited Jerusalem for the last time. He was soon in trouble with the unbelieving Jews, from whose violent hands he had to be rescued by the Roman garrison. When the soldiers had carried him up the stairs and were on the point of taking him into their barracks Paul asked leave to address their commander, who replied in astonishment: 'Do you speak Greek? Surely you must be the Egyptian who some time ago whipped up a revolt and led out into the wild country the four thousand Sicarians?' Like Josephus St Luke uses the hellenized Latin name. Like Josephus he implies that the Egyptian was still alive but his whereabouts unknown. But unlike Josephus he does not exaggerate the size of the Egyptian's following.[1]

[1] Acts xxi. 33-38.

CHAPTER 8

Ten Uneasy Years

SUCH WAS THE TUMULTUOUS STATE OF AFFAIRS IN PALESTINE AT
the beginning of the ten-year period that was to end in A.D. 66
with a violent clash between Jews and Romans, a clash which for
the moment brought a startling victory to the Jews, but which
brought in its train the destruction of that unhappy nation. Over
the countryside roamed armed bandits, plundering, destroying,
and holding honest men to ransom. Jews and Samaritans were at
enmity, Jews and Syrians in murderous conflict. In the Holy City
assassins lurked, and no man knew whether he would live to see
another sunrise. The Jewish authorities were powerless to restore
order: the Roman governors had neither the will nor the understanding. At Antioch was the *legatus*, clothed with the Emperor's
authority and backed by Roman legions, the most powerful
military force in that part of the Empire. He exercised direct rule
over Syria, and was ultimately responsible for all its neighbours as
far as the frontier of Egypt. At Caesarea Stratonis was the procurator, ruler of Galilee and Peraea, Samaria and Judaea, with
cohorts of Syrians and Samaritans to enforce his desires. At
Caesarea Philippi, now renamed Neronias by the time-serving
Agrippa, that monarch reigned over Chalcis, Abilene, Trachonitis, and Ituraea. He was not a Jew and he had no political
authority in Palestine; but he had been given the right to depose
the high priest and appoint another—a right that he exercised
again and again—and from time to time he occupied the Hasmonaean palace in the middle of Jerusalem, accompanied by his
sister Bernice, with whom his relations were believed to be
incestuous. She was later to forsake two husbands, and after a
brief period as mistress of Vespasian to captivate the heart of his
son Titus.

Typical of the disorders and misery of the time was a violent disturbance that broke out at Caesarea under the nose of Felix. The Jews claimed the city as theirs on the doubtful plea that its founder, Herod the King, had been a Jew. The Syrians retorted that there had not been a single Jew in the old town of Strato's Tower before Herod rebuilt it, and that the statues and temples which he had erected proved it to have been meant for 'Greeks'. The two sides came to blows and pelted each other with stones: there were daily battles in which the 'Roman' forces—recruited in Syria—lent their weight against the Jews. The magistrates intervened, and arrests, whippings, and imprisonments followed. When the Jews seemed to be getting the upper hand in the fighting, Felix himself intervened and sent in his armed soldiers, who killed a large number and pillaged their homes, without, however, bringing the rioting to an end.

It was shortly after this that Nero recalled Felix to Rome and sent out as his successor Porcius Festus. It will be remembered that the Apostle Paul had been confined at Caesarea for two years by Felix, who, typical Roman that he was, had vainly hoped to persuade the stubborn prisoner to purchase his release with a bribe; and that Paul being now brought before Festus made his dramatic appeal to Caesar, and later, when Agrippa and his sister had been invited to hear his defence and advise the puzzled governor, retold in all its wonder the story of his conversion.[1] Luke, who had so mercilessly exposed the venality and indecision of Felix, makes no complaint against his successor. Nor does Josephus find any fault with him: he praises the vigour with which he dealt with the bandits of Judaea, and with the Sicarians whom an impostor had persuaded to leave Jerusalem and follow him into the wilderness. But Festus' friend Agrippa does not come off so well: our author describes how tactlessly he had added to his palace a vast dining-room where he could recline, and during the meal keep an eye on all that went on in the Temple courts. As this was a breach of the Law, the priests were incensed and built a high wall to block his view. This naturally enraged the King, and Festus ordered the Jews to pull the wall down again; but when they appealed to him he allowed them to send ambassadors to the

[1] Acts xxiv. 24–xxvi. 32.

Emperor. These showed their worldly wisdom by approaching Nero through the most hopeful channel—his wife, the murderous and lascivious Poppaea, whom Josephus describes as a religious woman. They were completely successful.

Festus, unfortunately, died in 62 after only two years, and his successor Albinus was a very different person, guilty, according to Josephus, of every possible misdemeanour. From this time on things went from bad to worse. Not content with imposing crippling taxation on the whole nation, Albinus countenanced robbery and looting. Revolutionary leaders bribed him to connive at their mischievous activities; those who suffered from the prevailing violence could obtain no redress, and free speech was a thing of the past. Meanwhile the procurator filled his pockets by the simple expedient of allowing bandits clapped into jail by Felix or Festus to be bought out by their friends.

Such is the portrait of Albinus which Josephus paints in *The Jewish War*. He had every chance to find out the truth; for he was now a man of twenty-five, and as far as we know was living in Jerusalem. But as usual he has more to tell us in his later work, where the portrait is somewhat different. We must go back for a moment to the time just previous to the procurator's arrival.

Agrippa had made yet another change in the high-priesthood, this time appointing Ananus, son of that Ananus, or Annas, who figures so prominently in the New Testament story. In the *War* Josephus expresses the highest admiration for the new high priest: in *Antiquities* he portrays him in a very different light. Taking advantage of the interval between the death of Festus and the arrival of Albinus, Ananus seized the opportunity to convene the Sanhedrin and to bring before it, in its judicial capacity, 'the brother of Jesus, known as Christ, by name James, and several others'. These he accused of breaking the Law and sentenced to be stoned. Both trial and punishment were, of course, offences against the Roman regulations, and leading citizens sent indignant protests to Agrippa, calling on him to take action against his latest nominee. At the same time some of them went to meet Albinus, who was on his way from Alexandria, and reported these illegal occurrences to him. The new governor, recognizing the danger to his authority, wrote an angry letter to Ananus, threatening him with punishment; whereat Agrippa deposed the fledgling high priest and appointed yet another, one Jeshua. But Ananus, whom Josephus, probably incorporating a snippet from some other source, here calls Ananias, was not finished with: he was 'a great hoarder up of money', with which he purchased the friendship of the grasping Albinus and of his own successor, thereby enhancing his prestige in the eyes of the public. He then, in alliance with other chief priests as rascally as himself, employed a gang of thugs to purloin by violence the tithes on which the humbler priests depended for their subsistence, with the result that some of them died of starvation.

Ananus was to afflict Jerusalem in a second and very different way. Albinus on his first arrival had made a vigorous effort to rid the City of the Sicarians; but now they slipped back under cover of the crowds arriving for the festival, and seized, bound, and carried off the secretary of Eleazar, the Temple captain and Ananus' own son. As ransom they demanded the release of ten of their imprisoned fellow-gangsters, and this Ananus succeeded in purchasing from Albinus. It was an invitation which the Sicarians could hardly resist: they proceeded to remove members of Ananus' entourage one by one, thereby securing the release of one batch of criminals after another, all of whom at once renewed their depredations in every part of the country.

Albinus, like Festus, remained in office for only two years; but it was not death that removed him. Where the government of the Empire was in question His Imperial Majesty was no fool, and Albinus' period of misrule was terminated by his recall. Remembering that the Jews had not hesitated to protest to Caesar about the crimes of Felix, he made a last effort to appease the citizens of Jerusalem. He ordered the immediate execution of all prisoners whose death was called for, and released the remainder, commuting their punishment into substantial fines—payable to himself.

At this point in the story Josephus, whose usual though not invariable custom was to base his arrangement on chronology rather than subject matter, inserts two notes on the religious activities of Agrippa. The first might seem trivial to us, but in our author's eyes it was significant. The Levites who formed the Temple choir requested the King to summon a meeting of the Sanhedrin and to seek official approval for the suggestion that to mark his reign the singers should henceforth be permitted to wear linen, a privilege hitherto confined to the priests. The councillors raised no objection and permission was granted. Josephus, whose thoughts constantly recurred to the theme of divine vengeance and who was always ready to pinpoint the connection between cause and effect, makes this comment, to which we shall have reason to refer in a few moments: 'Now all this was contrary to the laws of our country, which whenever they have been transgressed, we have never been able to avoid the punishment of such transgressions.'

The second note is about the Temple, the care of which had been entrusted to Agrippa by Claudius. The magnificent building was at last complete, leaving eighteen thousand workmen without employment. It had been begun by Herod, if Josephus' later statements are correct, in 20 B.C., and it was finished in A.D. 64. It had taken eighty-three years to build; and in six years' time it would be no more than a heap of rubble. Was this indeed the penalty for those linen robes? Josephus has another suggestion to offer.

We must go back two years to the death of James. About this we can learn nothing from the New Testament, which makes no reference to anything that happened in Palestine from the day when Paul, in the keeping of the centurion Julius and in the company of Luke, his biographer and the only Church historian then living, left that country for ever. But we know that James, though not one of the Twelve, had been chosen as the first Bishop of Jerusalem, the birthplace of the Church, and was regarded by Paul as a fellow-apostle, probably because of the special appearance with which the risen Christ had honoured him. We must be grateful to Josephus for lifting a corner of the veil that hides the fortunes of the Christian community in Jerusalem from the time that the First Council was adjourned. We have already noted his brief account of the arrest, trial, condemnation, and execution of

James. That is all that we find in the traditional text of Josephus; but Eusebius has preserved for us a fragment which he must have found in some reference to the later disaster: 'All this came upon the Jews as punishment for their crime against James the Righteous (who was a brother of Jesus, called Christ), because although he was a most righteous man the Jews put him to death.' After reading Josephus' comment on the linen robes we shall hardly question the authenticity of Eusebius' quotation.

Was Josephus a witness of this outrage? He certainly gives us the impression that during the period covered by the present chapter he spent most of his time in Jerusalem; and had he not done so it is hardly likely that he would have made those contacts which occasioned his only recorded departure, a voyage to Rome that we shall shortly have reason to recount. If he was a witness, he must as an intelligent man have been deeply impressed; for the reputation of James seems to have been as high among orthodox Jews as among Christians, and his behaviour while undergoing martyrdom was striking in the extreme. We have another and much longer account, again preserved for us in the *History* of Eusebius, who has drawn this time not on the memoirs of an eyewitness but on the writings of Hegesippus, a very careful Christian historian who was born some twenty years after Josephus' death. The accuracy of Hegesippus' account, so dramatic and fascinating, is stoutly defended in what seems to me the most scholarly of Guy Schofield's three recent popular works on early Christian history—*In the Year 62*—published on the nineteen-hundredth anniversary of the murder of James. Mr Schofield also believes that a Graeco-Roman tomb near the corner of the parapet from which James was hurled to his death deserves its traditional title of the Tomb of James, and that confirmation is provided by Professor Allegro's translation of one of the Dead Sea Scrolls. I must say no more on this subject: my readers will be well rewarded if they study Mr Schofield's pages and those of Eusebius.

The death of James had occurred at the very beginning of Albinus' short procuratorship; Josephus' first contact with the Romans on their own ground occurred shortly before its end.

Four or five years earlier, while Felix was still misgoverning the country, certain priests who were friends of Josephus and, according to him, were men of the highest possible character, were for some negligible offence clamped in chains and despatched to Rome to defend themselves before Nero. There they had remained, living on figs and nuts to avoid ceremonial defilement. Their piety so impressed their young colleague that he determined to find some means of rescuing them; and soon after his twenty-sixth birthday, which must have fallen either before or just after the end of 63, he set sail from Palestine on his mission of deliverance. Dare we guess that he also welcomed an excuse to visit the capital and place himself in Roman good books? His voyage was an unpleasant one: like St Paul four years before he got into difficulties in the Sea of Adria, between Crete and Italy. The ship went down, and, believe it or not, the six hundred men on board swam all night, till at daybreak a ship coming from Cyrene was providentially sighted and the eighty swimmers who reached it first were taken on board. Josephus, who throughout his life emerged unscathed from every tight corner, was one of the lucky ones, and landed safe and sound at Puteoli. There he made friends with a Jewish actor named Aliturus who was high in the Emperor's favour. All went smoothly—dare we say swimmingly?—for him. Aliturus introduced him to Poppaea, who was so impressed by his appeals that she not only persuaded her tyrannical consort to release the unfortunate priests but sent Josephus back to his own country loaded with gifts.

How long he had dallied in Rome cannot be determined for certain; but comparison of the account which he gives in the *Life* of the state of things which he found on his return to Jerusalem with the record of events set down in *The Jewish War* suggests a period of two or two and a half years. He found revolution afoot, and an eager expectation of a clash with Rome. He solemnly warned the people not to be such fools; but his appeals fell on deaf ears, and being, not without cause, suspected of siding with the enemy, he was forced to take refuge in the Temple, in the Court of the Priests, as the fortress of Antonia had already been seized by the rebels. It was not till the middle of August in the year 66 that this happened. What had he seen during that long stay in Rome?

Whatever he may have thought about that 'religious woman' Poppaea Sabina, he had no illusions as to the character of her husband, whom he regarded as a murderer and a lunatic, the chief evidence of his madness, in Josephus' Roman eyes, being his appearances on the stage. Nero, the last emperor of the Julio-Claudian line, and in all probability the Beast of the Apocalypse, was of the same age as himself, twenty-six at the time of Josephus' arrival in Rome. He had been on the throne since the age of sixteen, when his abominable mother Agrippina had won it for him by poisoning her uncle and husband, the reigning Emperor Claudius. Nero himself made it more securely his own by poisoning his half-brother Britannicus, who had a better claim than he. Then yielding to the suggestions of Poppaea, his mistress and of course another man's wife, he decided that his mother was of no further use to him and arranged for her to be murdered. His Aunt Domitia went the same way. Then he made Poppaea his wife, and as such Josephus, who arrived a year or so after, speaks of her. To make the marriage legal Nero had divorced his previous wife Octavia, and to avoid further trouble she too was murdered. It cannot have been long after the champion of the imprisoned priests arrived that a startling event occurred in Rome. On the 18th of July, 64, a mysterious fire broke out; the flames were fanned by the wind; and eight days later two-thirds of the City had been burnt to ashes. Josephus must have seen it happen; and he must have heard the rumour that was in every mouth, a rumour which nearly every later historian declared to be true, the rumour that the incendiary had been none other than the Emperor himself. Nor can he have failed to see the smoke-screen that Nero put up to hide his guilt. He laid his murderous hands on all the members he could catch of that strange new sect which had sprung up in Rome and was growing apace. Without a shred of evidence he fastened on them the blame for his own monstrous act, and to avenge the fire made living fireworks of them in his own pleasure-gardens.

Were Paul and Peter among those Roman candles? Apparently not; for their deaths seem to have occurred some years after the holocaust, and to have taken forms devoid of any symbolism suggestive of fire-raising: the one was beheaded, the other crucified. Josephus was by then back in the country of his birth; but he had certainly been in Rome while Paul was languishing in his second and more rigorous imprisonment, finding solace in the company of Luke, his one remaining friend.[1] For the deaths of the two apostles, whatever the charge against them, Nero was responsible. Yet surely none of his subjects could have been more loyal to him. To the Romans Paul had written that the existing authorities had been ordained by God, so that anyone who opposed authority was rebelling against the ordinance of God:[2] from Rome Peter had called on the provincials to submit to every human institution for the Lord's sake—to the Emperor as supreme, to governors as his deputies.[3] That emperor was none other than Nero.

It is impossible to doubt that as in his own country so also in Rome Josephus saw and knew far more of the Christians than he cared (or dared) to set down in black and white. He must also have seen some of the rebuilding that Nero carried out in the calcined city, and perhaps the lower courses of the Golden House which that ostentatious monarch erected for himself, paying for it with the plunder of Italy. Meanwhile he had no doubt, consciously or unconsciously, done much to prepare the way for that sudden transfer of allegiance that he was to make only a year or two later. But the priestly prisoners had been released, and he could not linger indefinitely. Can it be that his return was hastened by the death of his patroness Poppaea, kicked in the stomach by the father of her unborn child, who with his accustomed nonchalance proceeded to marry a new wife, Statilia Messallina, after getting rid of her inconvenient husband by his usual methods?

During the long absence of Josephus much water had flowed under the bridges of Palestine, and the state of affairs had rapidly deteriorated. A new procurator had arrived, Gessius Florus, in comparison with whom Albinus seemed to have been a paragon of virtue. Nero had made a fatal mistake in appointing him; but the choice was not Nero's own; the appointment had been

[1] II Timothy iv. 10.   [2] Romans xiii. 1-2.   [3] I Peter ii. 13-14.

secured for Florus through the agency of Poppaea. The new governor was heartless, dishonest, disgusting: he filled Judaea with misery, accepting bribes from bandits, ruining whole communities, denuding every district, and openly boasting of his villainies. 'It was he', says Josephus, 'who compelled us to take up arms against the Romans, thinking it better to be destroyed at once than by degrees.'

It is at this point that Josephus brings the twenty books of *Antiquities* to an end. He has reached the final cause of that calamity to which all his work has been leading up. From now on we must draw our information from *The Jewish War*, glancing occasionally at the parallel account which he later set down in the *Life*. Apart from these there are no sources on which we can draw: the fragmentary account of the war in Tacitus' *Histories* adds nothing to our knowledge.

Florus was subordinate to Cestius Gallus, the governor of Syria. When Gallus appeared in Jerusalem on the eve of the Passover, a crowd, which Josephus estimates at three million, assailed him with denunciations of Florus. But Cestius did no more than promise that Florus would behave better in future, and as soon as he had returned to Antioch his subordinate, to distract attention from his crimes, set himself the task of deliberately fomenting a revolt. Racial strife broke out at Caesarea, where the Jews gave Florus a huge bribe to protect them from Greek encroachments, only to be imprisoned for their pains. Then the acquisitive governor sent his minions to Jerusalem and purloined a much greater sum from the Temple treasury. When uproar followed, Florus appeared in person at the head of an army, which attacked the citizens as they tried to appease him and offered apologies on behalf of those responsible for the uproar. Urged on by their commander, the soldiers then sacked the Upper Marketplace, chased the Jews through the narrow streets, murdered many in their own houses, and dragged others before him to be scourged and crucified. In all nearly four thousand perished —men, women, and infants alike.

ᐧ Relations between the procurator and his Herodian neighbours were not what they had been in the time of Festus. Agrippa was in

Egypt, but his sister was in Jerusalem with shorn head fulfilling a vow. Disgusted with the conduct of the soldiers she sent appeal after appeal to Florus in an effort to stop the slaughter. But he was busy collecting his rake-off from the loot and took no notice, so that the soldiers would have killed her, queen though she was, had she not fled into the royal palace. It was now the middle of May, 66.

The next day the crowd poured back into the Marketplace, bewailing the dead, and cursing Florus. The chief priests, in terror of the consequences, made frantic appeals and restored some semblance of order. This was the last thing Florus wanted, so he informed the priests that the people must go out and welcome two cohorts that were approaching from Caesarea. The priests instructed the people to do so, and implored them to give no offence, lest the Temple treasures should be plundered anew. The people obediently marched out and saluted the approaching soldiers; but orders had been given that no acknowledgment should be made, and the Jews in their chagrin at once burst out in abuse of Florus. The soldiers knew what was expected of them: they charged the helpless mass, clubbing them and trampling them under their horses' hooves, then pursued them into the City and swept through the northern suburbs in an effort to seize Antonia and the Temple. Florus with his other troops attacked simultaneously from the palace, but the Jews lined the roofs and pelted the Romans so effectively that the troops hurried back to their camp. Finally the Jews cut through the colonnades joining Antonia and the Temple, so destroying Florus' hopes of reaching the sacred Treasury from the Fortress. He therefore negotiated with the priests and agreed to withdraw from the City, removing the troops that had done the damage, but leaving a more disciplined cohort to keep order.

Was it at this time that Josephus was making the impassioned pleas for peace and for submission to Rome for which he takes credit in the *Life*? It is curious that we find no mention of them, or of any other of his activities at Jerusalem, in the *War*. It would be unsafe to draw any confident conclusion from this silence, but a reason for the discrepancy is not hard to guess.

Still anxious to drive the Jews into open war, Florus sent to Cestius a mendacious report of their alleged rebelliousness and violence. The Jews and Queen Bernice countered this with letters exposing the criminal behaviour of Florus in Jerusalem. Cestius' response was to despatch the tribune Neapolitanus to investigate the rival accusations and bring back an impartial report. Agrippa, meanwhile, was on his way back from Alexandria, and at Jamnia he was met both by Neapolitanus and by representatives of the Sanhedrin. The latter laid before him their complaints against Florus, and Josephus gives a rather unconvincingly smug account of the King's tactful reply. Seven miles from Jerusalem the people, headed by the widows of the soldiers' victims, came running to welcome him and addressed passionate appeals for help both to him and to the tribune. Arrived in Jerusalem the two men were shown the wrecked Marketplace and the sacked houses, and the Roman investigator was taken on a tour of the City to see for himself how docile the citizens were. Having satisfied himself he assembled the people, praised them for their loyalty, and urged them to keep the peace. Then after reverently bowing to the Sanctuary he returned to Antioch to make his report.

The people now suggested the despatch of a delegation to Rome to bring their complaints before Nero himself. Agrippa felt that to do this would be to ask for trouble; but he realized the danger of another outbreak of violence in which he himself might be involved; so he assembled the people in the Gymnasium, perched his sister on the palace roof where all could see her, and delivered the long and elaborate oration to which reference was made in our first chapter. In it he pleaded for submission to Rome at all costs, reminding his hearers of their pathetic weakness in comparison with the strength of Carthage, Gaul, Spain, Germany, Britain, and other powerful states which had been overwhelmed by Roman arms; of the minute size of the military forces that sufficed to keep all parts of the Empire in subjection; and of their own total lack of allies. He enlarged on the horrors of war, and ended with a burst of rhetoric in which he called to witness their common Fatherland and the holy angels of God, enhancing the effect of this peroration with a flood of tears in which his sister joined. He was now in a position to suggest that the people should give evidence of their pacific intentions by restoring the broken colonnades and paying their overdue tribute to Caesar.

For the moment the King got his way. The restoration was begun, and the magistrates toured the surrounding villages till they had collected the whole of the arrears, amounting to forty thousand pounds. But when Agrippa further attempted to persuade them to obey Florus until a successor arrived, the exasperated crowd insulted him, threw stones at him, and proclaimed his banishment from the City; so His Majesty withdrew in high dudgeon to his own kingdom.

PART TWO

The Catastrophe

CHAPTER 9

The Outbreak of Hostilities

IN BOTH THE *WAR* AND THE *LIFE* JOSEPHUS CONTINUALLY STRESSES the cleavage within the Jewish people. On the one side was a small minority of revolutionaries, insurgents, bandits, and assassins, led by wicked tyrants and unscrupulous gangsters and bent on war with Rome; on the other the bulk of the people, peace-loving and submissive, led by influential citizens, prominent Pharisees, chief priests, men of parts, and property-owners, all of them bitterly hostile to the trouble-makers. Again and again he insists that the war was not the fault of the Jews in general, though by their laxity in religious observances they had forfeited the protection of the Almighty: It was brought about by two causes—the headstrong folly of the mutinous minority and the unbearable misgovernment of individual procurators.

Not long after the withdrawal of Agrippa the war party sent a force to the Herodian fortress of Masada on the Dead Sea, captured it by stealth, slaughtered the Roman defenders, and installed a garrison of their own. At the same time a very different action was taken in Jerusalem, an action which in the historian's opinion made war inevitable. The Temple Captain Eleazar, whom we met in the previous chapter, persuaded the Temple ministers that henceforth they should accept no offering from a foreigner, and that sacrifice should not as hitherto be offered for Rome and Caesar. The conservatives were horrified. The adornments of the Sanctuary had for the most part been paid for by foreigners, no gift being ever refused, and no man had at any time been debarred from sacrificing. How could Caesar, of all men, be shut out? And would he not retaliate by forbidding them to sacrifice even for themselves? Such were the arguments put forward at a meeting hastily convened in the Temple courts; but they were of no avail. So these patriotic leaders, anxious as Josephus says to establish their own innocence, sent urgent requests to Florus and Agrippa, begging them to bring large forces to the City and crush the incipient revolt. Florus, only too pleased to let the revolt develop, returned no answer; but Agrippa sent a substantial body of cavalry.

It was the beginning of civil war. The 'peace-lovers' and the King's troopers occupied the Upper City, the insurgents the Lower City and the Temple. Battle raged for seven days, neither side gaining any ground. Then under cover of the crowd which, since it was the Feast of Wood-carrying, poured into the Temple to present fuel for the altar fires, a number of Sicarians slipped in and reinforced the insurgents. The King's troops, already lacking in courage, were now outnumbered and forced to abandon the Upper City. Their opponents poured in, and not content with burning down the palace of Agrippa and Bernice and the house of the high priest set light also to the Record Office, to the great relief of the many debtors whose bonds were deposited there. The high priest and his associates, along with the troopers, barricaded themselves in the palace of Herod.

The next day—about the 15th of August—the insurgents assaulted Antonia, entering and firing the fortress two days later. It was at this point that Josephus sought refuge in the Temple court. Then, flushed with success, they assailed the Palace walls from two directions, and when the defenders put up a stout resistance attempted to starve them out. They were soon joined by an adventurer named Menahem, son of Judas the Galilaean, the originator of the Zealots. This man had gone to Masada, broken open King Herod's armoury, distributed weapons to his followers, assumed the role of king, and returned to Jerusalem, where he now took charge of the siege. There ensued a battle of wits. Pelted with missiles from the battlements and having no siege-engines, the besiegers burrowed from a distance till they reached one of the towers, pushed wood baulks under its base, set fire to the baulks, and withdrew. When the wood was burnt away down came the tower. But the defenders had been wise to what was going on, and had built another wall behind. Menahem's men were bitterly disappointed; but the defenders were unable to carry on any longer and asked for a truce. This was granted to Agrippa's men and to their Jewish allies, so that the Romans found themselves alone. Their position was impossible; so they abandoned their camp and sought refuge in Herod's three impregnable towers. The camp was promptly looted and fired by Menahem and his men. The next day the high priest Ananias was murdered and the towers were invested. But the self-appointed king behaved so cruelly and tyrannically that Eleazar's party refused to serve under him any longer and plotted his overthrow. As he entered the Temple in royal pomp he was violently attacked, and after a short struggle he and his band of Zealots fled in all directions. Most of them were caught and killed, the fallen monarch being subjected to one torture after another. It was now that Josephus, as he puts it himself, emerged from the Temple; but of what he did from that moment till his despatch months later to Galilee he gives us no indication. All we know is that he again attached himself to the chief priests and the leading Pharisees. But they could do nothing to curb the revolutionaries, and in their alarm and despondency their only hope was that Cestius would soon arrive with overpowering forces and put an end to the revolution. Much was to happen before he did arrive, and the result of his coming was to be very different from what they had hoped.

The destruction of Menahem and his followers did not, as according to Josephus the majority of the people hoped, mean release of the beleaguered Romans. The band of 'conspirators' who were now in the ascendant pressed the siege with ever-increasing vigour, until the Roman commander Metilius sent officers to ask Eleazar to guarantee the lives of the soldiers on condition that they handed over their arms and all they possessed. The offer was eagerly accepted, and three emissaries were sent to give them the hand of friendship and promise them safety on oath. Metilius led his men out, and at the appointed place they all laid down their weapons; whereupon Eleazar's minions surrounded them and murdered them all—all except Metilius himself, who was the only one to sue for mercy, and actually promised to become a Jew and submit to the indignity of circumcision. Though he alone survived, the number of the dead was so small—five hundred at most—that to the Romans the loss was negligible; but the provocation was beyond measure, and the Jews were filled with dread, seeing destruction looming before them. The horrible crime had polluted the City; and to make things worse it had been committed on the Sabbath. If the vengeance of Rome did not fall on them, the vengeance of heaven assuredly would.

Such at least are the thoughts with which Josephus credits the Jews, and he goes on to see the hand of God in the coincidence that on the same day—about the 17th of September—and at the same hour the Jewish colony in Caesarea, numbering over twenty thousand, were massacred by the Syrian population, the few who survived being seized by Florus and sent in chains down to the dockyards. This atrocity provoked a violent reaction throughout the country, and bands of armed Jews sacked the Syrian villages and burnt or wrecked more than half the cities of Decapolis. The Syrians on their side killed any Jews they could catch, but for the most part the slaughter was the work of the Jews, many of whom were as eager for loot as for vengeance. This is the impression clearly conveyed in the *War*, though in the *Life*, a work in which partisanship and self-justification are much more prominent, Josephus lays the blame entirely on the Syrians, even alleging that the Jews had given them not the slightest ground of complaint.

One particularly horrible incident is described in both works. The Jews made a descent on Scythopolis, the one city of Decapolis that lay west of Jordan. There the very considerable Jewish population, so far from welcoming the incursion, joined forces with their Graeco-Syrian fellow-citizens to resist their meddling compatriots. The Syrians, however, were afraid of double dealing, and ordered the Jews to prove their loyalty by going with their families into a neighbouring wood. Two days went by without incident; but on the third they attacked the Jews off their guard, slaughtered them all—more than thirteen thousand men, women, and children—and plundered all their property. At this point our author's passion for poetic justice overcomes him, and he tells a lurid tale of one Simon who, defying the Jewish convention that it was right and a duty to kill foreigners but an abomination to kill fellow-Jews, had wrought prodigies of valour in defence of his native city. But now, so far from defending his kith and kin from the Syrians who were so treacherously attacking them, he proclaimed his guilt for all to hear, then proceeded to punish his own foul deeds, prove his courage, and prevent his enemies from gloating over his death. He seized his aged father by the hair and ran him through with his sword. Next he killed his mother, wife, and children. Finally, mounting the pile of corpses to make himself as conspicuous as he could, he drove the blade up to the hilt into his own throat.

News of what had happened at Scythopolis caused all the other Gentile cities in Palestine, Phoenicia, and the one-time Philistia to take armed action against their Jewish minorities. The worst casualties were in Ascalon, where two thousand five hundred perished, and in Ptolemais, where the figure was nearly as great. Similar disasters befell the Jews in Tyre, Hippos, Gadara, and other cities without number, and only in Sidon, Apamea, and Gerasa were they spared. Even in Agrippa's kingdom a plot was hatched against them. The King had gone to Antioch, leaving in charge a friend whose name is given in the *War* as Noarus, in the *Life*, which transfers these events to a later stage in the story, as Varus. A delegation of seventy men came from Batanaea to ask for armed protection in case of a local rising. Noarus had all seventy massacred in the night, his object, according to Josephus, being the desire to secure the contents of their purses. Other outrages followed, and continued till Agrippa, informed of what was happening, deprived him of his office.

The strife which raged at this period was not limited to the efforts of Jews and Syrians to exterminate each other. The Jewish insurgents were trying at the same time to damage their Roman masters and prepare the way for a trial of strength. To this end they attacked the fortress which dominated Jericho. It had been built by Herod the King, who named it Cypros after his mother. This was now captured and completely destroyed, the garrison perishing to a man. At about the same time the Jews in Machaerus, the almost impregnable fortress on the cliffs east of the Dead Sea, which has already figured more than once in our narrative, put pressure on the Romans to withdraw under a truce, and when they did so took possession themselves and installed a garrison of their own.

But it was the struggle between the incompatible races which formed the population of that disunited land that was the chief *malaise* of the time. Differences of race and language made difficulties enough; but the fundamental divergence in religious outlook was a much more serious factor; for though religion counts for so little with many of us today, with the Jews it was a matter of transcendent importance, and they regarded the pagan Greeks and Romans as being outside the Law and outside the pale, while the pagans in their turn felt that Jewish religion, customs, and moral principles were incomprehensible and absurd. Many on both sides were to find that in Christ all these difficulties could be overcome, and that mutual animosity could be replaced by brotherly love; but by the unredeemed these things were not dreamt of. 'Here there is no place for Greek and Jew, circumcised and uncircumcised, alien, savage, slave, freeman; but for Christ, all and in all.' This ringing proclamation of a new spiritual unity had been written four years before by a fettered prisoner in Rome; it had been written to the Jews and Greeks of Colossae; it had not been heard in Palestine.[1]

The state of that tortured land at this time was indeed terrible; but the terror was not confined to her borders. It reached out, as we shall see in the next chapter, to the old capital of Syria, Damascus, in the north-east, and with a shorter time-lag to the much more distant Delta of the Nile in the south-west. In Alexandria there had for nearly four centuries been a thriving Jewish colony, forming a large and important section of the population and, as a reward for their valour and loyalty, enjoying ever since the foundation of the city the same rights as the Greeks. They occupied their own quarter, where they could follow their peculiar way of life protected from pagan influences, and calling themselves by the proud title of Macedonians. These privileges, conferred by Alexander himself, were confirmed by the Ptolemies and extended by the great Julius and the early emperors.

[1] Colossians iii. 11.

But Greek and Jews saw by no means eye to eye, and as communications between Jerusalem and Egypt were excellent, the racial strife in Palestine was soon followed by similar outbreaks in the Delta. The frightful story of what happened in the great city of Alexandria, which Julius Caesar had once with his usual imaginative far-sightedness and tactless radicalism dreamed of making the capital of the world, is told with such vividness and economy of words in *The Jewish War* that it will be better to let Josephus recount the incident in his own way:

'It happened that the citizens were holding a public meeting to consider a proposal to send an embassy to Nero, when there poured into the amphitheatre along with the Greeks a great stream of Jews. As soon as they caught sight of them their opponents yelled: "Enemy spies!" Then they sprang up and went for them tooth and nail. Most of them fled and dispersed, but three men were seized and hauled off to be burnt alive. The whole Jewish colony sprang to their defence; first they pelted the Greeks with stones; then they snatched up torches and rushed to the amphitheatre, threatening to burn to death every single person there. And they would actually have done it had not their ardour been checked by Tiberius Alexander, the governor of the city. He employed no force in his first attempt to teach them sense, but unobtrusively sent respected figures among them to appeal to them to desist and not provoke the Roman army to attack them. But treating this appeal with contempt the insurgents heaped abuse on Tiberius. He, realizing that nothing less than a major calamity would halt the rebels, let loose among them the two Roman legions, and with them two thousand soldiers who happened to have come from Libya, with fearful consequences for the Jews. He gave the men leave not merely to kill them but to plunder their property and pull down their houses. The soldiers rushed into the area called Delta where the Jews were concentrated, and proceeded to carry out their orders, but not without bloodshed on their own side; for the Jews stood shoulder to shoulder with their most heavily armed men in front and held their ground magnificently, but when once the line gave they were destroyed wholesale. Death came upon them in every form;

some were overtaken in the open, others driven into their houses, which the Romans first looted and then burnt down. They felt no pity for infants, no respect for the aged; old and young were slaughtered right and left, so that the whole district was deluged with blood and fifty thousand corpses were heaped up; nor would the remnant have survived had they not begged for mercy till Alexander, pitying them, ordered the Romans to retire. They with their habitual obedience broke off the massacre on the instant, but the populace of Alexandria through the bitterness of their hate were disinclined to obey and could hardly be dragged away from the bodies.'

Why was there this bitter hate? Why have the Jews—a people which has contributed so much to the human race—in country after country, in age after age, been hated and despised, herded into ghettos, concentration camps, and torture chambers, accused of monstrous crimes, and saddled with responsibility for the perplexities of nations? Have they deserved these things or have they been victims of misunderstanding, prejudice, and envy? Such a question is beyond the scope of this book, but it demands an answer.

The disaster at Alexandria was on an immense scale, and horrifying in character; but it was in Palestine itself that history was being made. For there the Emperor's legate took action, action that was to have momentous consequences. What the motive was that induced Cestius Gallus to invade the territory of the Jews we do not know: Josephus merely states that he felt the necessity of action now that on every side the Jews were involved in war. It cannot have been to re-establish order and bring tranquillity and prosperity to that war-torn and impoverished land. Had that been his intention, he would surely have shown himself impartial and given a fair hearing to both sides, punishing offenders in either camp, co-operating with native authorities, and making it possible to rebuild what had been destroyed; and in doing so he would have made it easier for himself and his successors to control and govern these turbulent peoples. But he did nothing of the sort: he took no action against the Syrians but directed all his efforts against the Jews, leaving a trail of death and destruction wherever he went. It is fair to assume that King Agrippa, who lent him enthusiastic support, not only furnishing troops but attaching himself to Cestius as guide and adviser, had failed to realize what that general's line of action was likely to be; for loyal as he was to the Romans, and alive as he was to his own interests, he seems to have retained some lingering regard for the people to whom in name he belonged, and of whom he was the most distinguished representative; so perhaps we may take it for granted that, as Josephus suggested on an earlier occasion, Agrippa was equally solicitous for the rebellious Jews and for their Roman enemies, and had set his heart on saving the Jews for the Romans and the Temple and Metropolis for the Jews.

The invading force was a very large one, and Josephus gives us an account of its composition and movements in such detail as to make it evident that he wished to stress the tremendous effect of the enterprise of Cestius and of its termination, so unexpected, and so disastrous—momentarily for the Romans, but ultimately for the Jews. Such detailed knowledge suggests that when he wrote his account he was able to draw on Roman sources; for though he was in Palestine when these startling events took place, he was surely not in a position to ascertain all the facts and figures that he here sets down, even though these figures are so recurrent and so obviously inexact that we can hardly regard them as anything but approximations. The only genuinely Roman troops under Cestius' command were the heavy infantry quartered at Antioch, and it was necessary for him to supplement these with large contingents supplied by client kings, and with levies raised among the Jew-hating population of the Gentile cities in northern Palestine. He left his seat of government at the head of the Twelfth Legion which was at full strength, two thousand picked men from each of the other three, six cohorts of infantry, and four troops of cavalry, with four hundred miles to cover before they reached Jerusalem. With them went the allied contingents—five thousand bowmen, two thousand of them mounted, from King Antiochus of Commagene, almost the same numbers of horse and foot from Agrippa, four thousand men, some of them mounted and mostly bowmen, from King Soaemus of Emesa. Cestius chose the coastal route and paused for a time at Ptolemais on the Phoenician coast, where he assembled the local levies, amounting in all to 'very substantial reinforcements', though their military efficiency left a good deal to be desired.

Ptolemais served as a base for the army's operations, which from the very beginning took the form of wholesale looting. Cestius himself led the way, first of all marching against Zebulon on the Galilaean border. The inhabitants had fled, but the deserted town was full of valuables; so Cestius gave his soldiers leave to plunder to their hearts' content, and then set fire to the town with a soldier's contempt for its unmistakable architectural beauty. This was but the prelude to what followed: he overran the whole district, looting right and left and burning the villages. This task complete he returned to Ptolemais, only to find that the Jews had taken advantage of his absence to make a daring raid on the units left at the base, killing two thousand of his men.

Cestius now advanced his headquarters to Caesarea. As it was here that Florus normally resided we might expect to find some mention of him at this point, but we find none: indeed he appears only once in the story of Cestius' advance and subsequent retreat, which is surprising, to say the least; for he had forces of his own which might have been expected to co-operate with Cestius in the campaign; and he was, after all, both legally and morally responsible for everything that happened within his borders. From Caesarea Cestius sent part of his army ahead to surprise and occupy Joppa, a task which they accomplished easily by means of simultaneous attacks by land and sea. The inhabitants were slaughtered indiscriminately—eight thousand four hundred in all —and the city was pillaged and burnt. Meanwhile Cestius employed his cavalry to mete out the same treatment to the villages round Caesarea, at the same time sending the commander of the Twelfth Legion, Caesennius Gallus, to 'deal with' Galilee. Caesennius was loudly applauded as he entered Sepphoris, the chief Gentile stronghold. This example sufficed to prevent any trouble in the smaller townships, and the malcontents took refuge in a mountainous area somewhere in the middle of Galilee, an advantageous position from which they repulsed the first Roman attack, inflicting considerable casualties; but when the Romans arrived by a roundabout route at a still more commanding position, the lightly armed guerrillas proved no match for the armour-plated legionaries, and as they fled they fell victims to the pursuing cavalry, suffering losses ten times those which they had themselves inflicted. Galilee now appearing to be pacified, the Roman detachment returned to Caesarea.

It was already mid-October and action was urgent. The Roman campaigning season, as readers of *The Gallic War* will remember, normally extended only from about March to September. Cestius set off again with his entire force, stopping next at the well-watered city of Antipatris, thirty miles due south, from which he sent out a detachment to burn Aphek and the surrounding villages. A shorter march in the same direction brought him to Lydda on the main road from Joppa to Jerusalem. This town— the place where, some twenty-five years before, the healing of the palsied Aeneas had been followed by a great influx into the Church of Christ[1]—was empty: the entire population were in the metropolis twenty-five miles away, celebrating the Feast of Tabernacles. With the minor inconsistency which is not unusual in his writings, Josephus immediately follows up this statement by informing us that a number of the townsmen appeared, of whom Cestius massacred fifty. Then after burning the town he continued his advance, climbed the Jerusalem road till he came within six miles of the City, and pitched his camp at Gibeon.

He was speedily given a foretaste of things to come. The Jews did not wait for him to act but seized the initiative for themselves. They abandoned the Feast, and unlike their predecessors of earlier generations they paid no heed to the fact that it was the Sabbath day, but relying on their numbers and enthusiasm charged down in no sort of order upon the Romans, broke through their line and, at a cost of only twenty-two of their own men, killed over five hundred of their trained and well-armed opponents; they might have obliterated the whole of the invading army had not the mounted men stopped the gap. Unable to make any further advance the patriots then withdrew to the City; but

[1] Acts ix. 32-35.

as the Romans turned about to retire to Beth-horon the opportunity for a further success was seized and exploited by Simon son of
Gioras, who here comes into our story for the first time. He was
to play a major part in the terrible doings of the next four years.
A man of exceptional resource, he now assailed the retreating
Romans from behind, gave their rearguard a severe battering, and
returned to the City with a useful haul of baggage-animals.

It was three days before Cestius recovered sufficiently to make
any further moves. Then an unexpected event opened the way for
a fresh attempt. Agrippa, afraid for the safety of his allies—for
after all he owed his throne and his wealth entirely to Rome—
sent two emissaries to plead with the Jews, guaranteeing that if
they laid down their arms Cestius would pardon their mis-
demeanours. But the insurgents, fearing that the majority would
accept these terms, murdered one of the ambassadors and
wounded the other, then violently attacked those citizens who
protested. The disunity of the Jews being now plainly revealed,
Cestius attacked the motley host of the defenders and drove them
helter-skelter to Jerusalem. He pitched his camp on Mount
Scopus—Look-out Hill—and again waited for three days. Then a
day or two before the end of October he marched his army into
the northern extension of the City while the demoralized insurgents retreated within the inner walls. After burning down parts
of the suburbs he encamped in front of Herod's Palace. He could
then and there have broken through the walls into the Upper
City, and all Jerusalem would have been his; and that, Josephus
adds regretfully, would have meant the end of the war, and have
averted irretrievable disaster. But Florus, who anticipated more
profit from prolonged hostilities, had bribed the chief of staff and
most of the cavalry officers, and they persuaded Cestius to make
no such attempt. Yet he had every inducement to do so; for a
number of prominent citizens sent invitations to him, offering to
open the gates. But the dithering commander put off his decision;
the negotiators were murdered by the warmongers; and though
the Romans attacked from all directions, five days' effort produced
no result. Cestius then assaulted the Temple from the north,
sending up a barrage of arrows which drove the defenders off the

roof of the colonnade, and undermining the walls under cover of the Tortoise with which every student of elementary Latin is familiar. Panic seized the insurgents; peace-lovers ran forward to welcome the Romans; and Jerusalem was at the mercy of Cestius.

Why did the victorious commander suddenly call off his men, abandon hope, and 'flying in the face of all reason' retire from the helpless city? The history of war is littered with chances of a lifetime left unseized. Cestius not only wasted a victory but brought disaster upon the unfortunate men under his command. The 'bandits' did not lose *their* opportunity: they instantly attacked his rearguard and destroyed numbers of his men. He stayed one night in the Look-out Hill encampment, then resuming his retreat exposed his rear to new assaults. The enterprising pursuers showered missiles from both flanks, the heavy legionaries not daring to leave their ranks and chase their nimble attackers. The casualties were all on the Roman side, and men who dropped behind were quickly despatched. By the time the column got back to Gibeon three senior officers were dead, and most of the baggage had been abandoned. There Cestius stayed helplessly for two days, till at last he realized that with Jewish numbers constantly increasing his position was getting more and more desperate. At last he moved off again, speeding his flight by casting off every encumbrance. The animals were slaughtered, except those required to keep the artillery from falling into Jewish hands. Then on, through defiles that were death-traps to an army given no respite from attack, to Beth-horon. There the demoralized fugitives spent the night, while the Jews encircled them and waited for the morning.

At last Cestius used his brains. Resolved on ignominious flight he posted four hundred of his bravest men on the roofs with orders to do everything they could to make the position appear fully occupied. The ruse succeeded. By the time the Jews discovered what had happened Cestius had got a lead of three and a half miles. The luckless four hundred were soon disposed of and the pursuit was resumed. Thereupon Cestius dashed ahead so fast that his military engines were left behind, later to be used against other Roman armies. When at last Antipatris was reached the Jews

called off the chase, collected the booty, and returned in triumph
to Jerusalem. They had killed five thousand seven hundred and
eighty of Nero's soldiers in an action fought on the 8th of November in the twelfth year of that monarch's reign; an action that
made inevitable the war which, as Josephus tells us in the first
sentence of his preface, 'was the greatest of our time; greater,
perhaps, than any recorded struggle'.

The Governor of Galilee

IN THE LAST TWO CHAPTERS JOSEPHUS—THE MAN, NOT THE WRITER— has made but fitful appearances. In the next part of the story he will be the chief character, for in *The Jewish War* he has a great deal to say about the part which he played during the months of preparation before the coming of the army that was to avenge Cestius' defeat, and during the weeks of actual warfare in which he was subsequently involved; and that part was so important in his eyes that in the *Life* he devotes the bulk of his pages to it. Told twice, and in very different ways, it is not an easy story to disentangle, and the motives both of Josephus himself and of those who refused to co-operate with him are far from clear. Both accounts were written for the purpose of justifying the writer and are unlikely to strike any reader as being objectively true; but in the absence of any other accounts of the same events it is hardly possible to determine how far from objective truth they depart. Where the two accounts are inconsistent it is obvious that one is inaccurate; but which one? or are both? Can we be sure that an author who admits that on many occasions he practised deception —nay, revels in the skill with which he did it, as pleased with the success of his cunning as Athene and Odysseus in the Odyssey—is not also deceiving us?

The defeat of Cestius was not received in Jerusalem, as might have been expected, with universal delight. Many prominent Jews, whether actuated by genuine patriotism and the realization that a heavy price would have to be paid for this insult to Rome, or anxious to make their own position secure by dissociating themselves from such dangerous proceedings, slipped out of the City and went over to Cestius, who gave them immediate employment as emissaries to Nero, then in Greece, busy collecting trophies of his prowess as an athlete. Their task was to avert the anger of that merciless potentate from the humiliated legate by convincing him that the war had been brought about purely by the incompetence of Florus. They were evidently successful; for Cestius was allowed to remain at his important post, and to play a further part in the affairs of Palestine.

And yet he had not only disgraced the reputation of Roman arms: he had utterly failed to end the cut-throat struggle between Jews and non-Jews. It was at this time that a blow, similar to that which had fallen on the Jews in Alexandria, fell upon their colony in Damascus. It is a curious story. The Damascenes had as a precautionary measure some time before shut up the entire local Jewish population, numbering ten and a half thousand, in the Gymnasium. They now decided to avenge the defeat of Cestius by massacring the lot, but were afraid of being stopped by their own wives, who with the proneness of their sex to fall for the latest religion imported from another country had almost all turned Jewesses; so, keeping their intentions strictly to themselves, they fell upon the helpless mass huddled together in the Gymnasium, and 'slaughtered them all in an hour without any trouble'.

Meanwhile, those who had so triumphantly routed Cestius returned to Jerusalem and won over any who still favoured Rome. New generals were chosen for the army, and responsibility for all arrangements in the City, including the completion of the northern wall, was entrusted to the high priest Ananus and one Joseph. Eleazar was appointed to no official position, but the booty and vast funds at his disposal combined with his own 'jugglery' to make him the unchallenged leader of the common people. Commanders were sent to take charge of the various districts of Palestine and Idumaea. Their names do not matter to us, with one exception: Upper and Lower Galilee, together with the fortress of Gamala, east of the Sea of Tiberias, were assigned to Josephus, son of Matthias.

Why was Josephus chosen, and what was he required to do? These are difficult questions to answer. It was a heavy responsibility for a man of twenty-nine who had never held office of any sort, and who was neither soldier nor statesman, but a member of the priesthood—a body so large that a member might be called on to officiate only once in a lifetime, and might remain unknown. Had he taken an active part in the rout of Cestius, a part he dared not later admit in writing? Had he, on the contrary, after emerging from the Temple, resumed his public warnings of the invincibility of Rome? Had he, while privately deprecating all provocation, like certain others remained silent and later been 'won over'? Or did he know the right people, and had a little money changed hands? In neither of his books does he give us the slightest hint. Nor does he tell us why he was offered this key appointment, or why he accepted it. But he does tell us, at least by implication, what those who appointed him had in mind. As they were the leaders of the war party it is obvious that they intended him to prepare the border province of Galilee to resist the coming onslaught; and that he understood his commission in that sense is clear from his statement in the *War* that he knew the Romans would invade Galilee first, and for that reason fortified the most defensible positions, which he proceeds to enumerate. It is clear too from the praise which he bestows on the citizens of Sepphoris, whose enthusiasm for the war needed no stimulus.

If we now turn to the later work we shall find there a very different picture. When Josephus wrote the *War* he was high in the favour of Vespasian and Titus, both of whom were fully conversant with the facts, and it seemed perfectly safe to admit that for a time he had made preparations intended, at least officially, to meet a Roman invasion. But years later, when his patrons were dead and he had been openly charged with fomenting rebellion in Galilee, it became necessary to maintain that he had been on the Roman side from the start. The statement in the *Life* is so astonishing in the light of what he had written earlier that it deserves to be quoted in full:

'After the defeat of Cestius the leading men in Jerusalem, aware that the bandits and revolutionaries had no lack of weapons, were afraid that having no weapons themselves they might be powerless to resist their opponents, as later proved to be the case. So when they learnt that not all Galilee had yet revolted from the Romans, a portion of it being still quite calm, they sent me with two other priests of the highest character, Joazar and Judas, to persuade the ill-intentioned people to lay down their arms and to convince them that it was better for these to be left in the hands of the best qualified members of the nation. They, it was decided, should have their weapons in constant readiness for what the future might bring forth, waiting meanwhile to see what the Romans would do. With these instructions I proceeded to Galilee. There I found the Sepphorites greatly concerned for their own city, which the Galilaeans were determined to pillage because of their friendly attitude to the Romans and the pledge of loyalty they had offered to Cestius Gallus, governor of Syria.' (My translation.)

From the first sentence to the last the later account flatly contradicts the earlier. Josephus, now furnished with colleagues, is appointed by different persons for an entirely different purpose. He goes, not as governor and military commander, but as commissioner for the Sanhedrin. As for the two statements about Sepphoris, they are obviously irreconcilable. Which account are we to believe? We have to choose between a history written five years after the events and an *apologia* written thirty-five years after. The choice does not seem difficult. It was fortunate for him, but it is unfortunate for us, that the extermination of all other prominent persons who saw the war from the Jewish side left no one in a position to expose any playing about with the facts.

When we go on to read of the measures that Josephus took after his arrival, we find one discrepancy after another. The safest thing that we can do will be to summarize the story as we find it, told briefly and in an orderly manner, in the *War*, rather than to try to find our way through the labyrinth of the later and much fuller account, on which we must be content to draw now and then.

On his arrival in Galilee the youthful governor set himself to gain the good will of all classes by sharing his authority with the leading men and using them as a channel for the issuing of his instructions. He chose seventy elderly men, 'the most sensible he could find', and put them in charge of the whole region. Then he appointed seven magistrates for every town to try petty cases, reserving judgment in more important matters for himself and the seventy. Next he turned his attention to military matters, and to preparations for resisting the expected aggressors, fortifying towns, caverns, and rocks all over Galilee and Gaulonitis. Sepphoris was walled by its own citizens, Gischala by John at the governor's request. (This was the John whose feud with Josephus was to be a prominent feature of the story, and for whom Josephus again and again expresses the utmost detestation.) Apart from these two places all the work was directed and assisted by Josephus himself. Next he set to work about building an army. He enrolled a hundred thousand young men and equipped them with old weapons. But he realized that the success of Roman arms was due to unhesitating obedience fostered by a multiplicity of officers, and to thoroughness in training. So he imitated the Roman pattern as closely as he could, appointing decurions, centurions, tribunes, and higher commanders. Then he taught them signalling, tactical movements, and the technique of relief and reinforcement. He laid stress on discipline, morale, and physical fitness, and emphasized that it was the conquering Romans whom they would have to fight. Finally he adjured them to put away their besetting sins, promising them the help of God if they went into battle with clean consciences—a typically Jewish addition to all that he had learnt, perhaps on the Field of Mars, about Roman military methods. He claims to have ended up with a trained force over sixty-five thousand strong, including his personal bodyguard. This force he maintained by keeping one half of the men with the colours while the other half worked in the towns and supplied their comrades with the necessary rations. Had Josephus been studying the German system described in Caesar's *Gallic War*?

But all was not to go smoothly for the confident and energetic governor. John of Gischala began to make trouble. John was an unprincipled, vicious trickster, a ready liar who made a virtue of deceit, a habitual murderer who put to death all advocates of just courses, an ambitious but contemptible bandit. But why should one expect anything better from a man who set aside the purifications observed by his Jewish ancestors? He was guilty of countless crimes, for which he later paid the penalty he richly deserved. So Josephus would have us believe, but it is obvious that his bitter hatred of the man was due not to the miseries he brought upon his country but to the fact that he was a dangerous opponent of Josephus. For Josephus was a thoroughgoing hater, as he showed again many years later when the publication of a rival history by Justus of Tiberias endangered his reputation and provoked him to produce his counterblast, the *Life*, in self-defence.

John had first attracted the governor's attention by his unusual energy, and it was for this reason that he was allowed to undertake the fortification of his home town. But his heart was set on money, and he managed to secure a handsome profit out of the contract. Then he put through a piece of financial jugglery startling in its sophisticated modernity. To save the Syrian Jews from using oil from tainted Gentile sources he obtained leave to provide them with this essential commodity at the frontier. Then he cornered all available supplies—and the Galilaean olive harvest had been exceptionally heavy—and resold at a profit of seven hundred per cent. This he used to finance large-scale raids by his bandits, his hope being that if Josephus interfered he could be ambushed and killed: if he did not he could be reported for neglect of duty. Not content with this he spread a rumour that Josephus was betraying the country to the Romans.

Then came an incident which nearly proved fatal to Josephus, and in which John again had a hand. It is a horrible story, which sheds a blinding light on the character of Josephus, his resourcefulness that was adequate to every emergency and his unspeakable brutality. Some young men from Dabarittha waylaid the chief minister of Agrippa and Bernice and despoiled him of all his baggage, which included valuable clothing, silver goblets, and gold coins. This they brought to Josephus at Tarichaeae, a city on the edge of the Lake near Tiberias, probably to be identified with Magdala, the home of Mary Magdalene. He condemned their violence and deposited the stolen goods with the chief citizen Annaeus, intending at the first opportunity to restore them to their rightful owners. The raiders could hardly be expected to stomach this loss of all their labours, and went in all directions denouncing him as a traitor.

The next day a hundred thousand armed men gathered to attack him. The crowd, lashed to fury by the villainous John, packed the Hippodrome at Tarichaeae and yelled for Josephus to be stoned or burnt alive. His friends and his picked bodyguard fled, except four men (one, according to the *Life*) who, finding him asleep while the howling mob were preparing to burn the house over his head, woke him and urged precipitate flight. But our hero showed no trace of fear. He sprang forward with his clothes rent, his head sprinkled with ashes, and his sword suspended from his neck. The Tarichaeans were moved to pity, but the country folk, deceived by his abject grovelling, demanded that the loot should be instantly handed over. He asked leave to speak, and when it was granted he assured them that he never intended either to return the plunder to Agrippa or to keep it for himself. He had planned to spend it on new fortifications for their city; for his whole desire had been to serve them. This piece of mendacity produced the desired result—a fierce argument between the two sections of his audience. Then, having won over the Tarichaeans to his side, he went on to promise similar fortifications to the other towns as well. The bulk of the deluded crowd (the words are his own) withdrew, but two thousand armed men chased him into the house and hammered at the doors. It was time for a second trick. He mounted the roof and informed them that if they sent in a delegation to talk things over he would do whatever they wished. In came the magistrates and other leading men. Their treacherous host took them into an inner room and flogged them all till their innards were visible. The crowd, waiting quietly outside in the belief that discussions were proceeding, were horrified to see the door suddenly flung open and the wretched, blood-drenched victims pushed out by their torturer himself. Their weapons fell from their hands, and they fled one and all.

This revolting story is told again in the *Life* and, however exaggerated in its details, is no doubt substantially true, but there Josephus, instead of springing forward with his clothes rent, to evade his enemies proceeds by another route to the Hippodrome clad in black, and there falls flat on his face and soaks the ground with his tears; and in the course of the second ruse he invites the delegation in, not to talk things over but to receive the proceeds from the sale of the booty, and opens his door not to a party but to a single man, whom he throws out with a severed hand dangling from his neck—a stratagem, he says, which required some courage. It may be argued that lies are excusable when one's life is at stake; but why was it necessary for our author to manipulate the truth in one or both of his accounts? Was it to titillate the palate of his public? And how did these and the many other discrepancies between the two books escape the notice of his original readers? Were the two books addressed to different audiences? Or was the earlier work out of circulation when the second was published? I must apologize for asking questions which I cannot answer.

To resume: John had suffered defeat, so he tried another line of attack. He wrote to say that he was unwell and desired to try the hot baths at Tiberias. Josephus generously gave his consent, and made arrangements for John to be accommodated and cared for. But the ungrateful wretch did all he could to provoke a rebellion against his benefactor, who, informed of the situation by the local governor, set out post-haste for the city with two hundred of his soldiers. The whole population came out to welcome him— except John, who sent a message that he was confined to bed. When, however, Josephus was trying to explain the situation to the citizens assembled in the Stadium, John sent armed men to assassinate him by means of a stealthy approach from behind. On hearing a warning shout the orator swung round, and seeing the sword points at his throat leapt from the top of the hillock on which he was standing on to the beach, jumped with two of his bodyguard into a boat and dashed for the middle of the Lake. Meanwhile his soldiers charged the conspirators, so that the city was in danger of being destroyed by civil war, and Josephus immediately sent a message to restrain them. The people rallied to his cause in their thousands, forcing John to escape a violent death by beating a hasty retreat to his home town. Josephus easily obtained from them the names of John's supporters in every city, to whom he issued a public warning that if they did not within five days detach themselves from John their houses would be burnt down with their families inside. Three thousand took Josephus at his word and changed their camp: two thousand proscribed Syrians remained with John, who for the moment contented himself with sending to Jerusalem warnings that the ambitious governor was planning a *coup d'état*.

We are again faced with irreconcilable features in the parallel account to be found in the *Life*. There the occurrences are placed before, not after, the incident at Tarichaeae, and a different motive is assigned for John's stratagem: instead of John being the only person who did not come out to welcome Josephus, it is expressly stated that he did; it is not from a hillock that the orator leaps, but from the cornice of a stone wall; and the five days have grown to twenty, the three thousand men to four thousand. It would be idle to hazard an explanation.

John's messages to Jerusalem produced a surprising reaction. The general public, who might have been expected to fall for his specious allegations, took no notice at all; but magistrates and leading citizens, the very men with whom Josephus had been most closely associated, were so jealous of him that they secretly supplied John with funds to raise a force of mercenaries and make war on their own nominee. More surprisingly still, even Ananus, the high priest to whom the responsibility for all arrangements in the City had been entrusted, was a party to the plot. The explanation is provided in the *Life*. John had sent his message to a friend of his own and personal enemy of Josephus, the distinguished Pharisee Simon, son, it seems, of the still more distinguished Gamaliel, the teacher of Paul. Simon put John's case before Ananus, to be met at first with a blank refusal; so Simon gave a hint to John's brother, who thereupon sent the necessary bribes to Ananus and his supporters: they saw no further objection to the removal of Josephus from his post. A decree to that effect was issued without reference to either the Sanhedrin or the National Assembly; but as it was clearly invalid the four commissioners detailed to convey the decision to Josephus were accompanied by

two thousand five hundred soldiers; or, as our author decided
when he told the story the second time, five hundred soldiers and
three hundred civilians. Josephus was to be invited to come
quietly: if he refused, he was to be killed without fear of awkward
consequences. But Josephus was not one to be caught napping.
Warning that an army was on the way came to him from his
friends—or, as the *Life* tells us, in a letter from his father, who was
evidently residing in Jerusalem, where we shall later find him
during the siege. Not being informed, however, of what that
army intended to do,—after all it was only a handful of men, and
did not he himself possess an army sixty-five thousand strong, all
trained on the Roman model?—he took no action until four
important cities went over to John. But Josephus was as wily as
ever; he recovered these 'without having to use force', and then,
having 'by stratagems' got hold of the four commissioners and
the best of their soldiers, he sent them back to Jerusalem, where
they were roughly handled by the indignant public.

Evidently Gischala had after all not been recovered, for John
was still sheltering within its walls. Then Tiberias revolted again,
aided by the chance arrival of a few Roman cavalrymen, and with
help promised by Agrippa. Josephus was in Tarichaeae, and his
soldiers were all out searching for food, so that he could not take
the field that day; and the next day would be the Sabbath. Once
more his ingenuity rose to the occasion. He shut the city gates so
that no warning should reach the rebels, then collected two
hundred and thirty boats, each with a crew of four or less, and
sailed at full speed to Tiberias. Then he ordered the vessels to stay
too far from the shore for their occupants to be seen, while he
himself with seven members of his bodyguard went into full view
of his enemies on the city wall. They, concluding that all the craft
were packed with soldiers, threw down their weapons, waved
olive branches, showered compliments upon Josephus, and
implored him to spare the city. He replied by taking them
fiercely to task for their folly in face of the danger from Rome,
and for their disloyalty to himself, the builder of their walls and
the only guardian of their safety. He was, however, prepared to
receive a delegation that would offer an apology and help him to

make the city secure. 'Will you walk into my parlour?' said the spider to the fly. The invitation was at once accepted, and the ten most important citizens of Tiberias came down to the beach, stepped on board one of the vessels, and were carried some way from the shore. Then fifty leading senators were required to come forward for the professed purpose of giving some undertaking. Others followed as on one pretext or another they were successively called upon, and group after group they were embarked and taken out to sea. At last the whole senate—as large a body as our own House of Commons—along with two thousand private citizens, had been put on board, and the whole convoy was on the move, making full speed for Tarichaeae, five miles away. There they were landed, and the doors of the evidently capacious prison closed behind them.

It was a triumph of astuteness: bluff had succeeded magnificently; and in both his works the ingenious governor relates the story with the greatest relish. But the sequel makes by no means pleasant reading. The remnant of the people shouted that the person responsible for the revolt was an impetuous youngster called Clitus, and urged Josephus to concentrate his anger upon him. Josephus felt that it would be an act of impiety to put a member of his own race to death, but without giving the accused any chance to defend himself he determined to make an example of him. He ordered one of his guards to step ashore and cut off both Clitus' hands. The soldier refused to go alone into a mass of enemies, whereat Josephus lost his temper and in another moment would have jumped out on to the beach to inflict the punishment himself, had not Clitus begged him to leave him one of his hands. Josephus agreed to this, on condition that he cut off the other himself. Thereupon the terrified wretch drew his sword with his right hand and cut off his left. If the reader chooses, he may accept the later version, according to which the soldier was ordered to cut off only one of the young man's hands, and when he dared not do so Josephus made no move to leave the boat, but in order to disguise the soldier's poltroonery turned to Clitus himself and addressed him in the best literary style: 'Inasmuch as you are worthy to forfeit both your hands, having acted so

ungratefully towards myself, act now as your own public executioner, lest by disobedience you incur a yet heavier penalty.' To
the offender's tearful entreaties to be left with one hand Josephus
unwillingly consented, at which the young man, delighted at not
being compelled to cut off both his own hands (*sic*), seized a
weapon and cut off the left only. We are not likely to disagree
with Dr St J. Thackeray, who calls this second form of the story
'confused and ridiculous'. In either form it is a revolting episode.
Of course it was a savage world in which Josephus lived, and he
was only doing the sort of thing that others had done before him;
but he so often takes credit for mercy, generosity, and piety that
we cannot but wonder at deeds like these, deeds which gave him
feelings not of shame but of immense self-satisfaction. He wrote
so eloquently in praise of Moses and his enlightened legislation;
but what would Moses have thought of conduct such as his?

Tiberias had been brought back to its allegiance, and Josephus
felt so safe that he entertained his prisoners, nearly three thousand
in number, to supper. During the feast he gave them a good deal
of advice mixed with commendation of his own unparalleled
considerateness, and in the morning he set them all free. His
triumph was short-lived; for a few days later Tiberias revolted
again, together with Sepphoris. In both cases he followed the
same curious procedure. To punish the citizens he gave up their
cities to plunder; then to recover their good will he collected all
the loot from the soldiers and gave it back to the owners, flogging
any soldier who attempted to retain what he had been encouraged
to seize.

In Galilee the disturbances were at an end, and the people
worked harmoniously together to build up their defences to
resist the coming Roman onslaught. So at least we gather from the
War. The *Life* has a great deal more to say, and gives us a very
different impression; but there is no need to inflict the tortuous
narrative upon my readers: we shall have to look at the book
again when the time comes to examine the four works which our
author bequeathed to posterity. The Romans were at the door,
and we have no time now to linger among the petty events
inside the house.

A Change of Camp

IT HAS BEEN REMARKED ALREADY THAT IN MATTERS OF FOREIGN
policy Nero was no fool. He now showed his acumen by placing
the duty of restoring Roman authority over Palestine on the
shoulders of Vespasian. He could not have made a wiser choice;
for Vespasian had experience, determination, and strategic
ability; and he was completely reliable. He was already fifty-seven
years old and had served in many campaigns, his outstanding
success, according to Josephus, being the addition to the Empire
of Britain, 'till then unknown'—a success which enabled Nero's
predecessor to celebrate a triumph without having lost one drop
of his own sweat. But age and long service had in no wise
impaired his vigour, and with the assistance of his two sons,
whom Josephus loses no opportunity of complimenting, he was
just the right man for this difficult assignment. Nero had good
reason to treat the situation seriously; for the news that reached
him from Judaea was alarming; and though he tried to put a bold
face on it 'the turmoil of his spirit was betrayed by his furrowed
brow'. The folly of Cestius had inflicted on Roman pride a wound
that must be speedily avenged. Some of us remember how when
British arms had suffered bewildering reverses in South Africa
the blundering commander was not recalled, but a much better
soldier, backed by a much bigger army, was sent to take complete
charge, and the situation was transformed. For Redvers Buller
read Cestius Gallus; for Field-Marshal Lord Roberts read Titus
Flavius Vespasianus.

At the time of his appointment the new commander-in-chief
was in Achaia, the Roman province better known to us as Greece,
where he occupied a position on the Emperor's staff. He lost no
time in getting to work. He despatched the elder and much more
gifted of his sons, Titus, to Alexandria to fetch the Fifteenth

Legion, while he himself, eschewing the hazards of a long winter voyage, crossed the Dardanelles and travelled by road through the length of Asia Minor till he reached Syria and its capital Antioch. There he found not only the legate Cestius, who must have been extremely embarrassed by the interview, but also the prudent King Agrippa, who had brought his whole army to support the Romans. Good news awaited him; for the Romans had won a considerable victory at trifling cost. Bursting with confidence after their astonishing defeat of Cestius, the Jews had embarked on an enterprise beyond their strength and completely unnecessary. Sixty miles from Jerusalem lay the old Philistine city of Ashkelon, which for reasons that Josephus leaves unexplained the Jews hated most bitterly. A quick success appeared certain; for the attack was led by 'three men of unequalled prowess and ability', while the defenders numbered only one cohort of infantry and one troop of cavalry, under the command of Antonius.

But Antonius had warning of their approach, and instead of sheltering behind the city walls went boldly out to meet the tired and disorderly Jewish host. What happened set the pattern for innumerable battles to come. Raw levies, untrained and undisciplined, ill-armed and acting on impulse, could not stand up to veteran soldiers, a disciplined and organized fighting-machine, splendidly accoutred and obedient to every command. And though Caesar had found his infantry more than a match for any cavalry—and, as veterans of the 1914 war will remember, 'infantry in extended order have nothing to fear from a cavalry charge'—foot-soldiers who lose their heads are easy meat for trained cavalrymen. Antonius had chosen to fight in the open and his troopers knew how to use their advantage. What followed was not a battle, it was butchery. When darkness fell ten thousand Jewish soldiers lay dead, among them two of their intrepid commanders, and the remnant, mostly wounded, had fled into Idumaea. Even so their fighting spirit did not desert them, and they soon returned with reinforcements, only to fall into ambushes and be again encircled by the cavalry, losing another eight thousand men. Roman casualties were limited to a handful of men wounded. This disastrous failure was but one episode in the long story of Jewish heroism and Jewish folly.

Heartened by the good news Vespasian, accompanied by his royal hanger-on, Agrippa, left Antioch at the head of all the assembled forces and marched rapidly to Tyre, thence to Ptolemais. There he was met by the people of Sepphoris, who alone of the Galilaeans were pleased to see the Roman invaders. They had already treated with Caesennius Gallus, the deputy of Cestius. Now they offered their active help to Vespasian and asked for a garrison. This he provided—six hundred horse and a thousand foot under the command of the tribune Placidus. Sepphoris was the biggest city in Galilee, and was likely to make an ideal base for operations in that country. The infantry occupied the town, the cavalry encamped outside; but both arms proceeded to make raids in all directions, doing great damage both to the countryside and to the forces of Josephus, which were worsted in every encounter. An attempt which he made to win over Sepphoris by force or persuasion inevitably failed, and the Romans retaliated by ravaging and plundering, by murder and enslavement. From end to end Galilee was filled with fire and bloodshed, and there was no safety to be found except in the fortified towns.

Meanwhile, in spite of the winter, Titus had made a quick crossing to Alexandria, from which he had rapidly marched the Fifteenth Legion to Ptolemais, there to be united with his father's Fifth and Tenth. Attached to these were twenty-three cohorts, mostly foot, and six troops of horse, and in addition large contingents contributed by Agrippa and three other monarchs. All these might well total forty-five thousand men: Josephus may possibly be right in giving the figure as sixty thousand, not including large numbers of servants trained to fight almost as well as their masters. Readers who are interested in the history of war will find Roman methods of training and equipment fully discussed in the long digression which Josephus inserts at this point, and which in my translation I have transferred for convenience to the end of the book. These methods were no doubt applied by Vespasian and Titus to the motley force which they now had to mould into a manageable army, a task which occupied them at

Ptolemais for a considerable time while Placidus continued his more active work in Galilee. To counter the use of fortified towns as refuges for Josephus' none too courageous troops he decided to attack the strongest of them all, Jotapata, two or three miles north-west of Sepphoris. If Jotapata fell the rest would surrender. But for the present it was not to be. The attacking force was seen as it approached, ambushed by the citizens, and routed. Casualties on both sides were insignificant, but Placidus beat a hasty retreat.

As soon as he was ready Vespasian marched his great army, accompanied by quantities of siege-weapons, to the border of Galilee, and prepared to besiege the strongholds. His appearance was the signal for the complete collapse of Jewish morale. The carefully trained army of Josephus, encamped near Sepphoris, instantly melted away, and their commander 'for the time being decided to keep as far away as possible from danger' and took refuge in Tiberias, to the alarm of the citizens, who rightly concluded that he had completely written off the war. He was confident that he himself would be pardoned if he went over to the Romans, 'but he would rather have died over and over again than betray his motherland and flout the trust reposed in him'. So he sent a letter to Jerusalem, explaining the situation and urging the authorities to sue for peace at once: if they were not prepared to do so they must send him adequate forces—a request which he must have known (and hoped) that they could not fulfil.

It was natural that Vespasian should wish to avenge Placidus' failure at Jotapata and to capture so important a stronghold. There was no road by which the cavalry and transport could approach, only a rocky mountain track; but road-making was an art at which Roman engineers had always excelled, and in four days the task was complete. A few days later, on the twenty-first of May in the year 67, Josephus left Tiberias and slipped into Jotapata. It was to be the final effort of his resistance to the Romans, and the story that must now be told presents us with the greatest problem of his strange career, a problem which must be faced but which will perhaps never be solved.

What was going on in that astute mind? What were the motives of his actions, so equivocal as to puzzle and torment those who endeavour to understand him? Did he, as at this point he suggests, intend to awaken new courage in the sinking hearts of the Jews? Was his action consistent with his earlier statement that he had completely written off the war? Did he intend to make a supreme effort before finally making up his mind that resistance was hopeless? Did he share the view expressed by the deserter who informed Vespasian of his arrival, that the city ought to be attacked at once, since its fall would bring about the submission of all Judaea, if only Josephus fell into his hands? Would the man have deserted Josephus if he had held him in such high esteem? Was he really a deserter, or is it possible that he was to convey this message in the hope that Jewish resistance would soon collapse and the war be brought to an end? Was the awakener of new courage in sinking hearts already resolved to put to an early test his confident belief that he would be pardoned if he went over to the Romans? How did Josephus know what the deserter said to Vespasian? How did he know that Vespasian thought it was divine Providence which had put the ablest of his enemies in his power? Did Vespasian really hold such a high opinion of the man whose armies, bigger than Vespasian's own, did not wait for a battle but, as their commander himself confesses, even before seeing their opponents fled in all directions while he himself took to flight? Was it really, as Josephus states so confidently, in order to catch *him* that Vespasian hastened to enclose the city in a triple ring of steel?

These are mere speculations; but once an autobiographer has raised doubts in the reader's mind as to his strict veracity, suspicion follows suspicion in quick succession. Whether such suspicions as these are justified can only be decided when the whole story has been read and studied. A summary is no substitute for the author's own words, and there are some who if they read them may not feel any of the doubts expressed here. Unfortunately we cannot check the record by comparison with any other source, for the story of Jotapata is entirely missing from the *Life*, and only one other man survived (for how long?) who knew what went on in that unhappy city. All that we can do is to read the one account that we possess, admire the heroism and resource displayed by the defenders, the determination of the attackers, and, if we will, the superlative ingenuity of the man who so exultantly survived the catastrophe, reminding ourselves as we read that in spite of all our doubts the uncorroborated testimony of a single witness may yet be true.

The Jews did not at once retire within their walls, so when Vespasian began his first assault he subjected them to a heavy bombardment with long-range missiles, while his infantry climbed the slope beneath the fortifications. Seeing disaster threaten, Josephus led out the entire garrison, which fell upon the advancing Romans, and animated only by animal courage and blind fury drove them back. The battle lasted all day, and Roman casualties were very heavy; but the Jews fared even worse, losing more than six hundred men. The Romans, ashamed of their failure, renewed the attack on the following day, and for five days the attacks grew fiercer and the counter-attacks more determined.

Jotapata could be assailed from one direction only, for it was perched on a cliff and surrounded on three sides by ravines so deep that it was impossible to see the bottom. On the remaining (northern) side the ground sloped up to a ridge, which Josephus had included within his new walls. Vespasian after consulting his staff decided to build a platform against the wall on this side; so he sent out the whole army to collect materials. The surrounding heights were stripped of their trees and a mountain of stones piled up, while hillocks were levelled to supply the necessary earth. Under the protection of a structure of hurdles the men were able to build the platform without suffering casualties from the missiles, including 'great rocks', hurled down upon them. Next the artillery was brought up, and from a hundred and sixty engines a barrage of lances, arrows, firebrands, and stones each weighing nearly a hundredweight, was launched at the defenders on the walls, many of the missiles falling inside the town. Unable to retaliate in kind the defenders made sudden sorties in small groups, wrenched away the protective screens, attacked the unarmed builders, broke up the platforms, and set light to the woodwork. These tactics were repeated until Vespasian by concentrating his forces brought them to an end. The platform was rising steadily and was almost up to the battlements. Action was urgent: if the platform could not be kept down, the battlements must be raised up; so Josephus called on the stone-masons to increase the height of the wall. As the hail of missiles made building operations impossible, he instructed them to fix railings to the wall and over these to stretch raw oxhides: off these hides stones would bounce and arrows would glance, while firebrands would be extinguished by the moisture. Thus, protected, the builders raised the height of the wall to thirty feet, fitted a stout parapet, and constructed towers at short intervals. To increase the despondency and bewilderment of the Romans sorties were resumed, and continued day and night until Vespasian, despairing of a quick success, called off his attacks and decided to blockade the town, in the hope that hunger would compel the inhabitants either to surrender or to give battle when their strength was exhausted.

Inside the town supplies of food, apart from salt, were plentiful; but for the most important commodity of all, water, the inhabitants depended on their rapidly emptying tanks; for they had no spring and could count on no rain in the summer now beginning. This shortage caused great despondency among the Jews and exultation among the Romans, who from a neighbouring elevation could see them drawing their ration and could shoot them down as they did so. Josephus responded in a manner both daring and imaginative. To delude the Romans he ordered numbers of heavy garments to be soaked in such water as was left and hung dripping from the battlements. The stratagem produced consternation in the Roman camp and Vespasian, completely deceived, reverted to active fighting, much to the satisfaction of the besieged. Such is the story. Dare we suggest . . . ? No: this is not the place for further speculation, but for renewed wonder at the resourcefulness of the Jewish commander who, finding a hidden gully in the western ravine, sent out messengers who delivered letters to the Jews outside and brought back not only the answers but ample supplies of everything required. To escape detection they were instructed to cover themselves with sheepskins and pretend to be dogs. But detected they soon were, and the gully was blocked. Is that all there was to it? Maybe.

The days of Jotapata were numbered, and Josephus invited the leading citizens to discuss a plan of escape—for himself and them. The people, seeing what was afoot, implored him to remain, not blaming him for his wish to escape but appealing to him as their only hope and comfort. He replied that he was going entirely for their sakes: if he stayed he could do nothing further for them; but if he went he could raise a vast army and draw off the attackers, who would no longer press the siege, since he was the one person they were anxious to capture. The people were deaf to all such arguments: with one accord they fell down weeping, grasped his feet, and assured him that if only he would remain they would feel perfectly safe. Shaken by their tearful appeals, and knowing that watch would henceforth be kept on his movements, Josephus resolved to stay, and calling for deeds of gallantry made sortie after sortie, scattering the guards, dashing right to the Roman camp, tearing the tents which sheltered the troops, firing the siege-works, and invariably getting back to the town before the heavily armed legionaries could catch him. Vespasian, unwilling to risk damage to his most valuable fighting men, withdrew them from the danger zone and substituted the more expendable Arab bowmen and Syrian slingers.

He now decided to bring up the Ram, a huge device which Josephus, evidently writing for a public not too familiar with Roman military equipment, describes in detail, adding that even the stoutest wall will give way if battered long enough. All the long-range weapons were brought nearer, and the defenders driven from the battlements while the monster Ram was pushed up to the ramparts and set to work. The very first blow rocked the wall, and shrieks were heard from within. Josephus knew what would happen unless he took prompt action; but his wits did not fail him. He ordered sacks filled with chaff to be lowered by ropes to the spot which was going to be struck next, so as to cushion the blow. For a time this was completely successful, every blow being intercepted; but the Romans were intelligent enough to counter these counter-measures—they simply fixed reaphooks to long poles and cut the sacks down. The wall now began to give way, and Josephus had to think again. He and his helpers set light to a mass of dry wood mixed with bitumen, pitch, and brimstone, rushed out in three columns, and in a single hour burnt up the engines, platforms, and screens, while the Roman soldiers stood helpless by.

Throughout the four years' war the Jews displayed astounding courage in their hopeless struggle against far more powerful opponents, and from time to time our author pauses in his narrative to recount individual deeds of enterprise and daring. One such occurs at this point. A Galilaean named Eleazar stood up on the wall and flung a great stone at the Ram with such force that it knocked off the head of that aggressive animal. The marksman leapt down into the midst of the dumbfounded Romans, picked up the head, and carried it in triumph back to the ramparts. Missiles rained down on his unprotected body and five arrows found their mark. Paying no heed to these he scrambled up the wall and stood erect for all to see; then writhing with pain he fell to the ground, his precious trophy still in his grasp. Second only to him in courage were two brothers, Neiras and Philip, who with superb audacity charged the renowned Tenth Legion and routed all who opposed them. Such heroism reanimated Josephus and the rest, who snatched up firebrands and again set light to engines, shelters, and other constructions, forcing the units not yet attacked to cover all their tackle with earth. But the Ram was re-erected and pushed forward for a fresh assault on the weakened wall.

It was then that one of the defenders performed the somewhat surprising feat of shooting an arrow into the sole of Vespasian's foot. The wound was trivial, but our author makes the most of his opportunity, waxing eloquent about the dismay of the Roman army, the filial solicitude of Titus, the magnificent fortitude of the wounded general, and the furious determination of every soldier to avenge him. Meanwhile the Jews were suffering heavy losses as they stood on the battlements in the full glare of the fires and continued their efforts to incapacitate the manipulators of the Ram. They formed a perfect target for quick-loaders and spear-throwers, which, Josephus assures us, were capable of sending a single projectile through a row of men. Josephus saw the head of the man by his side knocked off by a stone and flung like a pebble more than six hundred yards; while an unborn child was shot out of his mother's body and deposited a hundred yards away! All the time corpses were being thrown over the rampart; for men were dying by the hundred. The battlefield ran with blood, and shrieks filled the air. The battering continued all night, and in the morning, when the wall at last yielded, the Jews filled the breech with their own bodies.

Vespasian now assembled his forces for the final assault. Gangways were to be placed so that his storm-troops could force their way through the three gaps that had now been made. Each gap was to be assailed by groups of dismounted cavalrymen, encased in armour and carrying long spears. Behind them the best of the infantry was lined up; the cavalry were deployed to catch any who might escape when the town fell; and still further back the bowmen, slingers and artillery were placed where they could aim their missiles at the battlements. Other men with scaling ladders were to make diversionary attempts on the wall in the hope of drawing off the defenders from the breaches. Josephus' answer was to post his fittest men behind the breaches, each group headed by six officers, himself being one. When the enemy raised their shout the defenders were to stop their ears, and bend down behind their shields till the Romans had shot all their arrows. Then when the gangways were in position they were to charge down them and attack the Romans on their own ground. Jotapata was lost, but it could be avenged. When, however, the wives and children saw what was coming they raised such a united shriek that poor Josephus was obliged to lock them in their houses and threaten dire punishments if they did not keep quiet. Then he took his place in the breach. The trumpets blared and the battle began. For a time it went exactly in accordance with the plans of Josephus, who describes it with an eloquence worthy of William Napier. But the Jews could not replace their losses or relieve the exhausted: assailed by endless relays of Roman legionaries they were forced up the slope, and disaster was imminent.

Josephus now resorted to a weapon associated rather with mediaeval France than with ancient Galilee. Boiling oil had already been provided, and his men now tipped quantities of it on the enemy, cauldrons and all. It ran down inside their armour, scalding them till in their agony they leapt off the gangways and fled. But the respite was momentary and the relentless Roman advance began again. Josephus had one more shot in his locker. He had already produced oxhides, sheepskins, and boiling oil. Now he covered the gangways with boiled fenugreek—a sort of clover—on which the attackers slithered about, falling on their backs or tumbling off the gangway, to be shot at by the defenders. As dusk fell Vespasian called off his troops. The assault had failed and his losses had been heavy. So too had those of the Jews, though fewer had been killed.

The Romans decided to try other methods. They raised the platforms to a greater height, and erected three towers which were triumphs of Roman engineering skill. They were fifty feet high, and encased in iron so that they could be neither overturned nor burnt. These were pushed on to the platforms, and on top were placed bowmen, slingers, and even light artillery. Immune from retaliation these were able to rain missiles on the defenders, who in desperation sought comparative safety outside the walls. Vespasian evidently felt that time was on his side; for he detached considerable sections of his forces to deal with trouble in two other places. Ten miles south of Jotapata the small town of Japha revolted. Trajan, father of the future emperor, was sent with three thousand men to reduce it. He won a crushing victory in the field, attributed by Josephus to the direct action of God, and sent for Titus to put the finishing touches to his success. Titus brought another fifteen hundred men, who soon broke into the town and slaughtered all except women and children in arms, whom they sold into slavery. Over seventeen thousand perished. The other trouble occurred much further away. The Samaritans gathered on Gerizim, their sacred mount. They gave no indication of a war-like purpose; but to forestall possible trouble Vespasian sent Cerealius there with nearly four thousand men. Afraid to fight an uphill battle Cerealius surrounded the base of the mountain. The Samaritans were being burnt up by the midsummer sun and dying of thirst, so many of them deserted to the Romans, who thereupon climbed the mountain and enclosed the remainder in a ring of iron. These refused the terms offered by Cerealius, so he destroyed them all—nearly twelve thousand.

On the forty-seventh day of the siege Jotapata was ripe for plucking. The platforms overtopped the wall, and a deserter informed Vespasian that if he attacked just before daylight he would find the exhausted garrison asleep. The general accepted his advice, and his men advanced noiselessly to the wall. Titus climbed up first followed by a handful of legionaries, and stabbed the sentries. Aided by a thick mist other soldiers made their entry, and soon the citadel had been captured, the centre of the town was full of Romans, and the inhabitants at last awoke to find the massacre beginning. The invaders swept down from the citadel, killing without mercy. Many of Josephus' best soldiers died by their own hand. At a cost to themselves of one man killed by a Jewish trick, the Romans continued the slaughter for two days and then demolished the city. It was the first day of July. Twelve hundred Jewish women and babies went into captivity. The dead, from start to finish, are reckoned by Josephus as forty thousand.

We have now reached the climax of our story. Josephus' days as governor, soldier, and opponent of the Romans were at an end, and it was a question now of survival. The Romans sought him everywhere, believing—vain hope!—that when he was captured the war would be as good as won. But he, 'helped by some divine providence', had jumped into a pit communicating with a large concealed cave, where, wonder of wonders, he found forty important persons and ample supplies! There he hid till on the third day a woman of the party gave him away—very conveniently indeed; for Vespasian at once sent two senior officers to promise him safe conduct. Josephus at first demurred, but a third officer then arrived, who was an old friend of Josephus. Nicanor enlarged on the generosity of the Romans and on their anxiety to preserve so excellent a man. Josephus, a priest familiar with prophecies, was at this very moment inspired to understand some terrifying dreams which God had recently sent him, and offered up a secret prayer in which he solemnly declared that he was about to go over to the Romans, not as a traitor, but as God's servant.

But going over to the Romans was not so simple as that. His fellow-refugees crowded round him, reproaching him bitterly for his cowardice and threatening to run him through. But Josephus was never at a loss. He launched out on a long oration, praising death on the battlefield, but condemning suicide as a sin against God and a crime condemned by Moses. It was his duty and theirs to accept life when it was offered. The speech was plausible but hardly convincing. After all, life had not been offered to anyone but himself. He was again reviled and everyone seemed about to strike him. 'But addressing one by name—towards another assuming the aspect of command—taking a third by the hand—and softening a fourth by entreaties, he succeeded in warding off the blades of all. Some there were whose arms were paralysed by reverence for the general in his extreme distress, and whose swords dropped from their grasp; while many, in the very act of thrusting at him, unconsciously let fall their weapons.' (Traill.)

With a second prayer to God he now made his last gamble. He proposed that they should draw lots and kill each other in turn. Whoever drew the first lot should be killed by number two, and so on. The last man was to kill himself. The others agreed and the lots were drawn. Each in turn unhesitatingly offered his throat till it came to the last two, of whom Josephus was one. 'Shall we put it down to divine providence or just to luck?' How is it that in the Slavonic text to which allusion was made many pages back we find instead of this bit of cynical hypocrisy the plain statement: 'He counted the numbers cunningly and so deceived them all'? Can it be that this was what he wrote in his original version, being, as he shows again and again, delighted with his skill as a deceiver, and that he later modified the crudity of this frank confession? Whether he wrote it or not, we shall hardly question its truth. Anyway, the two were alive, and the man who but a moment before had declared that it would be outrageous if when the rest were gone one man should change his mind and save his life now 'used persuasion' and remained alive.

The last obstacle was removed. To enable one man to have his way thirty-nine had died; and Josephus was at last free to join his friends outside. Nicanor took him into Vespasian's presence, where he aroused a variety of emotions in the spectators, some clamouring for his death, others awed by his exploits. Titus, impressed by his brave demeanour and full of pity for his youth—though Josephus was four years older than himself—persuaded his father to spare him. Vespasian proposed to send him to Nero; but Josephus requested a word in private, and all except Titus and two friends were ordered to withdraw. Thereupon the prisoner assured them in the name of God that Nero and his successors would not remain upon the throne: Vespasian was Caesar and Emperor, lord of the human race; so also was his son. This prophecy he made the more convincing by declaring that he had publicly foretold that Jotapata would be captured after forty-seven days and he himself would be taken alive. As prisoners when questioned confirmed this statement Josephus was accepted as a true prophet, and though for the time being kept in prison received from both the future emperors great consideration and valuable gifts, one of which took the unusual form of a wife—he already had one in Jerusalem—who remained with him only during the short period of his imprisonment.

CHAPTER 12

The Conquering Advance

WE HAVE CONSIDERED THE FOREGOING EVENTS AT SOME LENGTH, because Josephus was both making history and being made by it. Now for a while he will be off the stage, and we can go ahead at a greater pace, even though he has left us much detailed information, collected either while the drama was proceeding or perhaps later when it was all over. But while he is still in the wings we must turn our attention to Jerusalem, and see how the people reacted to the news that reached them from Jotapata. When rumours of the catastrophe arrived many refused to believe them. Confirmation followed, but truth was mixed with falsehood and it was stated that Josephus was dead. His supposed loss caused more distress than the actual loss of brothers, kinsmen, and friends, as he tells us without undue modesty, and professional mourners were hired to bewail him. The lamentation went on for a whole month. Then at last the truth came out: Josephus was alive and with the Romans, receiving favoured treatment. Grief turned into rage and denunciation, giving birth to a passionate desire to get at the Romans and thereby punish Josephus.

It was now early July, and though much of the summer remained Vespasian began to make his arrangements for the coming winter. He marched his army back to Ptolemais, and from there to the predominantly Greek city of Caesarea, where anyone who wanted to fight the Jews was welcome. Two legions were to be quartered at this central and highly convenient base, while the third was sent to Scythopolis, which like Caesarea was comfortably warm in winter. Several tasks remained to be done before they could settle down. The first place that claimed attention was Joppa. It was barely twelve months since Cestius on arrival at Caesarea had sent a detachment ahead to capture this important town, which had been looted, burnt, and stripped of its inhabitants.

But numbers of refugees had settled there, and being unable to earn a living on land they had built a large pirate fleet which made the seas impassable. Vespasian now sent a body of horse and foot, which entered the unguarded town at night. The inhabitants, forewarned, had taken to their ships and were riding at anchor. Just before daylight a violent gale from the north struck them, dashing some of the ships together and driving others on to the rocks, while those further out were swamped by the mountainous waves. Men who reached the shore alive were butchered by the Romans, and soon more than four thousand lay dead on the beach. The town was again demolished, and made a base for a raiding force which proceeded to waste the whole countryside.

The scene of the other conflicts lay in the north-east. Agrippa had invited Vespasian to visit his kingdom, being anxious to ingratiate himself and also to secure help in settling his local troubles. Vespasian marched to Caesarea Philippi, where for three weeks while the troops rested he attended state banquets. Then he resolved to requite Agrippa by crushing the rebellious Jews in Tiberias and Tarichaeae, which were at this time included in Agrippa's domains. He sent Titus to fetch the two legions quartered in Caesarea, met him at Scythopolis with the third, and encamped with all three an hour's march from Tiberias. From this camp he sent Valerian with a mounted troop to offer terms of peace to the citizens. Outside the wall to show their pacific intentions the men dismounted, but a party of armed 'terrorists' headed by one Jeshua sallied out, and the Romans fled in a panic, leaving behind them six horses which were taken in triumph to the city. But the opposite party, who were in a majority, sent delegates to make their submission to Vespasian in the name of all the citizens; so Jeshua and his friends fled to Tarichaeae. After a precautionary reconnaissance Vespasian led his army to Tiberias, where he was received with acclamations. Plundering was forbidden, and at Agrippa's request the walls were left almost intact.

When Josephus had been captured no successor arrived to organize continued resistance; yet the Galilaeans were in no mood to surrender tamely. Insurgents poured into Tarichaeae, relying on the strength of the walls which protected it on three sides, and on Lake Tiberias which not only protected the fourth side but would facilitate evacuation; for they had numbers of boats, and if necessary were prepared to fight a sea battle. The Romans pitched a new camp between the two lakeside towns, and were building extra strong fortifications when the intrepid Jeshua struck again, scattering the working party and tearing down part of the rampart. When the legionaries formed up to repel the raiders, they took to their boats and showered arrows on the Romans. A much greater body of rebels was lined up in front of Tarichaeae: Titus was sent with a powerful cavalry force to deal with them. The troopers were somewhat taken aback by the numerical superiority of the enemy; so Titus was forced to send for reinforcements, and in the meantime to deliver one of those long exhortations with which Roman commanders were wont to rouse the fighting spirit of their men. Perhaps a reporter took it down in shorthand: at any rate Josephus manages to reproduce it in full. The soldiers must remember that they belonged to a race of conquerors; that they were a disciplined, trained, and experienced army, their opponents nothing but a rabble and a mob of raw recruits. They had full armour, horses, and commanders: the enemy had none. Numbers therefore counted for very little. They were fighting for glory, the Jews merely for liberty. And they were all on trial— Vespasian, Titus, and the soldiers. With Vespasian victory was a habit; Titus would not let him down; the soldiers must not fail their leader. Then victory was certain.

Roman soldiers, as Caesar had been well aware, were highly emotional and very responsive to rhetorical appeals. Titus' men were now bursting with enthusiasm, and resented the participation of the reinforcements—four times their own number—sent by Vespasian. Josephus, who liked nothing better than singing the praises of his younger patron, thoroughly enjoyed himself as he wrote both the speech and the description of the ensuing battle. It was Titus, Titus all the way. While two thousand bowmen from the vantage ground of a neighbouring hill made it impossible for Jewish helpers to leave the town, he galloped to the front and charged the enemy, followed by his cheering troopers, who trampled their opponents underfoot and chased the survivors off the field. 'Titus, pursuing them hotly, cut up their rear, now breaking through their dense masses, and now pushing in advance of them he charged them in front: many he drove confusedly together, and dashing in upon them as they fell one over another trod them down: all he intercepted in their retreat to the ramparts and turned them back to the plain; until at length by their numbers they forced their way through and escaped in a body into the town.' (Traill.)

From within the Romans heard the sound of recrimination and strife; so Titus, after making a second and shorter appeal, again leapt into the saddle, rode through the waters of Gennesaret and led his men into the town. There was no opposition. Jeshua fled across country; the other militants made for the boats and put out to sea; and the non-combatants were slaughtered until Titus had had enough. Vespasian on hearing the news was delighted with his son's prowess and hurried to the scene. The town was sealed off and rafts were hastily put together, loaded with armed men, and sent in pursuit of the fugitives. The Jews in their tiny craft had no chance against this heavy armament, and while they vainly pelted the Roman armour with stones they were transfixed with arrows and spears, and their boats sent to the bottom. The scene is described in vivid detail and makes very painful reading. Not a man survived, and Josephus estimates the total of killed at nearly seven thousand.

The sequel is a sordid story. Vespasian is regarded as one of the best of the Roman emperors, and so no doubt he was; but both he and his exemplary son were capable of gross excesses, and his conduct on this occasion could hardly have been improved upon by even the vilest wearers of the purple. He separated the surviving residents of Tarichaeae from the newcomers, and asked his staff whether the latter also should be spared. They advised against it, and Vespasian agreed, but was not sure how best to get rid of them. If he killed them in Tarichaeae the residents might be antagonized, and his scruples would not let him give them a safe conduct and then attack them. However, he was soon persuaded that Jews had no rights at all, and that morality must always yield to expediency. So he gave the men an equivocal guarantee and allowed them to leave by the Tiberias road. Off they went, suspecting nothing. But the road was lined with troops and they were herded into the Stadium of Tiberias. There Vespasian had twelve hundred old and useless people murdered, picked out the six thousand strongest young men to send as a present to Nero, who required navvies for the Corinth Canal, and put the remaining thirty-five thousand or so under the hammer. But what did it matter? The mob, as Josephus self-righteously observes, consisted for the most part of insurgents and fugitives whose disreputable conduct in peace had made war seem to them a pleasant prospect.

All Galilee now submitted except Gischala and Mount Tabor, supported by Gamala on the other side of the Lake, a city which had been transferred to Agrippa but had maintained its independence. The name was said to be a local variant of 'Camel', and had been given because the long sloping ridge on which the town stood resembled a camel's neck and hump. Round the face and shaggy sides ran impassable ravines: the tail end was protected by an artificial trench. Along the flanks houses were piled on top of one another, and on the lofty head stood the citadel, perched over a precipice. Unlike Jotapata, Gamala did not lack fresh water. The tremendous natural strength had been reinforced by Josephus with a wall, trenches, and underground passages. Small wonder that in seven months Agrippa's besieging forces had made no impression at all. Vespasian now arrived, and when his three legions had pitched their camps on a commanding hill he set them to work constructing platforms at the tail end and filling in trenches and ravines. Agrippa chose this moment to approach the walls and invite surrender, but he was hit on the elbow by a sling-stone, treatment of which Josephus writes in shocked terms.

When the platforms were finished the engines were brought up under the usual curtain of missiles, and the wall was breached at three points. The Romans poured through and forced the defenders to withdraw to the upper parts of the town. Then came the counter-attack and the Romans were pushed down the slope and jammed in the alleys, where they suffered heavy losses. They tried to escape by climbing on the roofs, but these collapsed, knocking down those on a lower tier, and so to the bottom. Assailed from all sides with every weapon the exultant defenders could lay their hands on, they were well nigh desperate when at last they found the outlets and escaped from the town. Titus was away in Syria with Mucianus, who had at last taken the place of Cestius; but Vespasian, with the usual Flavian gallantry, had been in the thick of the fighting and had penetrated to the very top of the city, where he now found himself almost alone. 'Thinking it therefore neither safe nor honourable to fly, and mindful of his toils from early youth and of his character for valour, he, as if by a divine impulse, united in close barrier the bodies and armour of those with him. He thus sustained the tide of war that flowed down from above, and dismayed by the numbers neither of men nor missiles kept his ground until the enemy, struck with his supernatural intrepidity, relaxed in ardour. Being now less warmly pressed he retreated step by step, and without showing his back until he was outside the ramparts.' (Traill.) So writes his devoted admirer.

Roman losses had been heavy and morale was badly shaken, but the commander knew how to handle his men. He reassured them with carefully chosen words, complete with a quotation from Meleager rather surprising in the mouth of this earthy country-man, and gently rebuked them for their impetuosity in following the retreating enemy, apparently forgetting (or was it Josephus who forgot?) that he had himself advanced further than any. Meanwhile the Gamalans, who were by now feeling the pinch, lined the walls in readiness for the next assault; but when this came most of them tried to escape through the ravines and the underground passages. The rest held out as best they could, while the non-combatants died of starvation.

Vespasian was prepared to bide his time, and he took the opportunity to deal with the garrison of Mount Tabor. This rises some eighteen hundred feet above the Plain of Esdraelon, and the top forms a plateau three thousand feet long. Josephus, as Dr St J. Thackeray elsewhere remarks, and as the reader may have already suspected, is prone to exaggeration. Here he excels himself, and either through ignorance or to impress his Roman readers makes the height twenty thousand feet and the length three miles, claiming that he himself had in less than six weeks built a wall right round it. Within this wall great numbers had gathered; so Vespasian sent Placidus with six hundred horse to suppress them. Unable to make the ascent Placidus by offers of peace enticed them down to the plain where his cavalry had the advantage; then with typical Roman perfidy cut them to pieces, a remnant escaping to Jerusalem. The Romans then took possession of the mountain.

Now came the turn of Gamala. Very early one morning three members of the Fifteenth Legion succeeded in undermining a projecting tower. Unnoticed in the darkness they removed the five most important stones. Down came the tower, bringing the sentries with it. The other guards fled, and the startled population ran in all directions. Taught by recent experience the Romans were too wary to force an entry; but the next day Titus returned from Syria and took instant action. With two hundred picked men he noiselessly entered the town. When his presence was discovered some rushed with their wives and children to the citadel while others who faced the intruders were killed to a man, deluging the whole town with blood. Once more Vespasian led the way to the citadel, taking his whole army to finish off those who had congregated there. It was ringed with precipices down which the Jews rolled rocks and hurled every missile they could find, doing heavy damage to the Romans and suffering no losses themselves. But God, as Josephus so often tells us, was on the the Roman side, and He intervened at this critical moment. A supernatural tempest struck the Jews full in the face. The Roman arrows were carried up to them, while their own were blown aside. Overwhelmed by the blast they could neither see the enemy nor retain their foothold on the narrow ledges. The Romans were quick to seize their chance: they swarmed up the slopes and hemmed in the garrison, and in their furious determination to avenge their fallen comrades meted out the same treatment to resisters and non-resisters alike. Abandoning all hope the helpless defenders flung their wives and children down the cliff side and followed them into the depths of the ravine below. Suicide accounted for more than slaughter; for the Romans had killed four thousand, but five thousand took that terrible plunge. Any that lingered, even babes in arms, were slung from the crest by the merciless Romans. The sole survivors were two women, nieces of Agrippa's former army commander, who had remained in hiding until Roman tempers cooled down. New Masters now sat on the camel's back.

The revolt of Gamala had lasted exactly a month, and November was approaching. Only Gischala remained, so Vespasian determined to round off his campaign and complete the reduction of Galilee without delay. Gischala was a little town some way to the north, occupied mostly by farmers whose only desire was to gather in their harvest, a bumper one. But there was a Fifth Column in their midst, a powerful gang of 'bandits' who had corrupted some of the townsmen. The man behind this conspiratorial group was the wily, ambitious impostor John, whom Josephus sees as bent on war for the purpose of winning absolute power for himself. We have met a similar description before: in each case Thackeray cruelly points out that it is borrowed from Sallust's character-sketch of Catiline! Under John's influence the population were now preparing to offer armed resistance to the Romans. Vespasian was anxious to rest his infantry after the gruelling campaign of the last six months; so he sent the Tenth Legion into winter quarters at Scythopolis and accompanied the other two to Caesarea, where he knew that they would enjoy good living, and planned to subject them to strenuous training in readiness for the much harder task that awaited them in Judaea. The cavalry had taken a smaller part in the recent fighting, and he despatched a thousand of them under his very capable son to settle matters with John.

On arrival at Gischala Titus saw that the town would quickly fall to an assault; but his tender heart was grieved for the innocent people who would suffer with the guilty in the wholesale mass-acre which he knew that his supposedly disciplined soldiers would certainly carry out. He therefore attempted to persuade the people to surrender, informing the men who crowded the walls that even the strongest towns which had offered resistance had fallen at the first assault, while those which had surrendered had been left in peace. He offered the same terms to Gischala: if they were rejected the defiant inhabitants would find that to the Roman engines their boasted walls were mere toys.

Fear of the 'bandits' prevented any of the peace-loving towns-folk from replying to the invitation; but the wily John declared that he welcomed the proposals and would make himself responsible for their acceptance. However, it was the Sabbath, and Titus was surely aware that on that day the Jews were permitted to make neither war nor peace. The brief delay would not hurt Titus, for flight would be impossible. John was not really concerned with scruples but with his own survival, says Josephus, who was perhaps not the right person to offer such a criticism. Nor are we likely to accept his conviction that God saw to it that John did survive for the express purpose of destroying Jerusalem, and to encompass that desirable end induced Titus through John's mouth to remove his troops to a distance.

If John was really concerned only with his own survival, it is strange that in the night he sallied forth with not only his body-guard but a mass of non-combatants with their women and children—nearly ten thousand, Josephus tell us—in a bid to reach Jerusalem. For two miles he moved at the pace of the slowest; then he was forced to let them drop behind, and it became a case of every man for himself. At daybreak Titus returned to conclude the treaty; the gates were opened and he was hailed as a liberator and even invited to execute the rebels left behind. He sent a mounted posse to pursue John, who somehow managed to reach Jerusalem safely—an astonishing achievement for a man travelling a hundred miles on foot with only a few hours' start. The stragglers, however, were rounded up, some six thousand being slaughtered and the women and children brought back to the town. Had John hoped to save all these helpless people? Titus was vexed at his escape, but, says Josephus, he had adequate compensation in the mass of prisoners and heaps of dead. So he took no action against the remaining inhabitants, fearing that any penalty inflicted on the guilty might involve the innocent through the machinations of dishonest informers. He merely pulled down a small section of the wall as a token of capture and imposed a small garrison. He was to pay a heavy price for losing John. But Galilee was subdued at last.

CHAPTER 13

Jew against Jew: Roman against Roman

WE COME NOW TO A MELANCHOLY STORY OF FRATRICIDAL STRIFE
in both halves of Josephus' world. In Jerusalem and in the whole
region remaining to her the worshippers of the one true God were
at enmity with each other, injuring and killing their fellow-Jews,
weakening the nation's power of resistance, and making inevitable
the destruction that so manifestly threatened them. In Rome,
where already two emperors had been murdered, four more were
to die violent deaths in quick succession, and two terrible wars
were to be fought between the armies of the rival claimants
before stable government was at last restored. Rome did not, like
Jewry, destroy herself, but she inflicted grievous wounds upon
the body politic, and set a fatal example of emperor-making by
means of assassination and military force which after a brief
respite was to be followed again and many times again.

The blame for the dissensions and internal conflicts in Judaea,
as for the refusal to submit to the unconquerable might of Rome,
is unhesitatingly laid by Josephus on the shoulders of three men—
John of Gischala, Simon son of Gioras, and Eleazar son of another
Simon. The first two we have already met, and we know that
Josephus had personal reasons for hating John, apart from the
political reasons for which he condemns both John and Simon.
Eleazar was of less importance: he has come into our story last,
and will be the first to disappear. John, as you will remember, was
in love with despotic power, a fact that we are now told for the
third time, while he is also credited with the craftiness of a fox and
a long involvement in treasonable activities. It is with his doings
that we must begin.

When after his remarkable get-away from his own town John
arrived with his companions in Jerusalem, he was surrounded by
vast crowds clamouring for news. The fugitives explained that

the object of their flight had been to save their strength for the defence of the Capital, and John exerted all his energies to rouse the warlike spirit of the citizens, assuring them that an enemy who had suffered so severely in attacking the flimsy walls of Galilaean villages could never break through the mighty ramparts of Jerusalem. This evil initiative produced opposite reactions: like the counsellors of Rehoboam, the old men were sensible and fore-saw the coming disaster, while the young ones were headstrong and eager for violent measures. But if dissension in Jerusalem had been provoked by John, it was already raging in the country districts, where advocates of war and lovers of peace were engaged in a furious quarrel which divided communities and even families. Plundering followed, the scattered Roman garrisons being only too pleased to let the Jews ruin each other. Plunderers and plundered alike poured into Jerusalem, swelling the numbers both of the desperadoes who were already given up to banditry and murder and of the idle mob consuming precious supplies. Men in influential positions were imprisoned on the charges of seeking to betray their country to the Romans, and executed without trial. The terrorists then got control of the appointment of chief priests, introducing into the hierarchy creatures of their own, and behaving so insolently towards the Deity that they even entered the Sanctuary with defiled feet. They were resolutely opposed by Ananus, the man whom Agrippa had deprived of the high priesthood four years before, as we saw in Chapter 8, after three months of gross misgovernment. The portrait which Jose-phus drew of him when in *Antiquities* he described those incidents was anything but flattering; here, however, he finds him in every way admirable, as will soon become evident: after all, was he not opposed to the impious, sacrilegious Zealots, who had now made the Sanctuary their stronghold, and were able to draw lots and appoint what priests they liked? Thus one Phanias, not a descend-ant of chief priests but a boorish clodhopper, was dragged from his farm, dressed up in the sacred vestments, and told what he was supposed to do, to the amusement of the gangsters and the distress of the genuine priests.

This was too much to endure. Eminent citizens, such as

Gamaliel's son Simon—the man who had bribed Ananus to agree to the supersession of Josephus—together with Ananus himself and Jeshua, another esteemed chief priest, called public meetings and urged the people to clear the foul usurpers out of the Sanctuary. Zealots indeed! Zealous for all that was vile! The people approved the suggestion but no one had courage to act, so a mass meeting was held, which Ananus addressed in a speech of fiery eloquence worthy of Demosthenes, from whom indeed the speaker—or our author, who reports the speech *verbatim*—borrowed a notable metaphor. It was an admirable piece of oratory and makes most interesting reading, but there is no need to summarize it here. Suffice it to say that the peroration was so moving that the people clamoured to be led against the enemies they had heard denounced, and every man demanded a place in the forefront of the battle. Ananus began to enrol and organize the most suitable volunteers; but the Zealots were awake to what was happening and charged out of the Temple in murderous raids. The ill-equipped patriotic levies joined battle with them, stones, spears, and swords combining to cause heavy casualties on both sides. Wounded citizens were carried home; wounded Zealots retired to the Temple, leaving bloodstains on the sacred floor. At last numbers told, and the Zealots were slowly pushed back into the Temple. As Ananus and his men forced their way in too, they locked themselves in the Inner Court. Stalemate ensued; for Ananus had three reasons for advancing no further: the gateways were too sacred to be attacked; the enemy were throwing missiles from above; and he would have to purify his followers before allowing them to enter the hallowed precincts. So he set an armed guard six thousand strong to keep watch. This whole force was to perish later—thanks to John, to whom we must now return.

Ananus must have been very simple. He allowed the two-faced but obsequious John to accompany him when he attended important discussions and when he visited the guard-posts; and did not even suspect that his secret counsels were being regularly betrayed to the Zealots. When, however, it became obvious that someone was selling the pass and that no one was in a better position to do so than John, the Central Council called on him to swear that he would betray no secrets but would loyally assist them to destroy their assailants. The oath being cheerfully taken, Ananus felt happy again, and John was commissioned to negotiate a treaty with the Zealots. He went at once to the Temple, and informed the blockaded garrison that at Ananus' instigation the people had sent an embassy to request Vespasian to come at once and take over the City. Moreover, the next day there was to be a purification ceremony to enable Ananus' soldiers to get in under the guise of worshippers and attack the defenders at close quarters. Ananus had irresistible numbers at his disposal; so they must either obtain help from outside or sue for mercy; and that they were very unlikely to receive. The two leaders, Eleazar and Zachariah, were specially marked out for vengeance.

'Help from outside' could only mean the Idumaeans; so a letter was sent to inform them that Ananus was betraying the Capital to the Romans; that they, the defenders of freedom, were in a critical situation; and that only the immediate despatch of reinforcements could save them from Ananus and Jerusalem from the Romans. Further details were to be communicated to the Idumaean chiefs by word of mouth; so the two messengers despatched were chosen for both their nimble feet and their ready tongues. The Idumaeans were an excitable race, and on receiving the messages their leaders tore about the country proclaiming mobilisation. The people rushed to arms in defence of the Capital, and in a few days twenty thousand men had been enrolled and the army was on the way to Jerusalem, led by Simon son of Cathla and three other generals.

Ananus had not seen the messengers go, but he could not miss the arrival of the menacing host. He shut the gates and posted sentries, but to avoid a conflict he decided to try persuasion. Jeshua, his second in command, was put up to address them, and his eloquence in no way fell short of the example set by Ananus. It was a strange thing, he said, that a nation should have taken up arms to assist men utterly unlike themselves, the dregs and scum of humanity, drunken bandits and sacrilegious lunatics. They had been brought in by means of an accusation that was utterly false; for there was no intention whatever, now that war had been declared, of submitting to Rome. Was there a single shred of evidence that any letter or message had been sent to the nation's enemies? There were three courses open to the Idumaeans: they might defend the Capital and assist the patriotic citizens to extirpate these lawless, thieving, murderous, cheating ruffians; they might lay aside their weapons, enter the City, and arbitrate between the opposing factions; or they might dissociate themselves from both sides and watch the approaches to see who, if anyone, was in contact with the Romans. If none of these alternatives was accepted, the gates would remain fast barred.

Jeshua's speech had no effect. The Idumaeans were furious at being shut out and invited to lay down their arms; and Simon had difficulty in quietening the uproar so that he could make his reply, which was full of bitter sarcasm. The Idumaeans had come to defend Jerusalem and the Temple, from which, as they were Jews, it was illegal to exclude them. The Romans would have met with a very different reception! He and his men would remain in arms until Jeshua and his patriotic followers came over to the side of freedom.

The Idumaeans roared their applause and Jeshua retired in despair. But if the newcomers were indignant at their exclusion, they were bitterly disappointed at the failure of those who had summoned them to lend them any assistance. Their discomfiture was enormously increased by a terrifying thunderstorm, accompanied by violent earth tremors and a deluge of rain, all portending an unparalleled catastrophe. Both sides felt sure that this would fall on the Idumaeans. How wrong they were! The target of the divine wrath was the people within the City. The Idumaeans suffered little, for they huddled together beneath a roof of shields. The Zealots were eager to help them and thought of attacking the guards and opening the gates. But no fighting was necessary. Fate put the sentries to sleep, and unheard amid the tumult of nature a little band of conspirators sawed through the bars, first of the Temple doors, then of the City gates, and the Idumaeans streamed in. The first objective was the Temple, where they combined with the Zealots to knife the sleeping sentries. The guards in the colonnades, roused at last, seized their weapons and

offered a stout resistance until they realized that they had Idumaeans to fight as well as Zealots. Most of them at once gave up the
struggle; and though the younger men fought with the utmost
valour their shouts for help brought no response from the rest of
the citizens except groans and shrieks. The Idumaeans, blood-
thirsty by nature and battered by the storm, took merciless
revenge for their exclusion from the City. Eight thousand five
hundred of the citizens perished at their hands: those who
escaped were more unfortunate still, thought Josephus; for a
worse fate was in store for them.

Still thirsting for blood the Idumaeans left the Temple area and
roamed the streets, killing and plundering at random. Then they
concentrated their ferocity on the chief priests, and both Ananus
and Jeshua paid the price of their resistance, their bodies being
treated with contumely. 'I should not be wrong', comments
Josephus, 'in saying that with the death of Ananus began the
capture of the City, and that from that very day on which the
Jews beheld their high priest and the guardian of their safety
murdered in the midst of Jerusalem, its bulwarks were laid low
and the Jewish state overthrown.' Then follows an eloquent
encomium on the two dead priests. Wholly honest and unselfish,
and utterly devoted to freedom and democracy, Ananus had he
lived would have brought hostilities to an end; or if compelled
to fight would have proved a most effective leader. Jeshua,
though perhaps not to be compared with him, was far superior to
the rest. 'Virtue herself groaned over the fate of these men,
lamenting that she should have been so completely overcome by
wickedness.'

There was no one left to stand between the citizens and destruction, and the combined forces of Zealots and Idumaeans indulged
in an orgy of butchery. Their particular target was the young
nobles, whom in the hope of securing their co-operation they
refrained from killing but put into prison. One and all these men
rejected every overture, though the penalty was the lash, the rack,
and finally the executioner's sword. In this way twelve thousand
died, over whose bodies no mourners dared to utter a groan.
Then came the next stage—faked trials before sham courts, in

which the juries were required to pronounce an automatic verdict of guilty. Should they dare to do otherwise, as happened in the case of one Zechariah, whose fearless tongue had lashed his accusers as audaciously as long afterwards Dimitrov's was to lash the terrible Goering, the accused was simply murdered and the bold jurymen beaten.

The Zealots had gone too far, alienating thereby the sympathies of their allies, whose indignation was now exhausted and who, as one repentant Zealot pointed out to them at a secret meeting, had found no evidence of a plot to betray the City to the Romans: they had, moreover, been treated with scant respect by those whom they had come to assist, and by whom they had been tricked into sharing responsibility for the inexcusable atrocities that had been perpetrated. Regretting that they had come, the Idumaeans now set free some two thousand imprisoned citizens, who immediately fled from the City and took refuge with Simon son of Gioras. He will be playing a large part in our story before long. Then without more ado the Idumaeans left Jerusalem and went back to their homes. The result of their withdrawal was doubly surprising. The citizens, unaware that it was the less implacable of their enemies that had gone, felt safe again; and the Zealots, freed from the embarrassment of disapproving allies, became bolder than before. They made a dead set against all who roused their envy by possessing superior social status, or caused them fear by showing courage and enterprise. Niger the Peraean, who had performed prodigies of valour in earlier battles against the Romans, was dragged through the City and out at the gates, then murdered as he called down on them the vengeance of Rome, of heaven, and of their fellow-citizens. Death was the penalty for every offence, heinous or trivial, real or imaginary. Only those whom humble birth or poverty made insignificant went in safety.

All this was, of course, known to the Romans, and it produced an acute difference of opinion between the commander-in-chief and his staff. The generals were all for an immediate advance on the Capital, arguing that the Jews might at any moment patch up their quarrels and present a united front to their opponents.

Vespasian retorted that such a proposal did little credit to their commonsense. If they marched now the enemy would certainly unite to oppose them; if they waited the Jews would destroy themselves, a process which it would be wiser for the Romans to watch from a safe distance. The generalship should be left to God, who would make them a present of victory without danger to themselves. Why should they court disaster by plunging into battle when they could win without a fight?

If Vespasian really argued thus, he was wildly wrong. But the speech as reported by our author is unconvincing. Did this practical soldier, this rough-hewn pagan really propose to leave the generalship to God, or is it yet another attempt of Josephus to show that it was the Romans who were pious, the Jews who were impious? The generals too had announced that Providence was fighting for them. And was Vespasian sanguine enough to expect victory without danger and without a fight? The Jews were to be left for three more years to destroy themselves, and at the end Titus might have had something to say about victory without a fight! However, for the time being the policy seemed to be justi-fied by events; for numbers of people left the City, some eluding the Zealots, others purchasing their liberty by heavy payments, while those who could not pay were slaughtered. Dead bodies were heaped up along the roads and left to rot; for burial was forbidden. Yet even these dead were envied by the wretches tortured in the gaols.

We have for some little time lost sight of the wicked John. But now he re-emerges for a moment, intent, as we are told yet again, on establishing himself as sole sovereign. He had gradually separated himself from the Zealots and built up a following of his own, some of them subservient to him through fear, others won over by his oratorical tricks. The two gangs kept a wary eye on each other, but for the present they were too intent on looting to come to blows.

Meanwhile, terrorism was rampant on every side. During the Feast of the Passover the Sicarians who had seized the fortress of Masada took advantage of the inactivity of Vespasian's legions to make a night raid on the little town of Engedi ten miles further

north. The men escaped from the town, but seven hundred helpless women and children were butchered. The houses were
stripped bare and the crops seized as booty. All the villages in the
area were looted, and the fields ravaged. The same sort of thing
went on in every district of Judaea, small gangs plundering their
own villages and then joining forces in the wilderness, so that
raids could be made on sanctuaries and cities without fear of
retaliation.

This too came quickly to Vespasian's ears; for though the
insurgents killed anyone caught attempting to leave the City,
some few escaped unnoticed and fled to the Roman camp, where
they protested their loyalty to Rome and begged Vespasian to
save what was left of the Jewish people. Winter was over and it
was now the spring of the year 68, so the legions were ready to
move. Vespasian's first task was to reduce all remaining centres of
opposition, so that when he invested the Capital he should be safe
from any interference from without. He therefore marched to
Gadara—not the city of Decapolis but the fortified capital of
Peraea—which thanks to the co-operation of the well-to-do, who
dreaded any interference with their present comfortable tranquillity, he entered without trouble. After murdering the presumed
leader of these collaborators the dissentient element fled from the
city, while the rest of the population pulled down their walls,
welcomed Vespasian with loud cheers, and received a garrison to
protect them. The fugitives were not allowed to get away. Chased
by a large mixed force under Placidus, on whom Vespasian
clearly placed great reliance, they took refuge in a village to the
south-west, armed the local youngsters, and boldly rushed out to
attack the Romans, who first gave ground to entice them away
from the walls, then surrounded and slaughtered them. Those
who escaped from the trap forced their way into the village and
shut the gates; but after fierce fighting Placidus broke through the
defences, destroyed all who failed to escape, ransacked the houses,
and set the village on fire. Those who did escape alarmed the
whole countryside, and the terrified inhabitants fled in a mass in
the direction of Jericho, the only defensible city within reach.
But the Jordan was swollen and impassable, and when overtaken

by the cavalry they were forced to give battle. The Roman missiles and lances did terrible execution, and fifteen thousand perished on the bank. Over two thousand were taken prisoner, with quantities of livestock, and an unknown number leapt into the water, rendering the river impassable with their bodies, though thousands were later seen floating on the Dead Sea. Placidus then proceeded to occupy all the Peraean towns and villages as far as Machaerus.

While this was happening Vespasian had taken most of his forces back to Caesarea. But they were not to remain idle long; for news arrived of troubles in the far distant west. Nero's power was cracking, and his fourteen-year reign was nearing its end. Julius Vindex had headed a revolt in Central Gaul, and though his army had been destroyed by the forces of Virginius Rufus it was plain that civil war was imminent. In readiness for this it was essential to liquidate the Jewish problem with all speed, and Vespasian set about the formidable task with his usual relentless efficiency. He left Caesarea with the bulk of his forces, stayed two days at Antipatris, then, destroying every village as he went, pressed on to what was left of Lydda and Joppa and from thence to Emmaus, north-west of Jerusalem. Leaving the Fifth Legion there he moved south, burning and destroying in southern Judaea and northern Idumaea, where he put ten thousand of the inhabitants to death and enslaved another thousand. Then he returned to Emmaus, next moving north to Neapolis, the modern Nablus, in Samaria, where he arrived in June. Thence to Jericho, where he was joined by Trajan, whose forces had by now subdued all Transjordan. Jericho was empty, as the whole population had fled; but many people had stayed in the environs, and these were put to death. Garrisons were placed in Jericho and at other strategic points, so that Jerusalem was now hemmed in on all sides except the south-east, and any who eluded Zealot vigilance and escaped from the City must needs walk into the arms of the Romans.

Vespasian returned to his general headquarters at Caesarea, and was on the point of marching against Jerusalem when the expected news came. Nero was dead. On the ninth of June he had committed suicide, and Galba had been recalled from Spain to take his place. Vespasian at once called off all military activity pending the receipt of new instructions and sent his son, accompanied by Agrippa, whose throne was once more in danger, to pay homage to the new emperor. It must have been a very slow journey; for in the following January they had not yet got beyond Greece when they learnt that after a seven-month reign Galba had been assassinated. Agrippa went on to greet the newest claimant, Otho, but Titus 'by a divine impulse' made a speedy return to Caesarea, where it was again decided to hold up all operations against the Jews.

For the Jews, however, there was to be no respite, since they had enemies enough at home. Simon son of Gioras was less crafty than John but superior in strength and audacity—and, in Josephus' eyes, only a little less detestable. Driven away by Ananus from the neighbourhood of Jerusalem, he had attached himself to the Sicarians in Masada and joined in their plundering forays. When Ananus was dead he embarked on the pursuit of royal power, establishing himself in the hills at the head of a formidable army of bandits, which he got together by the device so common in the Graeco-Roman world of proclaiming liberty for slaves and offering large monetary incentives to freemen of all classes. With these he was soon strong enough to overrun the upland villages; and as his forces grew and with them his own authority he mastered the whole area north-east, east, and south of Jerusalem, using a number of caves to accommodate his commandoes and safeguard the loot. Had not the young outlaw David done very much the same thing a thousand years before?

It was clear now that his real objective was the Capital, so to forestall any further increase in his power the Zealots marched against him in full force. In the ensuing battle they were defeated with heavy loss and the survivors fled back to the City. But just as Vespasian was unwilling to attack Jerusalem till he had reduced every outlying stronghold, so Simon thought it better to postpone his attack till he had conquered all Idumaea. After all, he had only twenty thousand men. Against these the Idumaeans were able to deploy twenty-five thousand, and when they met in battle a whole day's fighting proved so inconclusive that both sides withdrew. Simon, however, soon returned with larger forces and encamped at Tekoa only a dozen miles south of Jerusalem, from which he sent yet another of the many Eleazars to Herodeion three miles away, to induce the Idumaeans to surrender that fortress. But the unfortunate envoy was chased away and forced to take his own life. Before risking a battle, however, the Idumaeans decided to reconnoitre the enemy forces. An officer who volunteered for the task went straight to Simon, and in return for the promise of an influential position undertook to help him conquer the whole of Idumaea. Then he returned to his own lines, reported that Simon's army was many times its actual size, and having thereby destroyed the confidence of all ranks urged them to place themselves in Simon's hands. Meanwhile he sent messengers to tell Simon that the time was ripe. When the bandit forces approached, he and his confederates leapt on their horses and fled, causing the whole Idumaean army to scatter in a panic. Simon, following up his success, advanced to Hebron, where he captured vast booty and quantities of corn. From there he went on, plundering and ravaging on every side to supply the needs of an army now doubled in size, and likened by Josephus to a swarm of locusts.

With such a formidable enemy the Zealots were not disposed to try conclusions a second time; but they achieved a notable success by ambushing the commander's wife, whom they carried off to the City in the belief that for the return of such a hostage Simon would lay down his arms. Their guess was wide of the mark. The enraged husband encamped close to the walls and seized and tortured all who ventured outside the gates: he was ready to feed on their dead bodies, says Josephus in one of those wild denunciations so irritating to the modern reader. Some he treated in the same way as his critic had treated the unfortunate Clitus, and sent back to report that if his wife was not instantly restored to him he would break down the wall and treat the whole population in the same way. Even the Zealots were terrified by this threat, and sent the lady back to her husband. Horrible as were the means he had adopted, it is pleasant to find that in that brutal age there was a husband whose wife counted for so much.

It was now the spring of the year 69, and we must leave Simon for a moment and see what had been happening on the Roman side; for sedition and civil war were not confined to one half of Josephus' world. In mid-January Galba had been assassinated in the open Forum, and his place taken by the much younger Otho. But Roman emperors enthroned as the result of murder were as insecure as the ancient kings of Israel. 'Had Zimri peace, who slew his master?' Or if you will, 'We but teach Bloody instructions, which being taught return To plague the inventor.' It was only three months before the legions in Germany named Vitellius emperor, and at Bedriacum in Cisalpine Gaul defeated the army of Otho, who on learning of the disaster committed suicide, leaving Vitellius free to claim the throne. Soon after news of this event arrived in Palestine, Vespasian marched out of Caesarea once more and occupied regions and small towns north of Jerusalem, taking many prisoners. Meanwhile Cerialius with a small body of horse and foot ravaged Upper Idumaea, and after capturing a number of less-known places forced his way into the ancient city of Hebron, once the capital of David, which he burnt to the ground after massacring every single inhabitant. Only three strongholds remained unreduced—Herodeion, Masada, and Machaerus; and the eyes of the Romans were fixed on Jerusalem.

That city once more becomes the focus of our attention; for Simon, who on recovering his wife had returned to what remained of Idumaea and forced most of the population to flee to the Capital, presently reappeared outside the walls. He was more terrifying than the Romans; but the Zealots inside caused more agony still. They had given control to John, and he in return gave them freedom to do as they liked. They looted, murdered and ravished; dressed in women's clothes, used scent and cosmetics, walked with mincing steps; and turned the City into a den of unnameable vice. But if they looked like women they murdered like men. John had lost control, and all the Idumaeans in the City turned on the Zealots, killing some and chasing the rest into the Temple. John rallied his supporters and prepared to counterattack. The Idumaeans, fearing his craftiness, conferred with the chief priests who, thought Josephus, were led by God to choose a remedy worse than death: they sent the high priest Matthias to invite Simon into the City. It was April when Simon entered. He at once led the citizens in an assault on the Temple; but John had the advantage of position, and with his customary ingenuity had raised four great towers on which, like Vespasian at Jotapata, he had placed archers, slingers, and light artillery. Simon's forces suffered severely.

At this point Josephus once more switches our attention to troubles in Rome, of which, being intensely interested in that city, he gives a detailed account. A brief summary will be sufficient for our needs.

It was not till his return to Caesarea in June or July that Vespasian heard of the accession of Vitellius and of his outrageous behaviour on arriving in the Capital. He was tempted to interfere, but was afraid both of the long journey and of the onset of winter. His soldiers, however, fancied the part of emperor-makers, and considered that they had a much better candidate than Vitellius. Vespasian protested his unwillingness to accept nomination, but under physical duress was at length compelled to agree. Mucianus urged him to assume imperial honours forthwith; but for three reasons Vespasian thought that the first necessity was to get control of Alexandria: it was the chief granary of Rome, whose citizens he was quite prepared to starve into submission; there were two valuable legions there; and if things went wrong he would be safe in a country with such strong natural defences. So he sent at once to the governor of Egypt and Alexandria, Tiberius Alexander, requesting his assistance. Alexander obtained the eager support of soldiers and civilians too, the legions being delighted. Vespasian moved to Beirut, where he received congratulations from all directions.

It was a fortunate occasion for Josephus. Vespasian recalled how when Nero was still on the throne he had dared to call him Caesar; he was shocked to think that the mouthpiece of God should be still in captivity; and he ordered the prisoner to be brought and released. Thereupon Titus suggested that as the recognized sign that the punishment had been unjust the fetters should be cut through, and Vespasian ordered them to be severed with one blow of an axe. Rehabilitation had come after two years, and the favoured turncoat was free to accompany his master to Alexandria, there to marry his third wife. More had to be done before they made the journey. Vespasian appointed various governors, then proceeded to Antioch, whence he despatched Mucianus to Italy with a large army to settle affairs in Rome. Mucianus, chary of sailing in the depth of winter, made the tremendous journey overland.

Meanwhile, Antonius Primus was marching on Rome from Moesia, much nearer at hand. To oppose him Vitellius sent Caecina, the conqueror of Otho's generals. The two armies faced each other at Cremona; but Caecina, feeling certain of defeat, urged all his officers to transfer their allegiance. For the moment they agreed, and the whole army with them; but a few hours later the soldiers changed their minds and bound the traitor, with the intention of sending him to Vitellius. Primus, learning of this, made an immediate attack and the mutineers turned tail, only to be encircled and destroyed by the opposing cavalry. Vitellius' loyal army of over thirty thousand trained soldiers perished in the battle, while Caecina was released, to be honoured by Vespasian to whom he was sent with news of the victory.

In Rome all was not yet over. Sabinus, Vespasian's elder brother, seized the Capitol and was joined by his young nephew Domitian. Vitellius, more disturbed by this than by the destruction of his army, flung the rest of his troops against the Capitol, which after a most sanguinary struggle was captured and set on fire. Domitian escaped in feminine disguise, but the garrison was annihilated and Sabinus hauled before Vitellius and executed. Next day the army of Antonius marched in and destroyed the victors of yesterday to the last man. The gorged and drunken emperor was dragged through the crowd, insulted, and stabbed to death, fifty thousand others perishing with him. On the next day, the 22nd December, Mucianus arrived, and after putting a stop to further bloodshed secured the appointment of Domitian as acting head of state pending the arrival of his father, who was acclaimed emperor.

Alexandria was soon overflowing with envoys come from all over the world to congratulate Vespasian. He, being eager to embark for Rome as soon as winter was over, could spare no more time for the Jews. He therefore deputed Titus to destroy Jerusalem, allotting him the best of his troops. Titus, after sailing some way up the Nile, marched overland to Gaza, then by Ascalon and Joppa to Caesarea, where he proposed to concentrate his forces. He had just celebrated his twenty-ninth birthday, and before the next came round his task would be completed.

CHAPTER 14

The Agony of Jerusalem

ALL THE STRATEGIC PREPARATIONS NECESSARY BEFORE JERUSALEM could be assailed had already been made by Vespasian, and Titus had only one objective, the City itself, which he was determined to attack as soon as the campaigning season opened. Jerusalem, although as in Jeremiah's day there were some who felt sure that the Lord would never allow His Temple to fall into Gentile hands, was in no condition to resist a magnificently equipped and thoroughly trained army under a careful and enterprising commander with everything in his favour. The state of the City was appalling: Josephus likens her to a maddened beast devouring its own flesh; for instead of preparing to resist the coming attack she was engaged in three-cornered intestine warfare. The Inner Court of the Temple was occupied by the Zealots, headed by Eleazar son of Simon and three others who had broken with John. Their numbers were small compared with John's, but he was awkwardly placed, occupying a lower level from which it was difficult to retaliate when pelted from above. Simon was master of most of the City, but had to attack John from beneath, John having the advantages as well as the disadvantages of the middle position, and being well provided with artillery, which in endeavouring to dislodge Eleazar's men often caused havoc among the worshippers in the Temple courts. All three factions were well supplied with provisions; for Eleazar did not scruple to raid the Temple stores, and the other two plundered the City, seizing what they wanted. In doing so they recklessly burned down both houses and granaries, so that between them they destroyed enough grain to support them through many years of siege. Jerusalem was committing suicide.

Titus was on the move. With the men from Alexandria he had brought his father's old legion up to strength, adding the Twelfth

Legion, which was eager to avenge its defeat under Cestius, to the Fifth, Tenth, and Fifteenth. He had also the royal troops and other allied contingents. They were all to meet at Jerusalem, whither the Fifth was to march via Emmaus, the Tenth via Jericho, while Titus himself led the rest through Samaria. He pitched his camp near Saul's Hill an hour's march from the rendezvous. From the hill he led a cavalry patrol six hundred strong to see if the Jews would surrender at the sight of him. But when he was approaching the north-west corner of the City a large party poured out and cut him off from the bulk of his little force. Finding his escape route closed the fearless commander charged the middle of the foe, scattering them in all directions. His incomparable prowess—but why trouble the reader with these adulatory heroics? We shall have plenty more. Titus got back to his men, and the Jews returned full of confidence.

'When ye see Jerusalem compassed with armies, then know that her desolation is at hand. Then let them that are in Judaea flee unto the mountains; and let them that are in the midst of her depart out; and let not them that are in the country enter therein. For these are the days of vengeance.'[1] Such was the warning given by Jesus on the day before His death; and all Christian tradition agrees that it was heeded; the little flock found shelter in the Peraean town of Pella and survived the destruction of the Capital; and the bishop who had been their shepherd since the martyrdom of James, Symeon son of Clopas, lived to be crucified in extreme old age.

To get a clear picture of the events that must now be related it is necessary to have some knowledge of the topography of Jerusalem. Of the various descriptions we possess, that of Josephus is by far the most valuable and should be carefully studied: we have space here for only the briefest summary. Anyone familiar with modern Jerusalem should remember that the ancient city extended further to the south and not so far to the north and west, and that the valleys and ravines of Josephus' time have been largely filled in. The old city was built on three hills, respectively occupied by the Temple in the east, the Lower City in the south,

[1] Luke xxi. 20-21.

and the Upper City in the south-west, the Upper City being separated from the other two by the Tyropoeon Valley. The three were surrounded by a wall, outside which ran deep ravines except on the north. At the north-west corner of the square formed by the wall stood Herod's Palace and his three great towers. The city had gradually extended northwards, and a second wall ran from Herod's Palace to Antonia, the fortress which towered up to the north-west of the Temple area. Beyond this lay Bezetha, the New City, and an area as big as the Old City had been enclosed within the wall begun by Agrippa I and never properly finished. Anyone wishing to capture the City must of necessity attack from the north or north-west, and break through the three walls in turn; and Antonia and the Temple must be the object of a separate attack.

The Temple hill, which had its own fortifications, had been built up into a large plateau. The original Temple of Solomon had been replaced by one of similar design, consisting of two halls, the oblong Holy Place and the square Holy of Holies, with priests' chambers attached to the walls on the outside. This block, which we shall call the Sanctuary, formed only a small part of the whole Temple, which was made up of a series of courts at different levels. The Outer Court was the lowest, and was surrounded by immense colonnades—the 'porches' of the Authorized Version—their combined length measuring three-quarters of a mile. This court, the Court of the Gentiles, was separated by a balustrade and terrace from the Inner Court, round which ran more colonnades. This was the Court of the Women (to which both sexes were admitted), separated by a flight of steps and a magnificent gate from the Court of the Israelites, within which again was the Court of the Priests on the highest level, containing the great altar and behind it the Sanctuary itself. It was a temple without parallel in those days and in these, and its huge size must always be borne in mind: it covered some twenty-five acres.

During the night Titus, whom Josephus now regularly calls Caesar, was joined by the Fifth Legion; and in the morning he advanced to Look-out Hill, an eminence overlooking the City, and pitched his own camp three-quarters of a mile from Agrippa's wall with the Fifth Legion six hundred yards behind, while the Tenth, which now arrived, pitched theirs the same distance to the east on the Mount of Olives beyond the Kidron. The Jews reacted swiftly. Patching up their quarrels they tore across the ravine and caught the labouring Tenth off their guard. Men trained to fight according to the book and in obedience to orders are, as Josephus correctly remarks, most quickly demoralized by unorthodox tactics. The legion turned tail, and disaster would have followed had not Titus rallied them, charged the Jews, and driven them down the steep slope. Then a mass of fresh men appeared from the City and caused renewed panic in the Roman lines. Titus was left almost alone; but deaf to all appeals from his few loyal friends he stood his ground, made a second successful charge, and drove the Jews into the ravine.

It was now the 14th of Nisan, and Eleazar opened the Temple gates to admit citizens who wished to celebrate the Passover. John's followers, their weapons concealed, slipped in with them, then suddenly threw off their disguise and seized the inner courts. The Zealots scurried into the Temple vaults, but later emerged to put themselves under John's command. The three factions were now reduced to two, eight thousand men under John holding the Temple and Ophel to the immediate south, while fifteen thousand under Simon occupied the rest of the City. John now had Eleazar as second-in-command, while Simon's lieutenants included Simon son of Cathla, the Idumaean.

Josephus now reappears in our story. He had returned from Alexandria with Titus, with whom he remained to the end, hated by the Jews and suspected by the Romans. He was employed as an intermediary, and it was now that he made his first vain appeal to the Jews to surrender. They were far too confident to think of yielding, and engaged the Romans again outside the walls, inflicting such heavy casualties that Titus had to make drastic changes in his dispositions. He pitched a new camp only four hundred yards from the north-west corner of Agrippa's wall, and deployed his forces in massive strength opposite the northern and western sections, making sorties almost impossible.

While Josephus was again endeavouring to put peace proposals before the sentries his companion Nicanor was struck by an arrow. This spurred Titus to begin the siege at once, and having chosen a weak spot in Agrippa's wall not far from the traditional Golgotha he embarked on the construction of platforms for his engines, stripping the suburbs of all available timber. Simon replied by mounting captured Roman artillery on the wall and pelting the builders as they sheltered behind their wicker screens, the Romans retaliating with much heavier missiles. The Rams were now brought up and the battering began. The frightful din had an electrifying effect within the City. All animosities were forgotten and the two factions united to counter the imminent danger. Weapons were showered on the Romans, and parties dashed recklessly out to attack the crews of the Rams; and in spite of Titus' tremendous efforts the wall suffered little damage. A lull followed; and then the Jews suddenly poured out, bent not only on burning the engines but on reaching the Roman defences. They fought with the utmost fury and might well have been successful had not Caesar charged with the flower of his cavalry, killing twelve men with his own hand and driving the rest into the City.

In addition to the platforms, Titus had three towers constructed, each seventy-five feet high, and though one of these fell down in the night the weapons hurled from the top floors did so much damage that the Jews abandoned the battlements, and the Romans worked unmolested until Victor, the biggest Ram, knocked a hole in the rampart. The Jews retired to their second wall and the Romans, pouring through the breach, opened the gates and let in the whole army. It was the 7th of May, and the fifteenth day of the siege. Titus spread out his men from one side of the New City to the other and at once began to probe the second wall. The Jews resisted strenuously, John being in charge of Antonia and the northern colonnade, and Simon manning the wall itself. There were endless sorties and the Jews showed no sign of giving way.

Titus now applied a Ram to the middle of the second wall, and four days after breaching Agrippa's he broke through this one too and entered with a thousand legionaries. As he wished to keep the City intact he refrained from breaking down more of the wall, an act of 'kindness' which was to cost him dear. The partisans attacked the small Roman force as it passed through the narrow streets. The Roman guards posted on the wall fled to their camps, and Titus' infantry would have followed them had they been able to get through the narrow gap towards which they were being driven. As it was they escaped destruction only because the heroic Titus, firm as a rock, pinned down the Jews by a stream of arrows till his men were clear. He then again tried to force an entry, and though the Jews stood their ground with superb courage for three days they at last gave way and Titus, entering a second time, avoided further trouble by demolishing half the wall.

Two walls had been captured in such quick succession that Titus might have been expected to attack the third and weakest immediately; but he decided to suspend operations until the citizens had had time to discuss surrender, a process which he hastened by a curious device. He ordered a pay-parade in full view of the Jews. On such occasions Roman soldiers always appeared in the equivalent of Guards' dress uniforms and were drilled with full ceremonial. We should hardly think of trying to strike terror into our enemies by Trooping the Colour, but Titus' scheme worked admirably, and the dazzling spectacle filled even the boldest defenders with consternation. For four days this softening-up continued; nevertheless, the citizens made no overtures for peace. So the siege began again, and Titus decided to raise four platforms, two facing Antonia and two the middle of the third wall; for if Jerusalem was to be his both Temple and Upper City must be captured. The work made slow progress; for Simon's men carried out destructive sorties, and John had over three hundred engines which he used to good effect; so Titus tried persuasion again, and sent Josephus to make his third appeal.

How the ancients made themselves heard amid the din of battle is a mystery, and as Josephus circled the City he kept out of range of the defenders' missiles; but heard he was. He enlarged on the invincibility of the Romans, so merciful to those who surrendered, so relentless to those who resisted; on the helplessness of the Jews, their internal divisions, their imminent starvation. It was they, not the Romans, who would destroy the City. These arguments being received with howls of derision and execration, he treated his audience to one of those long expositions of the nation's past history of which Jewish orators were so fond. Pharaoh Necho, Abraham and Sarah, the plagues of Egypt, Dagon and the Ark, Sennacherib and Cyrus, Zedekiah and Jeremiah, Antiochus and Pompey, Herod and Sossius were all passed in review. It was still not too late to repent of their unspeakable crimes, and by throwing away their weapons to save their incomparable City and Temple which, stubborn fools that they were, they were in the act of destroying. 'I know that danger threatens my own mother and wife, and perhaps you think it is for their sake that I advise you. Kill them! take my flesh and blood as the price of your own salvation! I too am ready to die, if thereby you can learn wisdom.'

Neither this moving peroration nor the tears that accompanied it had any effect on the partisans; but the common people began to think about desertion. Some sold their property for the little that it would fetch, then swallowed their gold pieces to provide for their future needs. Titus allowed these deserters to pass through his lines unharmed, hoping thereby to encourage further desertions. Rich men who remained were killed for their money, and the hungry partisans broke into houses in search of food, torturing all who could not or would not produce it. The stealing of food soon became a universal practice: even those who crawled out in the dark to gather herbs were robbed as they returned. Simon and John became brothers in crime. 'They drank each other's health in the blood of their countrymen and divided the carcases of the wretches between them.' Titus did not show the same tolerance to foragers as he had hitherto shown to deserters. Every day five hundred or more fell into his hands, and after scourging and every kind of torture were crucified in full view of the defenders, while deserters were no longer spared but sent back without their hands.

After seventeen days of continuous effort the platforms were at last complete, and the engines in position; but the resourceful John tunnelled right under the two nearest platforms, keeping the galleries open with wooden props. Then he brought in faggots daubed with pitch and set light to them: the props were burnt away, the galleries collapsed and into them crashed the platforms. Flames shot up, which the despondent Romans made no attempt to control. Two days later Simon assaulted the other two platforms, and three men whom Josephus regards as the greatest heroes of the defence set the engines on fire, remaining till they were well alight. The Romans arrived too late to extinguish the flames, which soon spread to the platforms themselves, and beat a retreat to their camps, fearlessly pursued by Jews who poured out from the City and advanced right to the Roman fortifications. The situation was serious; but—has the reader guessed?—Titus appeared in the nick of time, sternly rebuked the waverers, charged the flank of the Jews, and would have captured them all had they not hastily withdrawn within their walls.

The supreme commander now held a council of war, at which one party advocated a full-scale assault by the whole army, another the immediate reconstruction of the platforms, a third complete inaction while the beleaguered Jews starved to death. Titus felt that inaction would undermine discipline, and that besides making damaging sorties the Jews would get supplies in somehow and prolong the siege; the only safe and speedy way was to enclose the whole City with a wall. Then, while resistance was crumbling, work on the platforms could be resumed. The generals were convinced, and the work was shared out. It was a stupendous undertaking: the circuit measured four and a half miles, the ground was very difficult, and thirteen large forts were to be built on outside. Yet such was the competition from legion down to individual that the task was completed in three days. The forts were garrisoned and at night the intervals were patrolled, each watch being taken by one of the generals, beginning with Titus himself. The fate of Jerusalem was sealed. 'The days shall come upon thee, when thine enemies shall cast up a bank about thee, and compass thee round, and keep thee in on every side, and shall dash thee to the ground, and thy children within thee; and they shall not leave in thee one stone upon another; because thou knewest not the time of thy visitation.'[1]

Jerusalem was filled with hunger and despair, and Josephus

[1] Luke xix. 43-44.

paints a vivid and terrible picture of her agony. The dead were too numerous to bury, and the valleys outside were choked with rotting corpses thrown from the walls. How many died we shall never know: but deserters put the number of pauper bodies thrown out in three and a half months at six hundred thousand, and stated that others had been stacked in the biggest houses and locked in. The exultant Romans delighted to display their own ample supplies of food to the starving inhabitants, who nevertheless showed no sign of submission. The partisans executed anybody suspected of favouring the Romans, Simon even condemning that Matthias who had invited him into the City, and his three sons; while Josephus' father was imprisoned. Titus 'in his anxiety to rescue the survivors' began constructing four new and bigger platforms, though timber had now to be fetched from ten miles away: this time all four were directed against Antonia. While the work proceeded Josephus renewed his attempts at persuasion. This time he was knocked unconscious by a stone, and the Jews rushed out to seize their prize. But Titus sent soldiers to the rescue, and after a struggle they carried him back to camp. The partisans, believing him dead, were cock-a-hoop, and Josephus' imprisoned mother uttered a lament which he somehow managed to put on record. However, he soon showed himself again, to the consternation of the partisans and the joy of all good citizens.

There now followed a new wave of desertions, but the wretched fugitives fared very differently from their predecessors. Arriving in the Roman lines with empty bellies many stuffed themselves until they burst; a few had repeated the old trick of swallowing gold coins, and when this was discovered in the case of one man two thousand were cut open in a single night and their bowels ransacked. Titus was so disgusted with this outrage that he was on the point of shooting down the perpetrators; but there were thousands of them, and he was unable to proceed beyond threats, and these proved unavailing; for 'avarice, it seems, scorns every penalty, nor is any emotion as strong as covetousness'.

The Romans took three weeks to raise the new platforms, in the process turning sixty square miles of beautiful woodland into a desert. On these hung the fortunes of both sides: if the Jews failed to destroy them they were doomed; if they succeeded the last hope of defeating them was gone, since no more timber was available and Roman morale was low. On the first of July John sent out a party with firebrands. But their usual vigour was missing; mailclad legionaries were massed to oppose them, and the attempt failed. The Rams were then brought into action, but made no impression on the stout walls. However, in the night came a windfall for the Romans: the remainder of John's old tunnel caved in and the wall collapsed. But John was no fool, and when the Romans explored the gap they had a nasty shock— John's men had built another wall behind, and none of Titus' soldiers dared attempt to scale it. It was time for another of those harangues so necessary for the temperamental Romans, and Titus was never at a loss for words. He stressed the dangers, promised handsome rewards, made numerous references to the Deity, and painted a confident picture of the bliss awaiting the souls of heroes, freed from the flesh, welcomed by the ether, and set among the stars. Well, well! The prospect, not surprisingly, did not appeal to the bulk of the army and they made no response; but a shrivelled little Syrian called Sabinus offered his services, and at midday, followed at a distance by eleven others, he strode towards the wall and despite a deluge of missiles climbed to the top, and would have routed the Jews had he not stumbled and been shot to pieces, fighting to the last. All the eleven were killed or wounded. The next attempt was more prudent. At two in the morning twenty-four men climbed up in silence, stabbed the sentries, who as so often happened with the Jews were asleep, and sounded a trumpet call. The guards fled and Titus led his picked troops to the top, while other Romans poured in through John's tunnel, and drove on towards the Temple. For eleven hours the partisans put up a furious resistance, and succeeded in pushing the intruders back; but they could not clear them out of Antonia, and Titus ordered his men to lay the fortress flat.

Josephus was again put up to address the defenders, this time inviting John to bring his forces outside the walls and settle the issue without involving the City and Sanctuary. John made a bitter retort, to which Josephus delivered a reply, full of sobs and groans, which caused a number of priests and other notable citizens to go over to Caesar, who received them kindly and settled them in Gophna 'in perfect safety and supremely content'. How different from his reception of the poor! This sensible treatment resulted in a wholesale flight to the Romans, until the partisans took violent action to stop it and the Temple courts were littered with dead bodies.

Titus, though anxious to save the Sanctuary, felt compelled to resume hostilities. He formed a task-force of men picked from every unit, and ordered it to attack the guardposts an hour before sunrise. He would have commanded it himself had not his friends held him back. This time the guards were not asleep, nor did they turn tail. There was a furious battle in the darkness and neither side gave an inch, till at noon the fight was broken off. The legions now began to construct four platforms outside the Temple walls, though timber now had to be carried eleven or twelve miles, and the Jews had resumed their effective sorties, and even made a powerful, though unsuccessful attempt to capture the Roman posts on Olivet. They also destroyed the colonnade linking Antonia to the Temple, and fired the western colonnade after trapping a number of Romans on the top. The Romans retaliated by burning down the northern.

All the while the sufferings of the starving citizens were daily increasing: they were driven to eat leather and old hay, and one woman devoured her own infant. The story is told in every detail, and shall not be repeated here. 'Behold, the days are coming in which they shall say, Blessed are the barren, and the wombs that never bare, and the breasts that never gave suck.'[1]

The Temple walls were immensely strong, and though the Rams, mounted on the newly completed platforms, pounded them for many days they made no impression; so the Romans set up ladders and climbed on to the colonnades, from which they were thrown down with heavy losses. Titus next ordered his men to set fire to the gates, from which the flames quickly ran along the colonnades, while the Jews looked on in utter helplessness. The

[1] Luke xxiii. 29.

next day they recovered their confidence and made a sally against the Romans in the Outer Court, and would have driven them out had not Caesar—yes, had not Caesar led his picked horsemen to the rescue and driven the Jews back into the Inner Temple. He was anxious to capture the Sanctuary intact, and was planning a full-scale attack for the morrow. But one of the soldiers who had got into the Inner Temple climbed on another man's back and 'moved by some supernatural impulse, threw a blazing firebrand through an aperture into one of the cedar-lined chambers on the north side. The flames shot up and the Jews, forgetting everything else, dashed to put them out. Titus, who had been resting after the battle, was quickly informed: he raced to the scene, followed by officers and men in a disorderly huddle. He shouted and waved to both sides to put out the fire, but no notice was taken: in fact his own men called for more firebrands to be thrown in. The flames were still confined to the chambers; so Titus, after taking his staff into the Holy Place, whose furnishings far surpassed his expectations, once more tried to persuade his men to extinguish the blaze, even commanding a centurion to flog the disobedient; but they were mad on destruction and looting: one man pushed a firebrand into the hinges of the gate, and the sacred interior was soon ablaze. Titus and his staff now withdrew, leaving the Sanctuary to its fate. It was, says Josephus, 'the most wonderful edifice ever seen or heard of, both for its size and construction and for the lavish perfection of detail and the glory of its holy places; yet we find very real comfort in the thought that fate is inexorable.'

Left to do as they liked, the soldiers indulged in a mad orgy of looting and indiscriminate murder, while the partisans fought their way out of their blazing stronghold, through the Outer Court, and into the City. Such Romans as were still amenable to discipline methodically set fire to the remaining Temple structures, deliberately burning to death six thousand non-combatants who had taken refuge on top of one colonnade, deceived by a false prophet. Josephus here takes occasion to remark on the stubborn refusal of the Jews to heed a whole series of unmistakable portents —stars, comets, strange lights, gates that opened of their own accord, chariots in the clouds, and even a cow that gave birth to a lamb in the Temple courts! Nor had they listened to true prophets, such as a yokel called Jeshua who proclaimed the doom of the City and persisted even when Albinus flogged him almost to death. The story, which will also be found in Eusebius' *History*, deserves to be read in full.

The Romans now showed their contempt for the God whose Sanctuary they had destroyed by erecting their standards in the Temple precincts and sacrificing to them. Delighted with the plunder with which every soldier was loaded they hailed their commander *Imperator*. That model of gentleness now got the last of the priests into his hands, and calmly informing them that the correct procedure for priests was to perish with their temple, ordered their execution.

'And as some spake of the temple, how it was adorned with goodly stones and offerings, he said, As for those things which ye behold, the days will come in which there shall not be left here one stone upon another, that shall not be thrown down.'[1]

The Temple had indeed gone, but the rest of the City remained. The partisans now invited the Roman commander to a parley; so he took his stand to the west of the Temple site and with the aid of his interpreter—unnamed, but surely Josephus—addressed the Jews massed on the other side of the Tyropoeon Valley. It was the usual historical diatribe, full of abuse for the crimes and stupidity of the Jews, and of praise for the patience and kindness of the Romans, who even now were prepared to spare their lives if they threw down their weapons and surrendered unconditionally. To this they replied by requesting leave to go with their wives and children right away into the desert. Regarding this surely reasonable plea as gross impudence the infuriated commander, who had no doubt hoped to round up thousands of human chattels to be profitably auctioned, declared that henceforth he would spare no one; and the next day he sent his men to burn and sack the City, a mission which they set about with a will. But when a number of prominent citizens appealed to him for protection, he 'lived up to his character'—or shall we say,

[1] Luke xxi. 5-6.

showed his customary partiality for the well-to-do—and granted them asylum. On the second day the whole of the Lower City was overrun and set on fire, and only the Upper City remained to the last-ditch defenders. This could not be mastered without platforms; so the troops began building these on the east and the west. It became expedient to encourage deserters once more; so Titus reversed his previous decision and accepted any number. Of these all who were not 'townsmen', including the women and children, were sold as slaves; but as the supply far outstripped the demand and they no longer fetched an economic price, forty thousand townsmen were given complete liberty—an excellent inducement to others to follow their example.

In eighteen days the platforms were ready and the Rams began their work. Opposition was slight, and a section of the wall soon gave way. The Romans were in the Upper City at last, and resistance was at an end. The partisans plunged into the sewers with which Jerusalem was honeycombed, vainly hoping to hide there until the storm was over. Horrified as the Romans were when they found streets and houses full of emaciated corpses, they had no mercy on the living; 'running everyone through that fell in their way, they blocked the streets with the dead and deluged the whole city with blood, so that in numerous instances it extinguished the flames.' (Traill.)

All that remained now was the mopping up. Titus was only interested in those Jews who could be useful to him: by his specific order the aged and infirm were butchered; known terrorists were executed; the youngest and handsomest were kept for the triumphal procession; others, if over seventeen, were sent in chains to do hard labour in Egypt, or presented to the provinces to make sport in the amphitheatres; those under seventeen were sold; eleven thousand were starved to death in prison. Does Josephus betray any disgust at the cold-blooded savagery of his patron, or any pity for his suffering countrymen? Not a trace. He goes on coolly to give the statistics: prisoners taken in the whole war totalled ninety-seven thousand; those who perished in the siege one million one hundred thousand. Perhaps nothing is more painful to read than his account in the *Life* of how, having received as solace for his personal misfortunes a gift of sacred books, he secured from Titus the release of his brother and fifty friends; then picked out from a great batch of prisoners one hundred and ninety of his acquaintances and got them also freed, magnanimously demanding no ransom; and finally, on seeing among a number of prisoners as they hung on crosses three further acquaintances, went weeping to Titus and begged for them to be taken down and cared for. No tears or pleas for any but his friends! And not a word about his father, his mother, or his wife!

There is little more to tell. Those who had hidden in the sewers, if still alive, were ferreted out. John, nearly dead from starvation, surrendered, and for reasons not stated escaped torture and death and was sentenced only to life-imprisonment; Simon, who was not yet caught, was to meet a much more terrible fate. 'God rewarded them both as they deserved,' writes the censorious and complacent historian. The outlying districts were fired and the walls demolished. The whole City and Sanctuary were razed to the ground, leaving only Herod's three towers standing 'as a monument to Caesar's luck', and a stretch of wall on the west to protect the legion which was to garrison the glorious city that was no more. 'No one visiting the spot would believe it had once been inhabited.' Or as Another had said: 'Behold, your house is left unto you desolate.'[1]

[1] Luke xiii. 35.

PART THREE

The Sequel

CHAPTER 15

Celebrations

THERE BEING, AS JOSEPHUS SAYS, NO ONE LEFT FOR THE SOLDIERS
to kill or plunder, and no more buildings for them to demolish,
Titus felt that the time had come to bestow compliments and
rewards, and to make his dispositions for keeping Palestine and its
neighbours 'pacified', as the Romans called it. On his old camp-
site he paraded the whole army, and mounted a dais to deliver an
address. He praised their unfailing loyalty and obedience (making
no mention of their complete disregard of his authority when he
tried to save the Sanctuary). Their heroic efforts had proved to all
men that no power on earth could hold out against Roman valour.
But not even their victorious termination of so prolonged a war
could equal their achievement in providing Rome from among
their ranks with such magnificent rulers, winning thereby the
gratitude of every citizen. All his soldiers were admirable; but
some had rendered outstanding service, and these would be
rewarded. The names of these heroes were then read out; they
came forward one by one; and their commander presented them
with golden crowns and torques, miniature gold spears and silver
standards, together with quantities of booty, besides promoting
every man to a higher rank. Then he stepped down amidst
thunderous applause and directed the sacrifices, which took the
form of a victory feast for the troops, while he and his staff
celebrated for three whole days. Next he announced the destina-
tions of the various units. The Tenth Legion had already been
chosen to keep order in Judaea. The Twelfth, in spite of its
excellent services to himself, was punished for its defeat under
Cestius by being banished to the upper reaches of the Euphrates.
The Fifth and Fifteenth were to stay with him until he arrived in
Egypt. With them he went down to Caesarea, where he dumped
the booty and arranged for the custody of the prisoners. The

purpose for which he required these was soon made plain; for at Caesarea Philippi, to which he moved next, he staged a series of entertainments in which he diverted the citizens by showing them prisoners thrown to the beasts or compelled to fight each other.

Here he received the joyous news of the capture of Simon. It was a story in keeping with all that we know of this enterprising rebel. When he had gone down into the sewers he had taken with him his most reliable friends, a team of sappers, and ample supplies of food. When they reached the tunnel's end they worked their way ahead in the hope of emerging at a safe spot, as some others succeeded in doing. But progress was slow and supplies ran out; so Simon, hoping to be taken for a ghost, somehow managed to dress himself up in fancy clothes and to emerge where the Temple had once stood. The sentries were startled, but only for a moment. They asked him who he was; the garrison commander was fetched; and Simon was kept in chains pending the receipt of instructions from Titus. Thus 'he was put by God beneath the heel of his most bitter enemies'. When Caesar returned to the coastal Caesarea he ordered the captured leader to be reserved for the delectation of the Roman public. Here too, on the 24th October, he celebrated the birthday of his brother Domitian by sadism on the grand scale; more than two thousand five hundred of the men who had put themselves at his mercy were devoured by savage beasts, killed in gladiatorial combats, or burnt alive. Next came his father's birthday, at which all records must be broken: there was 'a lavish display' at Beirut, and the shows were magnificent'. It was now the 17th of November. Titus' pleasure in his own doings was enhanced by reports of his father's enthusiastic reception in Italy, whither he had made his leisurely way during the siege of Jerusalem. It is all described by Josephus with fulsome adulation which I will spare the reader, together with his account of the revolt of the German chiefs Classicus and Civilis, who had been defeated by Petilius Cerealis and, it would seem, utterly routed by that teen-age military genius, Domitian.

After a somewhat lengthy stay in Beirut the elder brother resumed his triumphant progress through Syria, treating every town to the same bloody entertainment, till he arrived at the great city of Antioch. Men, women, and children poured out to welcome him, mingling their acclamations with vehement appeals for the expulsion of the Jews. Until three years before the local colony had been very large and prosperous, enjoying equal privileges with the Greeks, and making many converts. But soon after Vespasian's arrival on Syrian soil a renegade Jew named Antiochus had seized on the prevailing animosity against his people to accuse his own father, the rest of the colony, and some foreign Jews, of plotting to burn down the city. The foreigners were burnt alive; and when Antiochus had repudiated his religion, offered sacrifice to Greek deities, and persuaded the authorities that all Jews should be compelled to do the same, the majority refused to conform and were executed. He then used Roman soldiers to suppress Sabbath observance. Shortly before Titus' arrival another blow fell. Fire destroyed a number of public buildings and swept through the whole city. Antiochus charged the Jews with responsibility, and the credulous citizens rushed madly upon them. The acting governor, Collega, quickly intervened, and after careful enquiry found no evidence against any of the accused; but their position remained perilous. When an appeal was made to Titus, he listened impassively to all that was said against them and made no response; he then went to receive the congratulations of the Parthian king and feast his emissaries. On his return he was again bombarded with requests to take action against the Jews, but he refused to interfere in any way. He then set off for Egypt, pausing on the way to take a last look at Jerusalem, piously disclaim any responsibility for its destruction, and receive an account of the vast wealth still being dug out from under the ruins. Arriving at Alexandria by the shortest desert route, he sent the Fifth and Fifteenth Legions back to their old stations, packed off Simon and John, along with the seven hundred best physical specimens of their late followers, to be exhibited in Rome, whither he followed them, accompanied by Josephus and apparently by the seductive Bernice and her complaisant paramour-brother.

In Rome he naturally received a hero's welcome, and the people were rapturous on seeing him reunited with his father and brother. The senate decreed a separate triumph for each of the two victors; but they preferred to combine for a single celebration on the most grandiose scale, of which our author gives us a detailed description. It was the display of a lifetime, and the whole immense population lined the streets to witness it. Before dawn all the soldiers formed up near the Temple of Isis, where the generals had spent the night. As day broke Vespasian and Titus appeared, wearing wreaths of bay and crimson silk robes, and went to the Octavian Walks to be received by the Senate and magistrates. Then mounting a dais they seated themselves on ivory chairs and listened to the loyal tributes of the soldiers. The Emperor called for silence, and wrapping his cloak round his head offered the ceremonial prayers, followed by a short speech. The soldiers were dismissed to enjoy a grand breakfast; the generals donned their triumphal robes and sacrificed to the gods; and the procession moved off once more. Josephus finds himself unable to do justice to the magnificent spectacle—the works of art, varieties of wealth, rarities of nature, and masses of silver, gold, and ivory resembling a flowing river. There were crimson curtains and Babylonian embroideries, jewels, statues, and an assortment of animals in gorgeous trappings. The members of the huge escort, and even the great array of prisoners, were splendidly attired. Most wonderful of all were the great floats, many of them three or four storeys high, framed in ivory and gold and richly curtained. These carried tableaux realistically portraying the glorious sights of the war—smiling countryside laid waste, formations put to the sword, fugitives and prisoners, huge walls thrown down, armies streaming into captured strongholds, the reek of slaughter, temples on fire, rivers flowing through blazing countryside, and even a number of ships. A thrilling sight indeed, and one which we can hardly visualize; a real Roman holiday to delight the unpitying spectators, and to call forth from the smug Josephus the heartless comment: 'Such were the agonies to which the Jews condemned themselves.'

So vast was the booty that most of it was heaped up indiscriminately; but a special place was given to the Temple treasures—a heavy gold table, the seven-branched 'candlestick', a copy of the Law. Then by way of contrast came shining statues of Victory; and last of all Vespasian with his sons riding behind him. At the Temple of Jupiter Capitolinus the procession halted to await news of the enemy commander's death. So Julius had awaited news that his gallant adversary Vercingetorix, brought out from a dark prison after seven years, had been strangled. Who was the victim now? Not John but Simon, who was dragged by a noose to the Forum while his escort tormented him cruelly. The announcement of his death was received with shouts of delight, sacrifices offered, and the sophisticated savages dispersed to gorge themselves till bed-time.

But such joys must not be speedily forgotten. Vespasian, with unlimited wealth at his disposal, resolved to commemorate his triumph for all time by erecting a Temple of Peace. Four years later, in 75, it was dedicated. It was the ancient equivalent of our art galleries and museums; for it was filled with the works of the greatest painters and sculptors, and Vespasian brought into it treasures collected from every corner of the world. There too he placed the golden trophies from Jehovah's Temple, keeping the Law and the Sanctuary curtains in the Palace for his own delectation. Titus, in more boastful vein, was later to raise a triumphal arch on which with admirable skill parts of the great procession were depicted, and for our information the likeness of the Temple treasures is preserved for all time. The treasures themselves, alas, are no more: it is thought that they were carried off by the Vandals to Africa, to be later transported thence by Belisarius to Constantinople; but like the Ark of the Covenant which Nebuchadnezzar removed from the First Temple to Babylon they have long since vanished.

The Romans had been in conflict with external enemies almost continuously for eight hundred years: they had fought innumerable wars and had declared peace again and again. It was proof of the tremendous impact of the Jewish War that it was the one whose termination had been commemorated in a Temple of Peace 'surpassing all human imagination'. When had it terminated? Officially on that September day in the year 70 when resistance finally ceased in Jerusalem and Titus felt that his work was done. But the stubbornness of the Jews knew no limit, and the Romans had to battle for three more years before the last bastions fell.

Lucilius Bassus was the new commander in Judaea, and his first task was soon accomplished: Herodeion capitulated without any show of resistance. But two other of Herod's fortresses remained, Machaerus and Masada, and both were immensely strong. It was against Machaerus that Bassus determined to march, lest it should serve as a rallying point.

Herod well knew how to site his strongholds, and Machaerus stood on a tall and rocky eminence surrounded on every side by immensely deep ravines. Bassus decided to fill in the ravine to the east, though it was a hundred and fifty feet deep. While the work was going on, the Jews separated themselves from the 'useless' Gentiles and made a serious of sorties to test the seriousness of the threat. In many of these an energetic young man named Eleazar took the lead in the attack and was the last to withdraw. Finally he was caught off his guard by an Egyptian soldier, who picked him up and carried him to the Roman lines. Bassus, surpassing in brutality Titus' best effort, ordered him to be stripped naked and flogged with whips in full view of the Jews. His agony was more than they could endure to watch, and when Bassus set up a cross as if he would crucify the wretched man, they determined to save his life by offering to surrender. The Romans agreed to spare the Jews, but the Gentiles were excluded: their only hope was to steal away in the night. But the Jews betrayed them, and the Romans massacred seventeen hundred men and enslaved the women and children.

Bassus had two other tasks to perform. Hearing that Jews who had escaped from Jerusalem and Machaerus were sheltering in the forest of Jardes he encircled the area and began cutting down the trees. An attempted break-through failed, and three thousand Jews perished. Next, acting on instructions from Rome, he sold all the Jewish territory and sent the entire proceeds as a perquisite to the Emperor, while the old Temple Tax was levied from Jews everywhere and paid into the Capitol. Then Bassus died and was succeeded by Flavius Silva.

Silva led the whole army against the only fortress that still held out. Masada, like Machaerus, was perched on a height whose almost vertical sides ran down into deep ravines. Josephus has left us a fascinating description which before long we shall be able to compare with the results of archaeological research. It was occupied by Sicarians led by Eleazar, a descendant of Judas the Galilaean. Silva attacked his formidable task with energy. He established his headquarters in a commanding position to which food and water had to be painfully carried up from a distance; then, after throwing a wall right round the fortress to make escape impossible, he performed an almost incredible feat of military engineering. On the left of the hill was a rocky ledge four hundred and fifty feet below the level of the fortress. On this Silva made his men heap earth till they had raised a solid platform three hundred feet high. On this they built a pier of fitted stones, reaching seventy-five feet higher still. On this in turn they erected heavy siege-engines and a ninety-foot ironclad tower with light artillery on the top. While this drove the defenders from their battlements a Ram battered the wall until a section collapsed. Behind it, however, the resourceful defenders had built a second wall of most original construction. It consisted of a framework of great baulks tied together by crossbars and packed with earth. This absorbed the blows of the Ram and suffered no damage. Silva decided to try fire, and burning torches were hurled at it. It was soon ablaze, and though a change of wind momentarily threatened to destroy the Roman engines the whole bastion was ruined.

Eleazar realized that all was lost; and knowing that the Romans would pour in next day and that every man, woman, and child in the town was doomed, he assembled the toughest of his brigands, and after making it plain that all was indeed lost invited them to admit that by their sins against their fellow-Jews they had brought on themselves the vengeance of God. To God therefore they must pay the penalty, but they could preserve their freedom to the last and cheat the Romans of all their hopes if the fortress and everything that it contained went up in flames and they themselves died by their own hand.

As might be expected, this brave suggestion had a mixed reception: not everyone, even if willing to die himself, is ready to kill his wife and children first. Eleazar tried again, and his speech makes a strange contrast with that delivered by Josephus in the cave at Jotapata. Josephus, in the name of God and His Law, had argued that suicide was a sin: Eleazar, in the same name, proclaimed that it was a duty. He mingled rebuke, scorn, and exhortation with history; he reminded his hearers of what had happened to those who had been captured in other strongholds, and depicted to them what they would see done to their own wives and children; he portrayed life as an evil and death as a good; he described in Platonic terms the relation of soul and body and the nature of immortality; he praised the Indians who to win the joys of a better life flung themselves on their own funeral pyres, and exhorted his hearers to show as noble a spirit. 'Let us deny the enemy their hoped-for pleasure at our expense, and without more ado leave them to be dumbfounded by our death and awed by our courage.'

The soundness of these arguments and the morality of self-murder may well be questioned; but of the nobility of what happened at Masada, as of the ignobility of what had happened at Jotapata, there can hardly be a doubt. The story is told in vivid detail by Josephus: how he obtained his knowledge will appear soon.

Eleazar's second speech produced such an overwhelming effect that every member of his audience was filled with a passionate desire to do as he had urged. Personal affection was very strong, but 'reason won the day'. They embraced their wives and took their children in their arms; but not one man failed to carry out his resolve. All their possessions were piled up and set on fire; ten men were chosen by lot to dispatch the rest; then they all lay down beside the bodies of their dear ones and exposed their throats to the knife. When only the ten remained, they again drew lots to choose their own executioner, with perfect confidence that there would be no cheating. The nine then followed the others, and the last survivor, after setting fire to Herod's Palace, drove his sword right through his body. Nine hundred and sixty men, women, and children lay dead.

How could Josephus bear to tell this story, so different from his own? And how did he know what had happened? By implication he gives us the answer to this second question; for he tells us that two women—who presumably had no husbands to assist them out of life—and five small children had hidden in the buried water-conduits. One of the women was of superior intelligence and education. She would need to be, if she was to memorize Eleazar's speeches and later repeat them to Josephus or his informant. But how from her hide-out under the ground did she witness that last tragic scene?

Early next morning Silva's troops entered the town, and finding no sign of life shouted aloud. The two women emerged and told the Romans the whole story, the intelligent one giving a clear report of Eleazar's oratory and the effect it had produced. Sceptical at first, the Romans found the lines of dead men and paid tribute to the nobility of their resolve. The fortress was garrisoned, and the rest of the army returned to Caesarea; 'for nowhere was there an enemy left'. The long war had ended on the 15th of April 73, and Vespasian, who had anticipated this day when two years earlier he had shut the doors of the Temple of Janus as evidence to all the citizens of Rome that nowhere in all her wide dominions was there a war, could without reservation rejoice as he watched the progress of his Temple of Peace. Peace did indeed last throughout his own short reign; but in the four centuries still left to her Rome was to be engaged in countless wars against barbarian enemies, and sometimes between rival emperors; while for Jerusalem, 'City of Peace', before two generations had passed there was to be the agony of another three years' war, the destruction of all that Titus had spared, and the building on her desolate site of a new city with a new name, a city from which all her children were shut out, and in which a Temple of Jupiter rose from the ruins of the House of the Lord.

However, Josephus has not quite finished the story of the Jewish War. In their own land, now the personal property of Vespasian, the agony was over. But there were many Jews elsewhere; and in Egypt, where they had suffered so severely a few years before, they were to suffer again. A number of Sicarians had escaped to

Alexandria, where they started an extreme nationalist and theocratic movement, endeavouring to persuade the whole Jewish colony to repudiate the authority of the Emperor. Prominent Jews whose one desire was to let well alone were murdered; so the leaders of the Senate called a mass meeting at which they denounced the meddling agitators and urged that they should be handed over to the Romans. The advice was accepted; six hundred were rounded up and subjected to every kind of torture to make them call Caesar lord. But with the fortitude of which only true martyrs are capable every single one, including little children, refused to utter the saving word. This disturbance Lupus the governor of Alexandria at once reported to the Emperor, who to deprive the Jews of a rallying point ordered him to demolish the temple which the priest Onias, a fugitive from the religious persecutions of Antiochus Epiphanes, had built in the district of Heliopolis. Lupus contented himself with shutting up the temple; but he died, and his successor Paulinus stripped the building of all its treasures, put an end to all worship, and locked the gates.

Another incident occurred in Cyrene, where a weaver called Jonathan led out a number of poor Jews into the desert to witness miraculous signs which he promised to produce. The leading Jews reported his movements to the local governor Catullus, who sent cavalry and infantry to attack the unarmed devotees. The few who survived the massacre were brought before Catullus, and Jonathan informed him that he had received his instructions from the wealthiest of the Jews. Delighted with this absurd accusation, Catullus ordered Jonathan to name a Jew called Alexander against whom he himself had a grudge. This done, he disposed of Alexander and his wife, and went on to murder three thousand of the wealthier Jews, confiscating their property for the benefit of Caesar, to ensure that Caesar should ask no questions. But it might be that Jews elsewhere would reveal his crimes; so he invited Jonathan to charge with subversive activities 'some of the most respectable Jews in Rome'—including Josephus! He brought his prisoner to the Capital to substantiate the charge, and Jonathan testified that Josephus had sent him weapons and cash; but Titus saw to it that his father found the accused not guilty, and Jonathan was tortured and burnt alive 'as he deserved'. Catullus got off with a reprimand; but shortly afterwards he became sick in mind and body: he was tormented by the ghosts of those he had murdered, and finally his bowels were eaten through and fell out. 'Such was his end, proof, if ever there was one, of the Providence of God.'

So, with a final tribute to the esteem with which his worthy self was regarded in heavenly places, our author brings his *The Jewish War* to an end.

CHAPTER 16

The Pensioner

IT WAS NOW THREE YEARS SINCE JOSEPHUS HAD COME IN THE train of Titus to Rome, where he was to spend the second half of his life. The first half had been exciting and stormy; the second was to be tranquil, comfortable, and prosperous, with few embarrassments to ruffle the placid surface of his content. Before there had been experiment, the open air, authority, a struggle for life, an attempt to serve two masters; now there was to be the satisfying but uneventful life of a writer, self-chosen confinement to the study, the wielding of the pen not the sword, and, as far as we know, no flights of oratory save those composed for inclusion in his histories. Josephus was a free man; to all intents and purposes a freedman; for like a manumitted slave he had taken the name of his master, and Joseph been Matthias had become Flavius Josephus. He had much to be thankful for. If it is true that at Jotapata he did the Romans all the damage that he claims to have done, it is remarkable that Vespasian and Titus, both of whom treated their helpless prisoners and thousands of non-combatants with such ruthless brutality, not only spared his life but showed him unique favours from the very first. Were they, as he would have us believe, the natural result of the esteem in which the commander and his son held him as the inspired prophet of their greatness? or were they the material reward for services rendered in the conquest of his unhappy country? At this stage we must content ourselves with the brief sketch of his good fortune which he gives us in his autobiography.

Titus, showing him the utmost respect, made him the companion of his voyage to Rome, where Vespasian carefully provided for him, assigning him an apartment in his own private residence, honouring him with Roman citizenship, and bestowing on him a generous annuity. These favours were continued till the day of Vespasian's death; and though the unfortunate Jonathan was followed by many others who, envious of the pensioner's good fortune, framed accusations against him, divine providence saw to it that he was invariably acquitted. He seems to have suffered from no lack of means; for previous to the grant of his annuity he had been compensated by Titus for the loss of his lands at Jerusalem with an estate on the plain, to which Vespasian shortly afterwards added a large tract of land in Judaea. And we must not forget the earning power of his pen. He had slaves of course: a Roman with means but no slaves was unthinkable. He had had slaves even in Palestine, where the constant use of the word *doulos* in the gospels—mistranslated 'servant' in our bibles— suggests that they abounded. In view of what Josephus had done to his victims in Galilee and was to do to his son's tutor in Rome we may guess that his slaves had anything but a happy lot.

Of the size and character of his *ménage* he tells us nothing, nor do we know whether it resembled those of his neighbours or was an island of Jewish life in a Gentile sea. Did he when in Rome do as the Romans did? or remembering the faithful priests whom in Nero's day he had come to rescue did he, himself a priest, follow the example of their piety and live on figs and nuts to avoid ceremonial defilement? He does, indeed, lift one corner of the veil to inform us, for the fourth and last time, of his matrimonial affairs. Though he was little more than thirty-five he had already had three wives—the one whom he abandoned in Jerusalem, the one whom he married at Caesarea on Vespasian's instructions and who declined to accompany him to Alexandria, and the one whom he there selected to fill the vacant position. This one bore him three sons, of whom only one survived; but her conduct failed to satisfy him, and he replaced her with a Jewess from Crete who 'came of a very aristocratic family, one of the most disting- uished in the country, and in character was well above the general level of her sex, as her subsequent behaviour proved'. She too obliged by presenting him with two sons. Whether the first two wives had borne any children, or whether the last two bore any daughters in addition to the five sons, he does not think it necessary to tell us: for the three who survived, the loyal Jew chose

no Jewish names, but Greek and Roman in equal numbers—the
first was called Hyrcanus, the second Justus, and the third, with
superb impartiality, Simonides Agrippa.

Vespasian's death in no way incommoded Josephus. Titus
esteemed him as highly as his father had done, and showed the
same contempt for the spate of accusations which continued
unabated. These must have been the golden years for Josephus;
for from the start it had been Titus who induced his father to trust
and befriend the wily Levantine; it was to Titus that Josephus had
rendered his greatest services; and whereas Vespasian was old
enough to be his father, Titus was nearly but not quite his own
age. But Titus was destined to reign for only two years and a
quarter, and his younger brother Domitian was a very different
person, for whom Josephus had done nothing save to pay him
unconvincing compliments in *The Jewish War*. He had none of the
sturdy commonsense and rough sense of humour of his father;
none of the leniency and sweet reasonableness of his brother: he
was not a man to be admired and loved but a man to be feared
and avoided. Yet so far from interfering with Josephus' happy
state he added to his 'honours', by which we are presumably to
understand emoluments; and like his two predecessors he gave
short shrift to those who even when Josephus had occupied his
privileged position in the Capital for more than a decade continued to traduce that innocent personage. Various Jews were
'punished'—the word used is an ominous one—and the Emperor
authorized the same treatment to be administered to one of Josephus' own slaves, a eunuch whom he had chosen for the responsible post of tutor to his son. No man is a hero to his own valet;
but many men are held in respect by those most intimate with
their daily life. Must it be that all these unspecified accusations
were pure inventions, prompted by spite against one deemed a
turncoat and a traitor; or was there a little fire beneath this cloud
of smoke? We shall never know. One thing is clear: whatever
services Josephus may or may not have rendered to the new
emperor he was secure in the favours of that dangerous potentate;
for Domitian went even beyond his predecessors, and not
content with disposing of Josephus' enemies he exempted his

Judaean estates from taxation, which was, as Josephus modestly affirms, the greatest honour that could be conferred on any man. We note, moreover, that his relations with the court were not merely official but personal also; for just as during his first visit to Rome he had got what he wanted from Nero by winning the support of Poppaea, so now he was in the good books of the Emperor's consort Domitia, who never ceased to load him with favours.

And there 'for the present' he brings the story of his life to an end. There is no mention of Domitian's assassination; of the accession of Nerva, so different in every way that the friends of the hated tyrant might well have been in the greatest danger; or of that emperor's premature decease which brought the mighty Trajan to the throne. Consequently we can never know what changes if any the end of the Roman Flavii brought to the Jewish Flavius: we can only assume that he was left in peace; and we know that he was able to continue his labours with the pen, perhaps beyond the turn of the century. May we not conclude from the imperial favours that remained unbroken for thirty years, and from the constant succession of Jewish attempts to undermine his position, that both parties were satisfied that he had been the friend of the Romans and the enemy of the Jews? And dare we say that they were mistaken?

Concerning the world in which Josephus spent the second and, as far as we know, uneventful half on his life we have in the writings of other authors a vast amount of information, which in such a work as this it would be impossible even to summarize; but it will be helpful to glance briefly at some of the features of life in the Capital that seem to have been of special importance in the last thirty years of the first century, and that can be seen in relation to our newly-begotten Roman. And first let us take a closer look at the five emperors whose favours he so continuously enjoyed.

After nearly five centuries of senatorial rule the principate, as we have seen, had been established by Caesar Augustus, backed by the professional soldiers who to the very end were to remain the makers and unmakers of emperors. Nothing was less congenial to the young emperor's temperament than to rely on the naked support of military force: by supreme tact and political acumen he got all real power into his hands, while showing the greatest respect for old institutions and traditions, and keeping up the appearance of senatorial authority and the pretence of a desire to lay down the powers which had been 'temporarily' bestowed upon him. The system worked admirably in Augustus' lifetime; but few of his successors had qualities resembling his own, and it was inevitable that a polity so largely based on fiction would be adapted to the realities of the situation and modified in the direction of autocracy. The semblance of senatorial authority was maintained till the assassination of Caligula, when it received its death-blow from the refusal of the Praetorian Guard to allow any candidate to be elevated to imperial power other than its own nominee, Claudius. When with the suicide of Nero the Julio-Claudian line came to an end it was the soldiers who, at the cost of civil war and enormous bloodshed, set up in rapid succession four emperors, culminating in Josephus' first imperial patron Vespasian.

Vespasian, who reached the age of sixty in the year of his accession, was no statesman; but he was a vigorous and efficient administrator, who saw what needed to be done and did it. Contemporary estimates of his character sometimes cancel each other out: his conduct as governor of Africa is described by Suetonius as upright and most honourable, by Tacitus as infamous and odious. Both writers agree in accusing him of avarice; but the evidence suggests, not that he was concerned with feathering his own nest—he must have made a pretty pile already out of the sale of all Jewish territory, which he had 'treated as his own property'—but that he applied himself to securing the greatest public benefits at the lowest public cost, a practice not often to be observed in Roman imperial history. In his short reign he accomplished much that would have been impossible to a weaker man: instead of yielding to the soldiers' demands for more ease and higher pay he subjected them to hardship and stern discipline; instead of distributing largesse to the civilians he levied new taxes and increased tribute; and in his own household he set an example of simple living that was a visible protest against the luxurious self-indulgence of a largely idle population. To secure efficiency in government he greatly developed the Civil Service which Augustus had started in a tentative way. (It is strange that such a practical people as the Romans should ever have thought it possible for an empire to be run by magistrates changed annually and without any previous experience of the duties they were required to perform.) Having by his prudence restored the public finances to a healthy state he was able to leave his visible mark on Rome by a vast programme of building. Much of the city that had met the eyes of Josephus on his first visit had disappeared in Nero's fire, and Vespasian's first task was to rebuild what had been destroyed, to replace mean alleys by streets to be proud of, and to repair the damaged aqueducts. But Vespasian went much further: he enriched the City with a new forum and with buildings of dazzling magnificence—the Temple of Peace already described, public baths on a lavish scale, and his supreme architectural achievement, the Flavian Amphitheatre or Colosseum. Josephus, who had been so impressed by the splendid buildings that were the memorials of Herod the Great, must have watched with eager eyes as this huge edifice arose on the site where he had once seen Nero's Golden House—an edifice over two hundred yards long and four storeys high, in which fifty thousand citizens or more could be seated at a time to watch the spectacles in the vast arena. But Vespasian's life was not to extend beyond the allotted span, and he had been in his grave one year when this, the greatest of his works, was solemnly inaugurated by his son and successor.

That son was cut off by fever when he was little more than forty; but he had had time to show that he was no slavish follower of his father, whose stern economy he abandoned in favour of lavish spending and public munificence, which combined with his fine presence and winning ways to make the citizens forget how strongly they had disapproved of his affair with the promiscuous 'Jewess' Bernice, with whom he had parted with notorious reluctance when she, who had already had three husbands and at least three paramours, was anxious to be his third wife. He now became so popular that he was called the beloved and the darling of all mankind—an estimate, as Dr Edward Salmon pungently remarks, derived from his lavish spending and his short reign, in which much of the surplus built up by Vespasian's thrift was dissipated, bequeathing a serious problem to Titus' brother and successor, Domitian. That popularity was further increased by the banishment of professional informers, an action which must have enabled many citizens to enjoy more peaceful sleep, though it made no difference to the Jewish accusers who caused Josephus so many headaches. Titus had time also to leave his mark on the outward appearance of Rome and to increase the amenities of the citizens; for in addition to his Triumphal Arch with its superb reliefs (completed like the Colosseum a year after its originator's death) he added yet another to the number of great public baths, communal bathing being a social pleasure to which fashionable Romans were greatly addicted.

It was in Titus' reign that Vesuvius erupted, raining destruction on Pompeii and Herculaneum and causing the deaths, among many others, of that encyclopaedic writer, the elder Pliny, who only two years before had dedicated to Titus the thirty-seven volumes of his fantastic *Natural History*, and as an experienced soldier of about forty-five is thought by some to have been on Titus' staff in Palestine. It was presumably there that he made the acquaintance of the Essene community on the western shore of the Dead Sea, of which in that all-embracing work of erudition he has left us a famous description, to be set alongside those of Philo and Josephus, who, as the reader will remember, had for a time been an Essene himself. It was that same insatiable scientific curiosity that brought him with fatal results to investigate the disaster in the Bay of Naples—a disaster which drew the Emperor himself to survey the scene of desolation and to open his purse for the relief of the survivors. Did Josephus go with him? Did he at any time leave the security of the Capital to visit other places, risking an encounter with some of his own countrymen, slaves in mine or field or quarry, who hated him still as the man who had helped in their undoing and had alone reaped the benefit? He tells us nothing, and no ancient writer found cause to add anything to his own account of his life.

Titus had no heir, and it had been Vespasian's intention from the beginning that his two sons, separated in age by eleven years, should reign in succession. It is surprising therefore that although Vespasian—anticipated years before by Josephus—gave Titus the title Caesar and associated him in the government of the Empire, neither he nor Titus gave the title to Domitian or conferred upon him any military command or administrative office. To deny to a future Emperor, and a man whose nature was morose and suspicious, all responsibility, experience, and worthwhile activity was a psychological blunder of the first magnitude. The result was that this repressed young man on finding himself in a position of absolute power exercised it despotically, was ostentatious in his appearance, and, defying the rule of all his predecessors, save the mad Caligula, that in Italy at least no divine honours should be paid to an emperor till they were voted by the Senate after his death, insisted on being addressed as *dominus et deus*. In his hands the Senate became even less of a political force than it had been since Claudius' time; for by making himself permanent censor he was able at any time, without appealing to the electorate, to appoint as senators any he thought fit, including Gauls and Spaniards. But he was an able and energetic ruler, who pursued a sound policy abroad and continued the work of his father and brother at home, beautifying the City, and building or rebuilding a multitude of temples; and if he did not deserve the fulsome flattery of the poet Martial, who identified him with Hercules, he ought never to have been the target of the satirist Juvenal, who rained envenomed shafts upon him when safely in his grave, or of the panegyrist Pliny the Younger, who to glorify Trajan by comparison blackened the memory of Domitian.

How interesting it would be if Josephus had told us something of Domitian's character and doings, for he was his dependant and neighbour for fifteen years—half his stay in Rome—and was far too clever and too well informed to be unaware of what was going on. But Domitian had maintained and increased his 'honours', and beyond that he saw no reason to include any facts or comments in his autobiography. And yet, in *The Jewish War*, his interest in everything Roman had led him to tell us far more about the earlier emperors than his theme demanded. The deaths of all except one of them, as of Pompey, Caesar, Cassius, and Mark Antony, were carefully recorded; but of the conspiracy against Domitian, ending in his murder at the instigation of his wife, Josephus' friend Domitia, there is not a word. In a later chapter we shall consider a possible explanation.

Gaius, Claudius, and Nero, the Julio-Claudians; Galba, Otho, and Vitellius, made and destroyed by the legions; Vespasian, Titus, and Domitian, the Flavians—all these had reigned since the birth of Joseph ben Matthias. Now at the age of fifty-nine he was to see the birth of a fourth era, the era of 'the five good emperors', that was to end only when the virtuous and philosophic Marcus Aurelius was fool enough to abandon his four predecessors' wise practice of nominating the best available men to be their successors, and let his son, the vicious and notorious Commodus, succeed him. First of the five was Nerva, an elderly lawyer, who was actually chosen by free vote of the Senate— by permission of the Praetorian Guard, whose commander was in collusion with Domitia, and whose threats he was later able to keep at bay only by the bold and imaginative stroke of adopting as his son and heir the most popular man in the army, Trajan. Nerva was an astonishing success, but like Titus he lived for only two years. It was a Spaniard who took his place, the first of many men who were called from distant parts of the Empire to hold sway in the august capital. Of him I propose to say no more than this, that he was a strong but tactful ruler, a daring and brilliant soldier, and one of the greatest of Roman builders. For though he reigned nineteen years we cannot say how much of his work was witnessed by Josephus, who is generally believed to have lived through two or three of those years, but whose death cannot be dated: we have no evidence that he lived beyond the year 100 or 101, though had he lived till the reign ended in 117 he would still not have exceeded the permissible four score years.

What sort of community was it over which these emperors presided? We must beware of picturing Rome as full of men of the type that prevailed in the days of Horatius, or Africanus, or Cicero: it was a cosmopolitan city whose population of a million or more was mixed in two senses. In the first place people of every race poured in from all parts of the known world to take up temporary or permanent residence in the capital city. Many of these came from Syria and Palestine, so that a disapproving patriot complained that the Orontes was flowing into the Tiber. In addition to those who came by their own wish there were thousands of freed slaves who had taken Roman names, adopted Roman ways, and in the second generation become Roman citizens. For slaves formed a large proportion of the population, and many of them were manumitted by grateful masters or used their carefully hoarded pocket-money to purchase their release, thereby becoming *libertini*—an ominous word—and slavemasters in their turn.

In the second place there was no impediment to marriage between men of these two classes and women of Roman or Italian blood; so that in addition to the many races that were living side by side in the great city there arose a new stock, much blended and, for better for worse, nondescript. The Romans were proud of their history; but they were not offensively race-conscious, and it would be a mistake to read too much into the oft-used word *barbari*, which implied neither hatred nor contempt. In Caesar's *Commentaries* the word has no more emotional significance than *Galli* or *Britanni*, with which it is freely interchanged; and if in admitting some of these *barbari* to the Senate he went beyond what old-fashioned Romans could stomach, we must remember that Cicero himself had been despised as a *novus homo*. In the century that followed change was very rapid. In the army not only were the rank and file almost entirely non-Roman, but good soldiers of foreign birth could even become generals; for instance, the elder Trajan, a Spaniard, was one of Vespasian's most trusted commanders in Palestine, while Tiberius Alexander, a Jew who had been governor of Alexandria, was Titus' chief of staff. Men from more countries than one were chosen to be senators; authors who came from Gaul, Spain, and Africa wrote some of the finest Latin literature and were held in the highest esteem; eunuchs and freedmen were the executives and confidential advisers of emperors; and from Trajan onwards it was actually a rare thing for anyone but a foreigner to ascend the imperial throne. Moreover class distinctions, based largely on wealth, cut right across racial divisions, and we find rich freedmen of doubtful origin looking with contempt on poor citizens of the purest Roman blood.

It has already been suggested that the foreign population included many Jews. How numerous they were we have no means of determining. A century before Vespasian's time they had caught the attention of Horace. A generation later they had evidently formed a substantial colony; for when Archelaus was in Rome pleading with Augustus for the inheritance of his father's kingdom he was involved in a dispute with fifty Jewish ambassadors 'backed by more than eight thousand of the Jews in Rome'. The total number must surely have been much greater. Half a century later Claudius, as we all know, expelled the Jews from Rome; but they must have been soon back; for it was only three or four years after his death that Paul wrote his epistle to the Romans, directed almost entirely to Jewish-Christian readers, who must surely have been numerous to justify the writing of so long and weighty a doctrinal exposition. Four years later when he himself arrived in Rome he at once found himself in conflict with non-Christian Jews.

We read of no further attempts to exclude the Jews from Rome, and it is likely that their numbers rapidly increased, so that important writers thought it worth while to investigate their history and beliefs and to make many critical comments about them, often misinformed and sometimes grossly unfair. 'The customs of the Jews,' writes Tacitus (Moore's translation), 'are base and abominable, and owe their persistence to their depravity. Jews are extremely loyal towards one another, and always ready to show compassion, but toward every other people they feel only hate and enmity. As a race they are prone to lust: among themselves nothing is unlawful.' Many Jewish habits and beliefs were beyond Roman comprehension. Sabbath observance was put down to sheer laziness; abstinence from pig's flesh caused as much amusement to pagan Romans as to the Venetian Christians in Shakespeare's comedy; circumcision filled them with contempt —so much so that Jews who could not endure to be mocked substituted a ceremonial incision for the real operation, to escape coarse jests in the baths and wrestling schools. The greatest puzzle was why the Jews worshipped only one deity, and him invisible and not to be represented by any likeness. The Spanish poet Lucan, who committed suicide in Rome while Josephus was there for the first time, had referred in his epic to 'Judaea given up to the worship of an unknown god'. Tacitus wrote that the Jews conceived of one god only, and that with the mind alone. Juvenal summed it all up in one short passage in which he is blaming fathers for the follies and vices of their sons. 'Some who happen to have had a father that revered the Sabbath worship nothing but the clouds and the godhead of the heavens, and think eating human flesh no worse than eating pork, which their fathers would not touch; by and by they part with their foreskins, and habitually flouting the laws of Rome they master the Jewish code, live by it, and revere it—every detail that Moses handed down in his mysterious tome—not to show the way to anyone who practised a different religion, and to guide to the spring they would visit none but the circumcised. But it is all the fault of the fathers, who gave up every seventh day to idleness and emptied it of every human activity.' (My translation.)

Had the Jews not insisted that their god was the only deity in the universe; had they like other nations simply worshipped a national god with a speakable name and a recognized image, they would not have seemed so strange. The Romans had many gods of their own and believed that those of other peoples were just as real. They had no objection to their being worshipped, and were inclined to accept them as additions to their own pantheon. Thus to the original Latin and Italian deities they had added all the gods and goddesses and heroes of Greek mythology, and from time to time they imported those of other races, such as Cybele, Isis, and Mithras. The immigrants who arrived in Rome in the early years of the Empire brought their gods with them, and the Romans had no objection. One deity did not exclude another, and the emperors, dead and sometimes alive, could be thrown in for good measure. But the Jews! they were different, and quite impossible. So it came about that recognizing the impossibility of compelling them to abandon their exclusiveness and conform to the State religion, the Romans with remarkable tolerance exempted them from the observances required of all others. This indulgence was not extended to the Christians, otherwise the catalogue of martyrs would be much shorter. They were not a nation, whose stubbornness was the result of their tenacious loyalty to age-old customs: they were a pig-headed assortment of heterogeneous upstarts, a secret society when all such were forbidden, worshippers of a dead criminal and, it was whispered, cannibals.

It was inevitable that as Josephus went about Rome, buying or selling books, visiting theatres and baths, playing with ball or hoop on the Field of Mars, escorting maybe his imperial patrons, or simply taking the air, he should frequently encounter his ubiquitous compatriots. What were his relations with them? Did he make any friends among his Jewish neighbours? Did they continue to accuse him to the end of his life, or did resentment die down as they began to realize that after all he had done his best and his advice had been sound, so that he deserved his good fortune? We may wonder too whether this Jew who believed in one jealous God, this Graeco-Roman who acknowledged the power of Fate and Fortune, remained faithful to the Lord Jehovah or compromised with Mars and Jupiter. Conformity with the State religion meant no more than attending the appointed ceremonies, and required no profession of a creed. There are strict Jews and liberal Jews; and did not one of the greatest of the prophets give his guest leave to bow down in the House of Rimmon?[1]

[1] 2 Kings v. 18-19.

CHAPTER 17

The Author

WHATEVER ELSE JOSEPHUS FOUND TO DO IN ROME, HE MUST HAVE spent most of his time in his study. For his literary output was by no means small: the four works that have come down to us fall not far short in bulk of the surviving books of Livy, one of them, as he himself emphasizes, running to twenty books and sixty thousand lines, while two more works were planned and probably part-written, even if never published. Furthermore, though the actual writing or dictating of a million words or so was a lengthy and laborious task, the preliminary work of collecting information from every source, studying and evaluating it, and reducing the available materials to manageable proportions and satisfying shape may well have been an even greater task. None of the works proceeded from the author's memory or imagination: all were based on written sources; and in the case of the longest work, as we shall see, those sources were very numerous indeed and must have taken a very long time to read and annotate. This necessary preparation was, of course, made much more difficult by the fact that the *codex* or folio, now thought to have been an invention of the Christians, was not yet available, and every single work to be consulted was written on a roll or rolls, without divisions and probably without an index; so that the tracking down of a wanted passage presented formidable difficulties. An added difficulty in the case of Josephus was that the authorities which he quotes or summarizes were almost all written in Greek, and in Greek he was himself obliged to write if his books were to be widely read; for Greek, which was in constant use among educated Romans, was employed for all purposes throughout the eastern half of the Empire, and any book intended for general circulation must of necessity be written in that language. But Josephus was not a Galilaean but a Judaean, and he thought in Aramaic and only used Greek when he was compelled. He himself tells us at the beginning of *Antiquities* that he hesitated and delayed turning so vast a subject into a foreign and unfamiliar language, adding at the end of the same work the plaintive comment: 'I have taken a great deal of pains to obtain the learning of the Greeks, and understand the elements of the Greek language, although I have so long accustomed myself to speak our own tongue that I cannot pronounce Greek with sufficient exactness.' (Whiston.)

How did an author so handicapped manage to write thousands of pages of Greek that is not only intelligible but for the most part correct and sometimes stylish and elegant? He himself gives the answer, telling us in his last work, *Against Apion*, that in his first, *The Jewish War*, he had employed some assistants to help with the Greek: Whiston is clearly mistaken in translating this: 'persons to assist me in learning the Greek tongue.' But these assistants did far more than correct the errors in the author's wording: though Josephus gives us no hint of the fact, it is plain that in many passages they themselves provided the words and to some extent the thought behind them. For by careful scrutiny scholars have detected such marked stylistic differences between sections of Josephus' writings that they can tell us with confidence where one amanuensis left off and another began. It is not just a question of words, though much can be learnt from the repeated use in some sections of words rarely if ever found in others. In the two longest works we find much dependence on earlier authors, who could not possibly be regarded as sources for works concerning Jewish history and beliefs, on Greek and occasionally Latin poets, philosophers, and historians, who provided ideas, figures of speech, stylistic graces, and memorable phrases, which served as embellishments for the works of an ambitious Jewish scribe. Apart from lack of time, that scribe is hardly likely to have possessed either the educational background for the familiarity with classical literature necessary for the absorption and utilization of such aids to good writing. For though a highly intellectual man such as St Paul, brought up outside Palestine, a Roman citizen by birth, and trained at a university, had no difficulty in illumining his epistles and addresses with apposite quotations from Aratus, Menander, and others, a priest from Jerusalem lacking any such advantages was in a different position.

But the notable thing is this: a change of amanuensis is revealed by a change in the models of which he made use in accordance with his personal predilection; thus one in chapter after chapter draws monotonously on Thucydides, while another, both by his words and by his grouping of ideas, reveals the dominating influence of Sophocles. Other authors drawn upon, not here and there throughout the work but only in particular sections, are Homer, Herodotus, Euripides, Xenophon, Demosthenes, and Epicurus. Josephus nowhere claims any acquaintance with Latin; but in *The Jewish War*, for most of which he seems to have employed the best of his assistants, there are unmistakable borrowings from Sallust, Virgil, and Livy. Moreover, it is to be observed that in the earlier books of *Antiquities*, in which there are fewest indications of literary assistance other than the provision of occasional adornments, translations of Scripture are newly made from the Hebrew text, a task within the powers of a Jewish priest who doubtless knew the language; but in the later chapters where the work of the amanuensis is more in evidence, translations are taken ready made from the Septuagint: it would appear that Josephus was doing less and less of the work himself. This need not surprise us. The greatest painters have allowed their pupils a share in the production of their masterpieces; and ghost writers are always with us. Pope's translation of the Odyssey bears the name of Pope; but how many of the couplets were written by that busy man? In his case the ghosts lacked the ability of the nominal author: with Josephus it was different, and the *Life*, the one book which he seems to have written unaided, is by common consent the least satisfactory of his works.

There is another and perfectly legitimate way in which we may surmise that the assistants made our author's task easier. It would have been impossible to write any of his books, except perhaps the *Life*, without constant reference to sources. In the case of a work on so grand a scale as *Antiquities* it was necessary to make a close study of a great many sources, some of them voluminous. It was right and natural that these should be collected and studied by persons who could read them easily and select the relevant passages for final acceptance or rejection by their employer. These could be summarized or rewritten in his own words: if desired they could be reproduced without modification; for there were no laws of copyright, and Josephus could copy Berosus as freely as Eusebius was later to copy Josephus. We shall not be far wrong if we picture a number of readers and writers busy at work in the study of Vespasian's former residence, while Josephus collated and directed their labours.

At this point the reader may well ask how Josephus, who in the preface to his first work informs us that he had gone to great trouble and expense, could afford to maintain a qualified staff through all these years. We can only guess at the answer. It may be that his assistants were all slaves; for it must not be forgotten that slaves from the Greek-speaking world were often better educated and intellectually more capable than their Roman masters. Even when the master himself was well endowed, he might like Cicero find a Tiro invaluable. Thanks to the wars slaves were plentiful and cheap, and required only food, clothing, and pocket money. Again, books were not as a rule written for a livelihood: Rome was full of amateur writers who had private means and wrote for the pleasure of writing, and of reading aloud to admiring friends, or in the hope of winning the praise of later generations, a thing for which so many Romans felt an overwhelming desire. Josephus, as we have seen, had adequate means; Vespasian had given him an annuity, both Titus and Vespasian had given him estates in Palestine, and Domitian had exempted those estates from taxation. We may hazard a guess that, again like Cicero, he had found marriage under Roman law financially profitable.

But there was something more. In imperial Rome as in eighteenth-century England authors basked in the sunshine of patrons, who in return for dedications and compliments gave books an influential send-off and subsidized their authors. Virgil and Horace had looked to Maecenas; and when Josephus had completed the earliest of his works he presented copies first of all to Vespasian and Titus and then to a number of their generals, and no doubt received the appropriate recompense. *Antiquities* was written when Domitian was on the throne, and Domitian offered no encouragement to authors; indeed the chief writers of the day stood in such fear of him that not until his death did they dare to publish their works. But Josephus found a patron, to whom he dedicated all the books that he wrote during that tyrannous reign. We do not know for certain who Epaphroditus was; he may well have been, as St Dr John Thackeray argues, a 'grammarian' or literary expert who is known to have lived in Rome from the sixties to the nineties and to have had a library of thirty thousand volumes, which were perhaps made available to Josephus. Finally, like so many writers of today, he may have found that though writing did not provide a living, it provided a useful addition to his income. For as readers of Martial are aware, there was a flourishing trade in books; and in the present case we have the author's own statement that after presenting copies of the *War* to selected recipients he *sold* others to many of his own countrymen, including King Agrippa, Agrippa's brother-in-law Julius Archelaus, and 'the most venerable Herod'. So now the picture is as complete as we can make it.

Why did Josephus give up half his life to writing? Why did he choose for his different works the subjects that he did? For what class of readers were those works written? Can we put them in order and say when they were published? Bearing these questions in mind, but without attempting any detailed summary or criticism, let us take a closer look at each in turn, first noting that the works which have come down to us are four in number; that a fifth which Eusebius believed to be his—The Fourth Book of Maccabees—is no longer so regarded; and that some years before he died he was planning to write two more, though whether they were ever written it is impossible to say.

Apart from the motives for writing which Josephus shared with other authors he had a pressing reason of his own. He himself, his compatriots, and his new friends in Rome were all open to attack because of what had happened in Palestine. His pen was the weapon with which he could defend them, and from the first page to the last his books were arguments for the defence. Rome might be criticized, but her position was unassailable; his own conduct had been ambiguous in the extreme, and his position was precarious. The first need therefore was to write an account of the defeat of his countrymen, and in so doing to present both himself and his own friends in the best possible light. Hence the first and most valuable of his works, which in most of the manuscripts is headed *Concerning the Capture,* but to which he himself in his later works gives the title *Concerning the Jewish War.* There is no authority for Whiston's quite unsuitable title *The Wars of the Jews.* This was one of many wars in Roman history, the war against the Jews; and just as Julius had written *Concerning the Gallic War,* so Flavius wrote *Concerning the Jewish War.* The author's standpoint is unmistakable. But Josephus had a genuine wish to write history, and with the exception of Thucydides ancient historians saw no need to circumscribe their subject and deny themselves the pleasure of digressions and irrelevances. So it came about that in its final form *The Jewish War* extended to seven books, containing much matter that is irrelevant to the nominal subject, such as the history of Palestine from the Maccabees to the later Herods, with full descriptions of the building activities of Herod the King, his sordid domestic life, and his miserable end, and innumerable digressions on a variety of subjects that happened to interest the author, such as Roman marching formations and the vegetation of the Arabah.

But the bulk of the work is given to the actual war, and the account is clear, effective, and moving. A special reason for writing it is more than once emphasized—the author wished to undo the damage done by rival accounts already published. For this reason we must not date the publication of his book too early, though he may have begun work on it very soon after settling down in his new home. Nor could he have written some of the military narrative until Vespasian's *Memoirs* or *Commentaries,* on which he claims to have drawn, were compiled and made available to him. For the date of publication A.D. 75 is as reasonable a guess as any.

The Jewish War as we have it was written in Greek, and was clearly intended for Gentile readers; for the author thinks it necessary to explain such familiar institutions as the Passover and Pentecost. Those readers were not all to be found in the Capital, where it would hardly have been necessary for a stranger from Jerusalem to explain in detail the organization, equipment, and training of Roman armies. He was aiming at a much wider public, writing, as in the case of his next work he expressly states, for the whole Greek-speaking world; and we cannot doubt that, determined like Thucydides, the historian on whose writings he drew most freely, to give the world 'a possession for all time', he was writing for the enlightenment and enjoyment of future generations too. Why else should he relate in detail so much that was known to everyone when he wrote, the story of the civil wars, the carnage in Rome, the succession of emperors? But it was not the Greek-speaking world at which he directed his first efforts: he states in his preface that he has decided to translate into Greek the books which he wrote some time before in his native language for circulation in the Middle East. Reasons for this procedure are not hard to seek. His Aramaic was fluent, his Greek was not; and it was important that the Mesopotamian Jews, whose Judaean brethren, as he informs us, had expected them to join their insurrection, should be impressed with the invincibility of Roman arms and effectively deterred from taking armed action themselves, perhaps in collaboration with Rome's most dreaded foes, the Parthians. It is most unfortunate that the Aramaic original is lost: its discovery would perhaps enable us to determine the source of the Slavonic version to which allusion was made in Chapter 11, and to determine at the same time the authenticity or fraudulence of the disputed passages. In that version there are some very bitter invectives against the perfidy, venality, and insatiable cupidity of the Romans. Were these passages, so true and so apposite in their context, forged in the Middle Ages, or were they taken from the original edition of Josephus' work? May we deduce that they were written for the Jews of Mesopotamia, and discreetly excised, along with his too-frank confession of his own perfidy at Jotapata, when the book was reissued for Roman readers? It is easy to ask questions about Josephus: it is very difficult to answer them.

While busy with the *War* Josephus had already determined to write a much longer work which he believed that every reader of Greek would find interesting, a work embracing all ancient Jewish history, politics, and law, or as he puts it in his final summary, containing everything recorded from Creation to the twelfth year of Nero's reign, the year in which Florus 'compelled us to take up arms against the Romans, thinking it better to be destroyed together than one at a time'. The author's purpose, in the words of St J. Thackeray, was 'to magnify the Jewish race in the eyes of the Graeco-Roman world by a record of its ancient and glorious history'. To fulfil that purpose he produced a work of great length—nearly three times the length of its predecessor—a *magnum opus* which, in spite of the great help which he received from his assistants, none of whom stayed the whole course, occupied him for some eighteen years. We cannot say exactly when his labours began, but we know when they ended; for he himself recorded in the last paragraph of the work the date of its publication—'the thirteenth year of the reign of Caesar Domitian, and the fifty-sixth of my own life'—as we should say, A.D. 93.

If eighteen years seems a long time, we must remember this. In writing the *War* Josephus had no need to go in search of authorities and to do a great deal of preliminary study: he relied mainly on the historical works of Nicolaus, on the *Commentaries* of Vespasian and Titus, on letters addressed to him by King Agrippa, and on his own diaries. But for the longer work he had to collect information from very many sources, including books by twenty-four named authors and several unnamed, letters by nine named writers, decrees and edicts of emperors, dictators, generals and public bodies, in addition to the Greek and Hebrew Scriptures, canonical and apocryphal—enough in all conscience to give a less determined writer acute mental indigestion. From these multifarious sources let us try to pick out the most important.

The work which we are discussing is known as *Antiquities*. The title, which is taken from the Latin, is a most unsatisfactory one, but it is too late to change it now. The author himself called it *Archaiologia*, meaning not *Archaeology* but Ancient History. In 7 B.C. Dionysius of Halicarnassus, another settler in Rome, had published his *Ancient History of the Romans* in twenty books. It was no accident that ninety-nine years later Josephus published his *Ancient History of the Jews*, also in twenty books. It is true that he brought the story down to quite recent events, but on the whole his title fits the subject-matter well enough. This being the case, it was inevitable that he should draw largely on what we call the Old Testament; but though he promises to add nothing to the sacred narrative he does in fact both reword it and amplify it from the resources of his own imagination, and also introduce stories entirely absent from the biblical account; in addition to which he refers to numerous secular authorities for verification. Bible history, of course, ends with Nehemiah, and the Apocrypha gives a very patchy account of the centuries that followed; so that it became increasingly necessary to draw information from secular sources, till with the later Hasmonaeans and the Herods there were no others to be tapped. If I were to go through the whole catalogue of these sources I should only weary the reader; but some of them demand special mention.

Covering as it does the whole period from the beginning of time to the middle of his own life the work naturally falls into different sections, each supported by its own group of authorities. These sections are four in number. The first—half the entire work —takes us from Creation to Ezra; the second and shortest from Ezra to Simon Maccabaeus; the third from Simon's death to the accession of Archelaus; and the fourth from that point to the misdeeds of Gessius Florus. Historically the last three sections are the most important, since they contain much information about events and institutions that can be obtained from no other source. The first adds little of importance to the biblical record and suffers from the same fault as the many modern rewritings of the gospel stories and parables: it is not nearly so well written as the original. The beauty, economy, and tautness have disappeared, and the added details supplied by imagination are superfluous and annoying. Anyone who will compare Josephus' account of Wrestling Jacob, of Samson's riddles, or of Nathan and David will appreciate what I mean. Again, he is open to criticism for disingenuousness; for in his desire to present his countrymen in the most favourable light before the eyes of Gentile readers he omits such discreditable incidents as the worship of the Golden Calf; while at other times he anticipates Dr Bowdler by making prudish excisions from the narrative; and if the scholars are right, he not only exaggerates numbers but to give the impression of accurate knowledge not infrequently invents them. Nor are many of the references which he makes to secular authors for the purpose of rendering convincing the biblical statements on such matters as primitive longevity of any great value. It is not likely that he had ever read their works: more probably he took over their names from later authors who had listed them.

The first of those who made major contributions to the wealth of Josephus' knowledge was Berosus, priest of Bel about three centuries before Christ. On the basis of the Babylonian archives Berosus wrote in Greek a three-volume history of Chaldaea, of which considerable fragments have been preserved in the works of later authors. The longest of these fragments contains one of the many Mesopotamian accounts of the Flood, from which Josephus makes his first borrowing; but Berosus provided him also with information about Abraham, Hezekiah, and Nebuchadnezzar. To the same century belonged another priestly author of a three-volume history, Manetho of Heliopolis. In his case too the original works are lost; but many chronological epitomes have come down to us, and enough of his statements have been verified to justify his being regarded as a very reliable witness. In *Antiquities* Josephus makes surprisingly little use of him, perhaps because, as we are told in *Apion Answered*, where he is quoted again and again for polemical purposes, Josephus considered that his testimony, though valuable, was vitiated by occasional mendacity. Thirdly, we must mention a very different author, Herodotus, the Greek historian of the fifth century B.C. From him Josephus drew confirmation of his accounts of Shishak and Hezekiah.

For the second section of his work Josephus was unable to find adequate sources of information to supplement Ezra and Nehemiah, Esther, 1 Maccabees, and the Apocryphal Esdras. But for international affairs between 220 and 146 B.C. he was able to use the authoritative and detailed history of Polybius, the Arcadian friend of Scipio Aemilianus, of which we, alas, possess only five out of forty books. It was a work which extolled the greatness of Rome, and Polybius, like Josephus and his friend Agrippa, was anxious to convince all who would listen that she was destined to rule the world. He was a writer after Josephus' own heart. For the third section our author had another good authority in Strabo, a Cappadocian Greek who, in addition to the famous geography that we still possess, wrote a long historical work as a continuation of that of Polybius. Of this only a few fragments survive; but Josephus had access to a copy and made good use of it. But there was another source far more important than Strabo; a source on which Josephus had been drawing from the very beginning of his twenty books, and which in the third section contributed more than all others put together.

Nicolaus, a Syrian of Damascus, an intimate and wealthy friend of Herod the Great and almost an exact contemporary, was closely associated with that monarch in his public and private business. He was employed by him to accuse his eldest son Antipater before Caesar in Rome, and later before the legate Varus in Caesarea. When both Antipater and his father were dead, and two other sons, Archelaus and Antipas, were disputing the succession, Archelaus took Nicolaus and his brother Ptolemy, who 'had been the most honoured of Herod's Gentlemen', to Italy to plead his cause before Augustus, the executor appointed in the dead king's testament. The dispute lasted for months, perhaps years; but Nicolaus lived long enough to see his employer installed as ethnarch of Judaea. He was thus in a position to record from personal knowledge everything that happened from Herod's first appointment as Governor of Galilee in 47 B.C. to the turn of the century. His pen must have kept him very busy; for while it is believed by some that he wrote a full-length biography of Herod, it is an established fact that he wrote a general history in no less than a hundred and forty-four books, comparable with Livy's enormous work. Readers who find themselves exhausted after struggling through the twenty books of *Antiquities* might well shudder at the thought of tackling those hundred and forty-four!

But others beside Josephus thought them valuable, and they remained in circulation for eight hundred years. Copies must have been plentiful in Rome when Josephus wrote, or surely he would not have told his readers in which volumes of Nicholaus' history they could find the passages quoted. Now we possess only the fragments enshrined in the pages of later writers.

It is plain that this shelfful of books embraced a very long period of time; for Nicolaus provided Josephus with material for his account of the long-lived patriarchs and the Flood, of Abraham, David, and Hyrcanus. But his chief service was to provide all the information required for the long account of Herod and his sons in the *War*, and the much longer account in *Antiquities*, accounts that in each case fill one-sixth of the entire work. It is not that Josephus is prepared to accept all the praise that Nicolaus lavished on his patron. He claims much more objectivity for his own writings. Here is his comment on Herod's pilfering of David's sepulchre, as rendered by Whiston. 'Nicolaus his historiographer does not mention his going down into the sepulchre, as knowing that action to be of ill repute; and many other things he treats of in the same manner in his book; for he wrote in Herod's lifetime and under his reign, and so as to please him and as a servant to him, touching upon nothing but what tended to his glory, and openly excusing many of his notorious crimes, and very diligently concealing them. As for ourselves, who come of a family nearly allied to the Asamonaean kings and on that account have an honourable place, which is the priesthood, we think it indecent to say anything that is false about them, and accordingly we have described their actions after an unblemished and upright manner. And although we reverence many of Herod's posterity who still reign, yet do we pay a greater regard to truth than to them, and this though it sometimes happens that we incur their displeasure by so doing.'

But the greatness of our author's debt to his predecessor is clearly shown by the amplitude of his information up to the accession of Archelaus, and the sudden drying up of the source at that point. Of what the ethnarch did after his return to his dominion, and of what happened in Palestine during the next twenty years we are told next to nothing. Perhaps that is why in the *War* Josephus inserts at this point his long and irrelevant dissertation on Jewish sects, and why in the corresponding part of *Antiquities*—the last of the four sections—so much space is given to a chronicle of the high priests, and to a very detailed and inapposite account of events in Rome under Gaius and Claudius, for which the authority seems to have been Cluvius Rufus. But the fourth section is a very poor piece of writing and scholars agree that Josephus, bored with his task, left its composition almost entirely to an inferior hack. He was already planning to write three other books, and was probably eager to make a start.

In addition to the two major works which we have been discussing Josephus wrote two minor works—little more than pamphlets—of which something must be said. In them we see him at his worst and at his best.

In the final paragraph of *Antiquities* he suggests that it will not be taken amiss if he treats briefly of his own life and career while there are still people who can disprove or support his statements. This he proceeds to do by writing the *Life*. It is a most disappointing work, belying the title; for though the first few pages and the last few give us a very sketchy account of his career, from which in earlier chapters we extracted all that is of value, the great bulk of the book is devoted to a detailed record of the few months he spent as Governor of Galilee, followed by a vehement diatribe against a rival historian, Justus of Tiberias. So far from being a genuine autobiography the book is an attempt to undo the damage done to Josephus' reputation by the recent publication of a history of the Jewish War that cast grave reflections both on the behaviour of Josephus at the time and on the trustworthiness of the account which he had subsequently published. His own new version of the stormy events is extremely muddled and, as all critics are agreed, differs fundamentally from his own earlier account. In it he tries to turn the tables on Justus by laying the blame on him for all that went wrong, beside defending his own conduct and veracity. It is a thousand pities that the rival history has disappeared, so that we can never know how far Josephus was justified in his denunciations and expostulations.

The *Life* shows every sign of hasty composition: it is violent in the extreme, completely out of proportion, and totally devoid of literary graces or any evidence of the saving help of the 'assistants'. It is customary to date its publication in A.D. 100 or 101, on the ground that it speaks of the death of Agrippa II, which according to Photius took place in the former year. But too much trust should not be placed in the unsupported statement of a ninth-century Byzantine writer; and Pauly-Wissowa-Kroll, followed by Ronald Syme in the *Cambridge Ancient History*, argues that Agrippa died in 93. No one after reading the *Life* could believe that its composition occupied Josephus for eight years; and there is no evidence for the view that the passage quoted at the beginning of the last paragraph was not in the 93 edition of *Antiquities*. I myself believe that the *Life* followed *Antiquities* after a very brief interval indeed, and that this is the explanation of the strange fact that it contains no mention of the emperors who followed Domitian. Josephus would have reason enough for losing no time in refuting Justus' accusations; for in the last years of his life the morose and suspicious emperor put to death men in a far better position than Josephus, and the most innocent went in constant fear. And fear, even more than anger and hatred, prompted Josephus to publish his passionate defence.

The second of the minor works is gratifyingly different. It is, as St J. Thackeray justly remarks, 'the most attractive of our author's works, exhibiting a well-designed plan, great literary skill, an intimate acquaintance with Greek philosophy and poetry, together with a sincere and impassioned zeal for his country's religion'. It is a noble defence of the author's nation, its antiquity, its history, its legal code, its morality. It protests against the neglect, prejudice, and malignant untruthfulness of Gentile writers and critics. One of these was Apion, a learned but ostentatious rhetorician who in the reign of Gaius had led a deputation from Alexandria to Rome to make an attack on the Jews, which was answered by Philo. This incident occurred some sixty years before Josephus wrote his own reply: it is this very absence of haste, in contrast with his immediate reaction to the criticisms of Justus, that enabled him to write with such care and good judgment. It is only in the second of the two books into which his work is divided that he answers Apion; so that the accepted title, first found in Jerome, is unfortunate. The manuscripts themselves entitle it either *Against the Greeks* or *The Antiquity of the Jews*, either of which would be less inadequate.

As to the date of publication little can be said. The prevailing belief is that *Apion*, like the *Life*, was issued at the beginning of the second century 'in old age', as Thackeray unkindly puts it, 'when the author was upwards of 63'. But the evidence is extremely tenuous: Josephus alludes to histories of the recent war, written and published by persons who had never been near the scenes of action, but put a few things together by hearsay and shamelessly passed them off as history. We have no idea to whom he is referring: if Justus is included we cannot say when his work had first appeared. All that we can safely assert is that *Apion* is later than *Antiquities*, to which it refers, and late enough to be in part a reply to published criticisms of that work.

Does all this shed any light on the final date, the date when the assiduous writer was at last compelled to lay down his pen? Is the fact that he lived to complete the two minor works, and that he outlived his friend Agrippa, all that we can say? Perhaps we should be justified in believing that he did not live much longer than that; for of the two other works which he purposed to write—a summary history of the Jews from the beginning of the war to the time of writing, and a four-volume work about the nature of God and the principles underlying the Mosaic laws—not a trace has ever been found. That the latest and most mature works of so eminently successful an author should vanish entirely seems unlikely enough; that they should vanish without so much as a mention from any ancient author either friendly or hostile seems almost impossible. May it not be that, as Cicero said of Plato, Josephus also *scribens est mortuus*?

CHAPTER 18

The Apologist

IT HAS ALREADY BEEN OBSERVED THAT ALL JOSEPHUS' WORKS ARE arguments for the defence. Whom or what was he defending? The first of several answers meets us at the very beginning of his earliest work. He wishes to establish the greatness of the Romans, not, like other writers, by decrying the Jews as feeble opponents, but by showing how by the vastness of their forces and the genius of their commanders, and by their heroic endurance of hardships, they finally overcame the most bitter and prolonged resistance, having right on their side, since for their misfortunes the Jews had only themselves to blame. With this object in view he has gone to great trouble and expense, though a foreigner, so that he may offer the Romans a permanent record of their triumphs.

The Jews were to blame not only because it was insane folly to do battle with Rome, but because they had committed such gross iniquities that God was determined to punish them, and the innocent Romans were the chosen instrument of His vengeance. God was actively engaged on the Roman side. During the siege of Jerusalem the wicked John of Gischala impudently cut up some immense baulks of wood which Agrippa had contributed for the purpose of increasing the height of the Sanctuary, and built mobile towers with them for military use. 'With the engines so constructed he hoped to defeat his enemies, but God made his efforts useless by bringing the Romans upon him before he had posted a single man on the towers.' In one of the tirades which Josephus addressed from outside the City to the 'stupid people' on the walls he voiced the same belief at greater length. After reminding his hearers of the destruction of Sennacherib's host when that monarch was in the wrong and the Jews in the right, he went on: 'Are the Romans behaving so like the Assyrian that

you can expect a like vengeance on them? They are only demanding the customary tribute which our fathers paid to theirs. It is
madness to expect God to treat the just as He treated the unjust.
If He had judged our generation worthy of liberty or the Romans
of chastisement, He would immediately have fallen upon them
as He fell upon the Assyrians. When? When Pompey meddled
with our affairs, when Sossius came against us, when Vespasian
was laying Galilee waste, last of all when Titus was drawing near
the City. And yet Magnus and Sossius not only suffered no set-
back but took the City by assault; Vespasian made his war against
us the stepping-stone to the throne; while for Titus the very
springs flow more abundantly, springs that had dried up for you!
So I am sure the Almighty has quitted the holy places and stands
now on the side of your enemies.'

The two crude beliefs implied by the last sentence are voiced
repeatedly in the *War*. Josephus declared more than once in the
same speech that God was the ally of the Romans, and it is plain
that he was as convinced as Homer or Virgil that God or the gods
took sides in human quarrels. He puts the same view in the mouth
of the pious Titus: 'Faction, hunger, siege, walls that fall when no
engine is at work—what else can be the cause but God's anger
with them and aid to ourselves? So to be outdone by our inferiors
and to betray God our ally as well would be unworthy of us.' And
later: 'God has been on our side; it is God who brought the Jews
down from these strongholds; for what could human hands or
instruments do against such towers?' As to God quitting the holy
places, so far from understanding as St Stephen had done that the
Most High dwelleth not in temples made with hands, Josephus
had not advanced beyond the primitive notion of gods tied to
localities which in certain circumstances they might quit in disgust.
And so after listing the portents foreshadowing the destruction of
the City he concludes by telling the familiar story, told also by
Tacitus, of how when the priests had gone into the Inner Temple
at night to perform the usual ceremonies they were aware, first
of a violent movement and a loud crash, then of a concerted cry:
'Let us go hence!' Josephus makes no bones about it: God had
migrated from Jerusalem to Rome.

If Josephus was eager to exalt the character, achievements, and unique destiny of Rome, he delighted still more to sing the praises of the two emperors or Caesars, Vespasian and Titus. Throughout the *War* he showers compliments on them both, doing his best to show them, even to Jewish readers, in the most splendid light. When Nero was wondering to whom he could entrust the East in its disturbed state, he found no one but Vespasian equal to the task. He had been a soldier all his life and was now a veteran; he had pacified the West and crushed the German rebellion; furthermore he had added Britain to the Empire—a statement that would have astonished Vespasian's old commander-in-chief, Aulus Plautius, if he had lived to read Josephus' imaginative pages. His sons, moreover, were hostages for his good faith, and could provide the hands if he provided the brains. The appointment was everywhere acclaimed. At Antioch Agrippa awaited his arrival with the whole of his army. At Caesarea the citizens of Sepphoris, the only people in Galilee who desired peace, gave him an enthusiastic reception and pressed him to accept their help against their own countrymen. Before Jotapata he was struck by an arrow: the wound was trifling, but the occurrence produced the utmost consternation in the Roman ranks; most of the men forgot the siege and in dismay and terror came running towards their commander. But Vespasian rose superior to his pain, showed himself to all who were alarmed on his behalf, and stimulated them to yet more furious onslaughts; every man in his eagerness to avenge his commander was anxious to be in the forefront of danger. At Gamala again he showed such superhuman courage that the enemy were overawed: the stirring tale has been told (in Chapter 12) in the author's own enthusiastic words, and need not be repeated here.

Two years later came the call to take the place of Vitellius on the imperial throne. The soldiers were insistent and clamorous, and Josephus somehow obtained a record of their informal talk. Vespasian, they agreed, was a candidate with the strongest claims, a clean liver and a kindly leader, a man of outstanding excellence and experience, the father of vigorous sons. He *must* be emperor! They would kill him if he refused! Reluctantly compelled to submit, and having Mucianus and Antonius Primus willing and eager to do battle for him against Vitellius (while he himself remained at a safe distance) Vespasian proceeded to Alexandria and thence to Italy. There he was greeted with delight in all the cities, and welcomed with matchless enthusiasm and splendour in Rome. The Senate regarded his appointment as a godsend; the people were still more eager for his coming; the soldiers pinned their faith on him and longed for him to be at their head. The entire population poured out to meet him and hailed him as benefactor, saviour, and the only worthy emperor of Rome. Then they turned to feasting, and prayed the gods that Vespasian might remain for very many years at the helm of the ship of state, and that for his sons and all the generations of their descendants the throne might be preserved unchallenged.

Such were the tributes that Josephus laid at the feet of Vespasian —ample enough, but slight in comparison with the wealth of praise bestowed on his elder son. It is a theme to which he returns again and again in the *War*, and it is obvious that one of his principal objects in writing the book was to win universal approval for Titus—and thereby to win the gratitude of Titus for himself. From the mass of relevant passages I must select only a few, classified according to the qualities they exemplify.

The Romans were justifiably proud of their unique achievements in centuries of warfare, and it is not surprising that Josephus did everything in his power to gratify that pride anew. More than half his references to Titus are concerned with his qualities as a soldier and a general, and in particular his heroism in hand-to-hand combat. Never holding back to control the battle from a distance, he was invariably in the van of the fight, leading his soldiers from the front, not driving them forward from behind. The reader will no doubt recall how in the final assault on Jotapata Titus was the first to climb up to the battlements, followed by only a handful of men; how when outnumbered at Tarichaeae he galloped to the front, charged relentlessly through the Jewish hordes, and led the way into the terrified city; how at Gamala he showed the same high courage and enterprise; how on his first appearance outside Jerusalem he hacked his way almost single-handed through the dense masses that hemmed him in; and how, when the time came to capture Antonia, it was he who led the way to the top of the wall.

Such a man as this could never be persuaded to retire when things went wrong. It was no use reminding him that he was not a private soldier but commander-in-chief and master of the world: he shut his ears, stood his ground, and boldly attacked the advancing enemy. Nor was he slow to go to the rescue when his troops were hard pressed. 'To the help of those in difficulty Titus never failed to come.' Thus, when the Jews were setting fire to the Roman engines he brought up the flower of the cavalry and charged the enemy, killing twelve of the leading Jews with his own hand. Again, when his soldiers had broken through the second wall and were cut off by a Jewish counter-attack, they would probably have all been cut to pieces had he not come to the rescue. Wherever he appeared his presence was an inspiration; the greatest inducement to valour was 'the fact that always, in every place, by every man, stood Titus. To show weakness when Caesar was there, fighting at their side, was unthinkable, while the man who fought valiantly did so before the eyes of the one who would reward him: indeed, he was paid already if Caesar had recognized his courage.' We are even assured that when men were being burnt to death on the blazing colonnade he was moved with human compassion, and it was a comfort to the dying men to see him so distressed. 'Taking with him that sympathy like a glorious winding-sheet every man died happy.'

There were other qualities too which showed the greatness of this youthful commander. Whenever his men were required to make a supreme effort he was able to deliver the speech, sometimes explanatory, sometimes sternly critical, sometimes powerfully stimulating, that fitted the occasion and aroused an ardour for battle and a readiness to die. 'As Titus delivered this address a sudden wave of enthusiasm swept the men off their feet.' Nor was he found wanting when great decisions had to be made: it was he who in the face of his generals' opposition insisted on enclosing Jerusalem inside a containing wall, and so sealed her doom. And he knew how to handle men: when they misbehaved he inflicted the severest punishment; when they showed discipline and valour he bestowed on them rich and imaginative rewards.

Josephus was writing for Jewish readers as well as Roman, and it was necessary to show that they too had reason to admire this paragon of virtue. Accordingly stress is laid, almost from the first page of the *War* to the last, on the pity which he had shown for the rebellious Jews, and on his reluctance to add to their sufferings or to destroy their city and temple. Whenever he showed forbearance and mercy, he is praised for it; whenever he behaved cruelly—and how cruel he could be!—no comment is made. 'Throughout the war he had pitied the common people, who were helpless against the partisans; and over and over again he delayed the capture of the City and prolonged the siege in the hope that the ringleaders would submit.' When he rode up to Gischala he saw that it would be easy to take the town by assault; but he knew that if it was stormed there would be a wholesale massacre of the population by his soldiers, and he was sick of bloodshed and grieved that the whole people, without distinction, must share the fate of the guilty. He was therefore anxious to persuade the town to surrender, and offered lenient terms, freely forgiving the truculence that had been shown. At Jerusalem he assaulted and broke through the second wall; then, hoping to shame the Jews by waiving his right to do them hurt, he refrained from widening the breach to ensure an easy retreat: he never imagined they would repay his kindness with treachery. After his entry he forbade his men to kill any prisoners or set the houses on fire; the partisans he informed that if they wished to fight they were free to march out; to the citizens he promised the return of their property, his chief concern being to preserve the City and the Temple. If only they would change the battle-ground no Roman should go near the holy places: Titus would protect the Sanctuary for them whether they wished it or not. When later the Temple gates had been fired by the soldiery he ordered the flames to be extinguished, and held a council of war at which the senior officers were unanimous in recommending the destruction of the whole building, since it served as a rallying-point for Jews all over the world. Titus replied that in no circumstances would he countenance such a course.

Here it may be whispered that Josephus' veracity on the point is open to question. 'It was apparently on the order of Titus himself,' writes Professor Momigliano, 'that the Temple was burnt by the soldiers and a terrible massacre began. Josephus' denial is clearly tendentious.' This accusation is not based simply on reading between the lines of our author's account: Sulpicius Severus, writing much later but drawing on a lost chapter of Tacitus, reverses the roles of Titus and his generals, making the supreme commander the advocate of destruction; and Sulpicius had no apparent axe to grind. However, Josephus' account is at any rate all of a piece, and we go on to read that when Titus learnt that a misguided soldier had set light to the Sanctuary itself he leapt up from his couch and ran to extinguish the blaze, shouting and waving to the combatants to put out the fire. But curiously enough, as mentioned in an earlier chapter, no notice whatever was taken of Caesar's peremptory command. 'Titus was either unable, or more probably unwilling, to restrain his soldiery.' Thus Dr Salmon. More curiously still Caesar and his staff withdrew, leaving the men free to start what fires they liked. Perhaps to an unsuspicious reader our author's account may seem sufficiently convincing; and the picture is complete when we read how Titus, while he later viewed the ruins, was pained by the City's destruction, cursing and cursing again those who had instigated the revolt and caused this retribution to fall on the City, and making it crystal clear that he would never have wished the terrible punishment that had been inflicted to serve as proof of his own prowess.

We have by no means exhausted all that Josephus has to say in praise of Titus, but it is time now to look at his younger brother, of whom our author has tried valiantly to present a pleasing image. It was a prudent thing to do; for it was already taken for granted that sooner or later he would be master of the world. There was little that Josephus could say. When first mentioned Domitian is coupled with Titus as a hostage for their father's good faith on being entrusted by Nero with such potentially dangerous military power. Later he is treated by the soldiers as an asset to Vespasian when called upon to assume imperial authority. Vespasian's brother Sabinus had been entrusted with control of the Capital; and his young nephew Domitian was popular enough to rally many young men of distinction to the cause. When Antonius Primus was approaching the City and Sabinus seized the Capital he was joined by these young nobles, and with them Domitian, 'the chief pillar of his hopes of victory'. Sabinus was captured by Vitellius and executed; but Domitian escaped, and when Vitellius had been knifed Mucianus arrived and put him forward, recommending him to the assembled citizens as Head of the State till his father arrived. Later came his dash to Germany, where he hurled himself at the barbarian hordes, who submitted without a blow. Then he returned to Rome, covered with glory and admired by all for his amazing exploits. As these appear to have been unknown to any historian other than Josephus, whose statements on such a subject, needless to say, no one would have dared to contradict, Domitian was no doubt very grateful for his admirer's efforts. As for Titus, it is no wonder that when he had read *The Jewish War* he was so anxious that from that work alone mankind should acquire its knowledge of the facts that he signed the volumes with his own hand and ordered them to be published.

The imperial trio were not the only persons whose prestige Josephus was eager to enhance. There was the 'Jewish' couple, King Agrippa II and his sister, Queen Bernice. Josephus makes no mention, of course, of the other and less reputable relationship between them, nor of the unpleasantness caused in Rome by the spell which the enchantress cast upon the susceptible Titus. (Nor, we may add in passing, has he ever dropped a hint that Vespasian was influenced by his strong-minded concubine Caenis.) There were other and more obvious reasons why Their Majesties' reputation should be buttressed by the apologist. They had behaved in a very dubious manner during the war. Agrippa was anxious to be regarded as a Jew. He had been given responsibility for the Temple and had contributed generously to its upkeep. He had the right to appoint and depose high priests, as we saw in the

case of Ananus, the murderer of James the Righteous. Yet in the
war he had come down openly on the Roman side and had put all
the forces under his command at the disposal of his country's
enemies. It was apparent that he stood in need of justification
before Josephus' Jewish readers, and that justification our author
provided, without in any way smirching his image as presented
to the Romans.

Agrippa's first action after his enthronement by Claudius had
revealed his love of the Jews. There was a sanguinary quarrel
between Jews and Samaritans, and Quadratus the Governor of
Syria had sent the leaders of both factions to argue it out before
Caesar. The Samaritans were backed by the procurator Cumanus. Agrippa came forward to plead for the Jews, and did it so
effectively that their opponents were sentenced to execution or
banishment—and Agrippa was transferred to a larger kingdom.
Next we find him in Alexandria, whither he had journeyed solely
to congratulate Tiberius Alexander on his appointment as
Governor of Egypt. Why? Because Alexander was a Jew. Bernice
now appears upon the scene. During her brother's absence she
was in Jerusalem, performing a vow, like any pious Jewess in
sickness or distress, by a month of self-abasement. Cut to the
heart by the sight of the criminal conduct of the Roman soldiers
she repeatedly sent her officers to the procurator Florus to implore
him to stop the slaughter. When he took no notice she herself
went barefoot to appeal to him; but she barely escaped with her
life. Yet she had courage enough to join the Jerusalem magistrates
in sending to Cestius Gallus in Antioch detailed reports of his
subordinate's misdeeds.

When Agrippa returned, the leading priests and citizens went
down to the coast to welcome him and pay homage, though he
was not king of Judaea. He was shocked by the tale they had to
tell, but he discreetly turned his indignation on the Jews he
inwardly pitied, wishing to humble their pride and damp their
ardour for revenge. Arrived in Jerusalem he was pressed to send
an embassy to denounce Florus before Nero, but being the last
man to stir up trouble he chose rather to instruct, soothe, and
warn the people; and, associating his sister with his efforts to save

the Jews from themselves, he delivered the notable speech already summarized at the end of Part One, finishing with an appeal to rebuild the broken colonnade and pay the arrears of tribute to the Emperor. The ungrateful Jews drove him out of the City, and he was very hurt; but his determination to help them was unshaken, and when Simon's victory at Beth-horon brought the imminent possibility of a flare-up, he sent ambassadors to urge the foolish citizens of Jerusalem to make their submission to Cestius, guaranteeing them favourable terms if they did so. As the reader already knows, the Jews replied with a murderous attack on the ambassadors, having no longer any use for the man who had tried so hard to help them.

Agrippa might well be as pleased as Titus when he read his pre-publication copy of the *War* and saw what efforts the author had made on his behalf. Josephus received his reward; for the king wrote no less than sixty-two letters of congratulation to his 'dearest Josephus'.

Josephus, as we have seen, gives a great deal of space to an eloquent and reiterative *apologia* for the Romans, for his patrons, and for his friends. But he never ceased to be a Jew, and in spite of their sins and follies he desired to defend them, and to let it be seen that he was loyal to them. He knew that they had behaved perversely, but understandably, under great provocation; and though in general he praised the conduct of the Romans so highly he made no attempt to whitewash such unsatisfactory and disreputable procurators as Pilate and Albinus, or to hide the appalling brutality and corruption of which Florus had been guilty. He was always ready to criticize the Jews: in the *War* he lashed them unsparingly. But it was a particular misguided generation that excited his indignation: to the race in general, the race that had known God and had produced the great lawgiver and the inspired prophets, he was always ready to pay tribute. Even in the *War* he emphasizes their devotion, their endurance, and their fantastic courage. But in two of his later books, one of them—the *Antiquities*—of monumental length, the praise of his race is almost the sole topic. Apart from his ambition to be hailed as a great historian, his one aim was to rehabilitate his people in the eyes of their Roman conquerors, who though they had suffered so much at their hands were genuinely interested in their curious beliefs and customs, but through grievous misunderstanding were prone to despise them, especially as Apion and many other Greek authors whose works were read by educated Romans had traduced this splendid people so abominably. That is why in *Antiquities* he not only upholds the Jews on the basis of their history and their own writings, but shows what high opinions others have had about them by quoting at length the official tributes paid to them by Athens, Sparta, and other Greek cities, and over and over again by Rome herself.

Was there anyone else for Josephus to defend? There was indeed—Josephus himself. Of the need to do that he must never lose sight. His conduct and his veracity—both invited attack. His veracity he defended in every one of his works, protesting, it may be felt, too much. Was he not scrupulously honest and far more accurate than other historians? In the first paragraph of the *War* he tells his readers that persons with no first-hand knowledge, accepting baseless and inconsistent stories on hearsay, had written garbled accounts; while those of eyewitnesses had been falsified either to flatter the Romans or to vilify the Jews. He goes on: 'I am determined therefore to respect the truth of history, though it has been neglected by the Greeks.' In the very last sentence of the book he declares that he does not hesitate to make the emphatic assertion that from the first word to the last he has aimed at nothing else but truth. In the *Life* he scornfully contrasts his own unimpeachable truthfulness with the demonstrable dishonesty of Justus, emphasizing as proof of his strict adherence to the facts both his use of official sources and the warm commendations of Titus and Agrippa, and propounding as his own guiding principle the dictum: 'The first duty of a historian is to tell the truth.' From *Antiquities* I have already quoted his declaration that he thought it 'indecent' to say anything false in defence of the Herods, and that he paid a greater regard to truth than to them, even at the cost of their displeasure. In *Apion*, when denouncing the calumnies of Posidonius and Apollonius Molo, he proclaims that to high-minded men the most disgraceful thing of all is to tell any kind of lie.

The defence of his conduct is confined to the *War* and the *Life*, since he took no part in the events related in the other two works. On this score little need be added to what has, I hope, been made clear enough in several of the preceding chapters. From the moment when he negotiated with Nicanor at Jotapata he was vulnerable to attacks from every quarter, and from the first page of his narrative of the events in which he had taken so puzzling a part it was necessary to convince his readers in Rome, in Palestine, and throughout the Diaspora that his part had been innocent and commendable. He had foreseen coming events; he had done his utmost to save both Jews and Romans from the imminent calamity; until war broke out he had striven hard to avert it; when the crimes of Florus drove the long-suffering Jews to raise the flag of revolt, and he had been entrusted, though so young, by the most responsible men in Jerusalem with the task of organizing resistance in Galilee, he had felt it his duty to bow to their judgment and accept the dangerous assignment; in Galilee, in spite of the opposition of John and other traitors he had laboured to carry out his orders; he had taken enormous personal risks, had shown incredible ingenuity, and had fought heroically to the very last. Then he had done the only sensible thing: unable to resist the enemy any longer he had made his submission, and winning the favour of the Roman commander by his dignified bearing and his inspired utterances he had put himself in a position to help his misguided countrymen, and had striven to the limit of his powers, as he had shown when, disregarding the perils of misrepresentation and of physical injury, he had time and time again ridden round beleaguered Jerusalem in dangerous proximity to the walls, explaining to the deluded defenders the hopelessness of further resistance, and pleading with them while the tears ran down his face to yield to the merciful Roman whose one desire was to end their agony.

In the *War* all this amounted to only one feature, albeit a very important feature, of the defensive scheme: in the *Life* it is the top, middle, and bottom, the *raison d'être* of the whole unbalanced structure. *Cet animal est très méchant: quand on l'attaque, il se défend.* Josephus defends himself with a vengeance. He was soldier enough to know that the best defence lies in vigorous counter-attack, and there is no lack of vigour in his assault on Justus. Not only was his allegation that Josephus caused Tiberias to revolt utterly false, but while all Josephus' actions had been defensible and proper, Justus's had been mischievous in the extreme. There was a strain of madness in him; he was eager for revolution, ambitious for power, a clever demagogue who countered the wisdom of his opponents with trickery and deceitful words, a depraved creature who was almost entirely responsible for the catastrophe—and in league with the unspeakable John! The *Life* is a polemic indeed.

Thus, then, for thirty years our author plied his busy pen arguing the case for the defence—defence of his ancient nation, of the great empire of which he was now a citizen, of his patrons and friends, of his own life and writings—in fact, of all that made up the world of Josephus.

CHAPTER 19

The Historian

JOSEPHUS, THEN, WAS PRE-EMINENTLY AN APOLOGIST. BUT HE WAS far more than that: he was a competent historian whose works have done much to enrich our store of knowledge. Those works may not entirely commend themselves to modern readers, and his historical method may not be all that we should desire; but his faults were not unique: they were shared by many other ancient historians. We no longer care for rhetoric but prefer a plain unvarnished tale; but the Greeks and Romans regarded rhetoric as the end and crown of all education. A modern historian would not dream of composing speeches from imagination and putting them into the mouths of historical persons; but the ancients expected it: they thought in terms of speech, and Herodotus, Thucydides, and Xenophon had set an example which Caesar, Sallust, and Livy had followed, and it was unthinkable that any writer should forsake the practice. Some of these, notably Livy, had overstepped the line between history and the historical novel, between factual record and imaginary reconstruction, two literary forms which we think it necessary to keep distinct. If we find the longest of Josephus' works dull reading, we shall find the same fault with many of the long-winded writers of ancient times; and *Antiquities* is not nearly as long as some of the many-volumed histories that have mercifully been allowed to disappear. The ancients themselves found many of their histories valuable enough to preserve, but too long for most people to read; and summarized versions of Livy and other authors were marketed for everyday use. Many of our modern historians have been treated in the same way. A writer may decide to write a 'definitive' history or biography which shall include every item of information on which he has been able to lay his hands. Such works are very valuable for purposes of reference, and have an honoured place on our library shelves. And such a work was *Antiquities*, into which was packed everything that Josephus could find to say about the history of his nation.

Nevertheless, with the exception of *Apion Answered*, which is hardly to be classed as history, the form of Josephus' works leaves something to be desired. The *Life*, of course, is a highly tendentious personal apology, and the historical matter that it contains is scarcely to be taken seriously. We must confine our attention to the other two works. Both suffer from the same fault of construction. A tragedy, says Aristotle, must have a beginning, a middle, and an end. This is surely true, if in a lesser degree, of a history. Josephus began the *War* with the Maccabees, simply because that was where the canonical scriptures left off: he ended *Antiquities* at the twelfth year of Nero, on the ground that what followed had been adequately dealt with in the *War*—a statement just as true of many of the later pages of *Antiquities*, to which the *War* cannot possibly be read as a sequel. The result is that the ending of the later work is abrupt, while what might reasonably have made a short introduction to the earlier occupies no less than one-third of the book, making the reader wonder when the author will reach his avowed (and quite sufficient) subject, the Jewish War. I am, of course, criticizing only the *form* of the book. The irrelevant pages contain a wealth of valuable information, but the right place for it is in *Antiquities*, where it is duplicated. The other two-thirds of the book keep to the subject, and the story goes relentlessly on, well-proportioned, lucid, vivid, exciting, enthralling, horrifying. Certainly there are interruptions. We have long descriptions of Jerusalem and the Temple, of Palestinian geography, of geological and botanical curiosities, of Jewish sects, of Roman armaments. All these are interesting and informative, and in some cases reasonably relevant; but to the reader eager to 'get on with the story' they are irritating intrusions. In my own translation I have taken the liberty of transferring the longer of these to the end of the book, the shorter to the foot of the page, convenient devices of which the ancient writers and copyists made no use.

Of the later work it is unfortunately impossible to say that it carries the reader along, or that it is vivid and enthralling. Much of it is far too drawn out and minutely detailed, and the speeches are too many and too verbose. Josephus had set out at the start to write as extended a work as Dionysius had written, and at the end he expresses his satisfaction at its length. There is no single dramatic theme like the Jewish Revolt with its terrible dénouement; only a long succession of events strung together chronologically, but with little correlation of substance or significance.

The exceptionally competent assistant who put *The Jewish War* into shape did not make this mistake of relentless adherence to chronological order: in telling the story of Herod he separated the glories of his victories, his buildings, and his generosity from the disastrous effects of his jealousy and suspicion and the utter ruin of his family life, emphasizing the painful contrast between the two. In *Antiquities* the lack of a central idea, other than the purpose of doing justice to the Jews, results in a serious lack of proportion between the parts—a defect still more likely to occur if an author farms out his work to a number of 'assistants' and fails to keep a tight hold over them. Some of these were more skilful than others; some could write stylishly and succinctly, others rambled on with their prolixity unrestrained. It may be too that stories borrowed from earlier writers were of different lengths in the various originals drawn upon, and were never reduced to the same scale in the finished work. Again there are many passages which we might wish that the author had omitted altogether. These are not, like the digressions in the *War*, interesting pieces of description which we should be sorry to do without, but slabs of history that concern Rome or the Middle East but have little or no relevance to the Jews, whose story is the avowed subject of the entire work. In Book XVIII, in between an account of the building of Tiberias by Antipas and the story of Pilate's provocative actions in Jerusalem we find a thousand words devoted to the matrimonial affairs of the King of Parthia, the incest and parricide committed by his son, the murder of another prince, a war between Parthia and Media, and a political upheaval in Commagene. A few pages later six thousand words are given to the doings of Agrippa in Rome and the last days of Tiberius, while in the next chapter eighteen thousand—a quite amazing number—are required in order to explain how Caligula was murdered and Claudius was placed on the throne. Then in the next and last book we are given another dose of the very unedifying history of Parthia. I can think of no justification for the inclusion of any of these passages.

The length of both the historical works is increased by the insertion of speeches which, as we have seen, were considered essential in Greek and Roman histories. But different authors handled them in different ways. Thucydides, a true Athenian, used them as did Euripides in his plays, to give a personalized exposition of opposing points of view. Livy provided them for occasions when speeches of some kind must almost certainly have been made, for instance the 'pep-talks' delivered by Hannibal and Scipio to their troops on the eve of their first encounter. There is no pretence that these speeches are authentic: they are rhetorical exercises basically similar to the orations which students were required to compose as part of their training. Very different are the addresses and conversations recorded in the Acts of the Apostles, in which the author shows a complete familiarity with the thought, expression, and habitual terminology of the speakers, and because he writes at so short an interval of time is able to draw on the memories of speakers or auditors—and what memories the people of that time possessed!—if not on written notes, which we have reason to believe were commonly made.

Very different again, are the orations of Josephus. Perhaps the writer whom he most resembles in this matter is Herodotus. Like him he can provide speeches for all occasions, and is not in the least worried if a speech or conversation could not possibly have been recorded or reported. Would any reader imagine that Josephus really knew what Herod and Mariamme said to each other in their bedroom, while having intercourse? But many speeches attributed to living persons, Vespasian, Titus, Agrippa, and Josephus himself, are far from convincing; and any illusion of truthfulness is dispelled when the speeches of Mattathias and Judas, which Josephus has borrowed from the Apocrypha, are altered or amplified, and when speeches provided for Herod in the *War* are scrapped and replaced by new ones in the *Antiquities*.

Such departures from the accepted rule of modern historiography, that all statements must be based on knowledge firmly grounded in evidence, caused no raising of eyebrows in Josephus' world. Not only was he at liberty to report speeches which no one had overheard: there was no objection to describing incidents at which no one had been present. The long and minutely detailed horror story in the *War* of Mary the infanticide, and all that she said and did to her baby in the strictest secrecy, is an obvious instance; and in the last book of *Antiquities* we are regaled with a luscious account of the intimate experiences of King Monobazus of Adiabene, who married his sister and begot a child by her. 'As he was in bed with her one night he laid his hand upon his wife's belly and fell asleep, and seemed to hear a voice, which bade him take his hand off his wife's belly, and not to hurt the infant that was therein.' There is much more in the same strain. At Rome too our author seems to have been aware of much that had gone on in the Emperor's palace, and tells us at great length of the private doings of Tiberius, his conversations with Gaius, his private prayers, his emotions, and his secret thoughts. Many who have read the account of the siege of Jerusalem must have wondered how Josephus acquired such an enormous amount of information about what went on within those beleaguered walls. He himself realized that such wonderment would be aroused, and took the precaution of explaining that he habitually questioned Jewish prisoners in Roman hands. No doubt this is true; but it does not seem enough to explain the astonishing fullness and dramatic effectiveness of the story, and I cannot help thinking that his information was worked up by a lively and creative imagination, as had, I am sure, been the case with many exciting descriptions in Livy. Nor do I find credible the lurid account of the torments of mind which are said to have afflicted Herod after his murder of Mariamme, though Stewart Perowne is apparently convinced of its complete historicity.

Apart from such liberties as these, taken in the interest of 'fine writing', impressiveness, and dramatic effect, and apart from the frequent exaggeration, to some instances of which attention has already been drawn, can we regard Josephus as in essentials a trustworthy historian? With certain qualifications I think we can. For Roman affairs he evidently had reliable sources, and where his account differs from those of other writers it is by no means certain that the error is his. With so many Roman readers any wilful perversion of the facts or careless misrepresentation of what was known to have occurred would have been promptly detected and held up to ridicule. He was, of course, capable of making slips; and there must have been some broad smiles on the faces of his soldier readers when they saw that astonishing assertion that the Roman infantryman wore his sword on the left side! For the war in Palestine, at least from the landing of Vespasian, the publication of his *Commentaries* and those of Titus, together with the memories or diaries of the eminent generals who had served under them, made any serious departure from the truth impossible. For Palestinian history of an earlier period the sources used by Josephus were presumably at the disposal of his Jewish enemies, who would surely have been quick to pounce on any section of *Antiquities* not faithful to the facts.

At the same time there were certain factors that militated against complete objectivity in Josephus' narrative. We are too ready to trust the printed word. There used to be many who would believe anything if it was in the Bible: now there are many who will believe anything so long as it is not in the Bible. We even fall for the memoirs of generals, who, if they are to be believed, were personally responsible for all their victories and none of their defeats, and had to fight not only the enemy but the incompetence of their subordinates, the treachery of their allies, or the opposition and stupidity of politicians at home. Few writers who describe events in which they have themselves taken part see those events from outside with an impartial eye, and write with no motive but the calm presentation of a factual record; and yet many readers display a touching faith in the accuracy of what has been written. There was a time when I accepted all that Caesar had to tell me, even his condemnation of Gallic patriots and praise of Gallic quislings, and never doubted the rightness of Xenophon in any of his constant quarrels with other members of the Ten Thousand, any more than I doubted that Cicero's enemies, Catiline, Clodius, and Antony, were unmitigated scoundrels. Now, perhaps, I am prone to regard all auto-biographical writers with too much scepticism and ought, in the case of Josephus, to accept the verdict of Scaliger, whom Dr Whiston with good reason regarded as 'perhaps the most learned person and the most perfect judge that ever was', and who was well qualified to see both sides of the question, since his given names were Joseph and Justus! 'Josephus', he wrote, 'is the most diligent and the greatest lover of truth of all writers: nor are we afraid to affirm of him that it is more safe to believe him, not only as to the affairs of the Jews, but also as to those that are foreign to them, than all the Greek and Latin writers; and this, because his fidelity and his compass of learning are everywhere con-spicuous.'

What then were the factors that in his case militated against complete objectivity? The first was the motive of self-justification, so prominent in the writers referred to in the preceding paragraph. Much space was devoted to this in Chapter 18, and I only wish to point out here that when Josephus wrote his original account of his doings in Galilee he had no expectation that it would ever be questioned; for there were few Jews still alive to tell the tale, and those authors who had attempted to recount the war before he published his own version were all Greeks. He could write what he liked about events at Jotapata, for he himself assures us that he was the only survivor of the siege. Hence it was a terrible shock to him when Justus publicly impugned his honesty, and he fell over himself in his attempts to answer the impudent accuser, doing it so vehemently that I cannot help wondering whether Justus was still alive, or, like every single person condemned in the *War*, safely in his grave. Did Josephus take the risk of provoking another devastating counterblast? or did he like Tacitus, Sueton-ius, and Juvenal assail only the dead?

I will only add this: I have elsewhere expressed the opinion that, although when Josephus has no axe to grind and is not indulging in patent exaggeration he is an informative and reliable historian, we must nevertheless use the greatest caution in accepting at its face value any statement that he makes about himself or about his personal enemies. In holding this opinion I am in accord with the historian Dr Salmon, who declares that 'any references to his own exploits and behaviour are suspect', and with one of the greatest students of Josephus, Dr Thackeray, who held that though his narrative '*as a whole* (his italics) cannot but be accepted as trustworthy, Josephus, with all his boasted zeal for truth, shows on occasions, when his statements are subject to control, a lax sense of the meaning of that word.'

To what control can we subject his statements? To comparison of what he wrote at different times about the same thing. We need not be unduly worried by discrepancies between the *War* and *Antiquities*. They are in the main due to mistakes in the earlier work being corrected in the later on the basis of new information, though it must be confessed that altered figures seem to be sometimes due to a growing habit of exaggeration. But there is no getting away from the startling disagreements between the *War* and the *Life*, though in both he is describing his own doings. Hence Dr Cecil Roth in discussing the *Life* writes: 'the account of his part in the events between 66 and 70 given in this work differs fundamentally in many respects from that in the *Jewish War*'; while Dr Samuel Krauss makes the harsher comment: 'From the beginning Josephus represents himself as a partisan of the Romans, and therefore a traitor to the interests of his people, flatly contradicting his earlier account, which is more trustworthy.' These contradictions or inconsistencies betray, to quote Dr Thackeray once more, 'either gross carelessness or actual fraud'; and, if Dr Eisler is right, 'the latter alternative is a certainty'.

In addition to the doubtful character of his statements about himself there was a second factor, the tendency, so common in ancient authors of a rhetorical temperament, to exaggerate the virtues of their friends and the vices of their foes. Josephus' friends were the patrons to whom he owed everything. We have already seen how richly Vespasian, Titus, and Agrippa were repaid in chapter after chapter of *The Jewish War*, and how stoutly he championed the nation of whom he had become an adopted citizen. In *Antiquities* he returns to the same theme, going out of his way to praise Vespasian and Titus for their generosity and moderation. 'Flatterer' is an unpleasant word to throw at anyone, but Dr Krauss does not hesitate to write 'He pretends not to have flattered the Romans, though he is distinctly partial to them. He emphasizes his exactness; but his claim thereto is justified only when he states bare facts.' As for his foes, all that he has to say about them is said with such vindictiveness and malignancy, that his words can hardly be taken seriously. His character-sketches of John, Simon, and Justus have been quoted already; but his bitter hatred and determination to denigrate them permeate all his references to their actions.

Something must now be said about the almost innumerable written sources from which our author drew so much of his material for the two major works. That he collected and made use of so many and relied so little on hearsay and invention is greatly to his credit. In the *War* he continually avails himself of the labours of his predecessors without making any acknowledgment whatever. In *Antiquities*, in other respects a much inferior work, he names a great number of his authorities though not all, and in the case of some, especially Nicolaus, he gives his readers instructions where to look up the passages quoted. It is unfortunate that we, his modern readers, are not able to take advantage of this invitation; for the whole of Nicolaus' colossal history is lost, and the same is unfortunately true of nearly all the other authors quoted. We have the more reason to be thankful that by his quotations Josephus has preserved for us at least some samples of their writings, just as Eusebius was later to do on an even greater scale with his sources.

Of course Josephus' debt to his predecessors was not limited to his *verbatim* quotations: he draws to an enormous extent on the information they provided, sometimes making it clear that he is reproducing their actual words, at others summarizing or freely paraphrasing what they had to tell him. That he felt himself free to rearrange or reword what they had written is shown by the fact that the same chapters taken from Nicolaus' account of Herod the Great appear in one form in the *War*, and in another in *Antiquities*. But in addition to these rehashes of the original and the acknowledged quotations there are long passages where no authority is named or hinted at, which may well have been lifted without apology from an earlier document. This would explain the inordinate length of some of the passages which so strangely interrupt the natural flow of the later books of *Antiquities*: we can picture a conscientious but not very discriminating 'assistant' lighting upon them in some work allotted to him for study, and transferring them just as they were to these patchwork chapters without regard to any other consideration than chronological correctness. A minute examination of word-frequency, the application of other linguistic tests, or the presence or absence of words and phrases reminiscent of Sophocles, Thucydides, and the other favourite models, might indicate that these passages were or were not borrowed from an earlier writer; but the fact that *Antiquities* is admittedly the work of several hands besides that of the reputed author makes such tests inconclusive. Far more convincing evidence of unacknowledged borrowing is furnished by the fact that in a number of places allusions to incidents mentioned nowhere else in Josephus' writings are followed by such expressions as 'as we have already stated'. Similarly, in the *War*, one paragraph begins 'On an earlier page we referred to the Alani', although the Alani are here mentioned for the first time. Are we to explain these inaccuracies as due to mere carelessness on Josephus' part? or did his assistant stick too slavishly to the original wording of a borrowed passage?

A final point about Josephus' sources is that according to some of his critics he does not show discrimination in his use of them or make any real attempt to evaluate them. A source is simply a source. He cannot see that the apocryphal Esdras is a less reliable authority than the canonical Ezra, or that the Sibylline Oracles are not original and authentic but derivative and propagandist. But how many of the ancient historians came any nearer than Josephus to a critical approach?

The objectivity for which we look in a writer of history does not preclude the expression of opinions which in his eyes are a part, and an important part, of the truth. 'Comment is free: facts are sacred', declared a famous editor; and what is true of journalism is surely true of historical writing. Josephus certainly held some very decided opinions, which his professed and largely sincere devotion to the truth did not make him hesitate to utter; and he constantly offers comments on the facts. He held strong views on morality, philosophy, and religion, as every serious writer must; and though these particular views may not be shared by his readers he had every right to express them, as long as his comments were relevant to the matter which called them forth. It may be thought that he rubbed in the same philosophy too often, or that he moralized too much: that is surely a matter of taste. At least it should be agreed that moral judgments, and even moral dogmatism, are preferable to moral indifference. It must be remembered that to an earnest Jew morality was all-important, since it was the will and law of God. Sin was one of the great facts of history and the source of all human misery; and God punished sin even if it meant the destruction of His own chosen people. How could a man convinced that this was true fail to proclaim the terrible but inescapable truth? how could a man convinced that all things were in the hand of God and ordered by His providence write like a rationalist, a materialist, a coldly scientific annalist? Josephus could not: to do so would have been to deny his very nature. He wrote as he must; and if he irritates, perhaps infuriates us as we read, is it not all to the good?

CHAPTER 20

Last Thoughts

IN THESE NINETEEN CHAPTERS I HAVE ATTEMPTED TO DESCRIBE THE world of Josephus in its various aspects. We looked first at the geographical world with its two regions, so different in physical features, so many hundreds of miles apart, and in his experience with nothing between them but the hostile sea, crossed with such painful slowness and such ever-present danger. Then we looked at the historical world, divided likewise since the streams of Jewish and Roman history had so long flowed far apart, though there had been some mingling of the waters in living memory and a final fusion of the two streams in his own lifetime, witnessed by him in all its roaring tumult. We studied too some aspects of the world of thought—dichotomous again; for Jewish thought, especially in its attitude to religion, morals, and political philosophy, was poles apart from Roman thought; and Josephus, unable to pass wholly from one to the other, harnessed these uneasy yoke-fellows together as best he could. We have tried also to see how Josephus fitted into that double world in all its aspects, how he reacted to it, and what he accomplished in it. There are, I suppose, some who if they had been born in a different land or in a different age would have lived and thought and spoken in very much the same way as in their actual circumstances they did. Others are the children of the world in which they were born, and their whole life is moulded by their circumstances and environment. Such a one was Josephus, the unmistakable product of his country, his century, his parentage, and his contacts with friends and foes. What lay around him and what happened around him made him what he was, the veritable child of his world.

In that world he took a very lively interest. Both halves fascinated him, but it was to the Roman half that historical events and his own temperament alike attracted him. In that half he felt at home. Rome had his sympathy, and at Rome he could live without antagonizing his fellow-citizens. He lived among them and like them, and on the question that arouses the most dangerous human passions and divides men most fatally, the question of religion, he shared the Roman willingness to be accommodating, eclectic, and passion-free. His writings too were Graeco-Roman; not merely written in Greek for citizens of the Roman Empire to read, but conceived on the Graeco-Roman pattern. Thucydides had written *The Peloponnesian War*, Caesar *The Gallic War* and *The Civil War*; Josephus wrote *The Jewish War*. Dionysius had written *Antiquities of the Romans* in twenty books; Josephus wrote *Antiquities of the Jews* in twenty books. The Graeco-Roman trio had written history for history's sake, and in Caesar's case with the secondary purpose of justifying his own conduct in war; Josephus did exactly the same.

But Hebrew literature was very different. *The Jewish War* is five times the length of the longest book in the Old Testament, while *Antiquities* is as big as the entire canon of the Jewish Scriptures. But the difference was not confined to the number of words. The whole motive and tone of Hebrew historical writing was different; whereas Josephan history was adorned with a sprinkling of moral *dicta* and theological reflections which have their counterparts in his Graeco-Roman models, the whole purpose of the Biblical historians was so to present the historical facts that their moral and theological import would be the chief impression left on the minds of their readers. Nor had the authors a secondary motive: except possibly in a few chapters of Jeremiah and Nehemiah the writer had no thought (or need) of justifying himself, let alone complimenting and praising himself as Josephus often does. A third difference should be noted. The reader of this book has been reminded *ad nauseam* of the way in which Josephus sees the characters of his story as either black or white, exalting certain persons to the skies and trampling others in the mud. How different were the Biblical historians! Only Haman comes to mind as a thoroughgoing villain, and even he had only a small endowment of the vices so liberally showered on John, Simon, and Justus. As for the heroes, from Jacob and his sons to the great King David and his, their sins, crimes, weaknesses, and follies are mercilessly laid bare. The result is that while the bad men of Josephus are mere Aunt Sallys and resemble the black-haired villains of melodrama, and his good men are paste-board figures or stained-glass saints too angelic to be true, those of the Old Testament are creatures of flesh and blood, clothed with life and almost painfully close to us.

In respect of this third difference can we see any resemblance between Josephus and the Latin authors of his and earlier days? We can indeed. Cicero had regularly portrayed men in shining white or deepest black: a man was either *vir praeclarissimus omnibus virtutibus praeditus*, or *perditissimus et sceleratissimus homo*. We have already noted the extravagance of the flattery heaped on Domitian in the epigrammatic verse of Martial and on Trajan in the rhetorical prose of the younger Pliny. These were both contemporaries of Josephus. So too were those pastmasters in the art of denigration, the historian Tacitus, the biographer Suetonius, and the satirist Juvenal. How unreliable are the character-studies which such writers gave to the world, how much they are the products of obsequiousness or of spite, can readily be seen in the case of Antonius Primus, the man who destroyed the army of Vitellius and won Rome for Vespasian. He gave Martial a new toga, and complimented him on his verses. Martial repaid him by writing two short poems in which he is described as a virtuous man of noble character and distinguished mind, who at the age of seventy-five could look back at his past life without recalling a single day the memory of which did not cause him satisfaction; a man whose portrait the poet garlanded, like the image of a god, with violets and roses. Now turn to Tacitus, and you will read that Antonius was arrogant, avaricious, insolent, glib-tongued, and given to secret vices; that he had been guilty of robbery, bribery, scandal-mongering, and fomenting sedition, and had been condemned for forgery; and that in his determination to be on the winning side he had deserted from Galba to Otho, from Otho to Vitellius, and from Vitellius to Vespasian.

Josephus was certainly in good literary company. And while Antonius is in our minds we may perhaps wonder whether, in the readiness which, like him, Josephus showed to change sides for his own convenience and climb on the bandwagon, he was not more Roman than Jew. The Romans were inordinately fond of condemning perfidy in others, and the reason is not far to seek: they were prone to perfidy themselves and were secretly ashamed of the fact; so they flung vehement accusations of perfidy against other people. After the First Punic War they were guilty of the grossest perfidy against the Carthaginians; so from then on the Carthaginians were continually denounced for their alleged perfidy. To Livy, who provides no evidence, Hannibal was characterized by *perfidia plus quam Punica*; and when Martial went to law for the recovery of three stolen nanny goats his counsel insisted on declaiming against *periuria Punici furoris*. What happened at Jotapata may well seem *perfidia plus quam Punica*. It has been argued that in spite of his change of sides Josephus remained loyal to the Jews; that after securing his own survival he used his privileged position in the entourage of Titus to do all that he could to save his doomed countrymen; that it was for their sake that he implored the citizens of Jerusalem to surrender, and that the tears that rolled down his cheeks were tears of genuine sorrow. All this may be true; and there is no denying that in two of his works he did everything he could to enhance the reputation of his nation. But I have an uneasy feeling that the Jews of whom he wrote so warmly were an ideal, not a reality; an abstraction, not a compound of flesh and blood; a peculiar people belonging to the past, not human individuals alive in the present; and that his feelings about them were nostalgic rather than sympathetic. The idealized race was something to glory in; the Jewry he had known was something to condemn.

As I pointed out in my Preliminary Survey, both the character of Josephus and the truthfulness of his writings have been vehemently attacked and as vigorously defended. Such differences of opinion will undoubtedly continue, and wise students will feel that the question remains open, and that judgment should not be hastily pronounced. 'The personal character of Josephus', wrote Whiston many years ago, 'may be regarded as an historical enigma'; and a century and a half later Jacob Hart was still of the opinion that 'Josephus was and must remain to after generations an enigma'. Yet some commentators have felt a warm admiration and even affection for him: Whiston and Traill repeatedly refer to him as 'our Josephus'. Others have been impressed by his learning and historical accuracy. I have already quoted the great Scaliger's extravagant tribute, and Bishop Porteus, warmly approving this commendation, roundly asserts that 'the fidelity, the veracity, and the probity of Josephus are universally allowed; and Scaliger in particular declares that he deserves more credit than all the Greek and Latin writers put together. Certain at least it is, that he had the most essential qualification for a historian—a perfect and accurate knowledge of all the transactions which he relates; and that he had no prejudices to mislead him in the representation of them.'

As everyone who has studied this book will have observed, I find it impossible to recognize our author in these rosy pictures. Both Whiston and Traill, the latter of whom prefaced his translation with an enormously long dissertation on Josephus' character, pass over the last stage of the Jotapata story with no comment whatsoever; so does Perowne. I find myself in complete agreement with Dr Hart, who writes: 'When he was, as often happened, in danger, he took the meaner alternative, and saved himself at the cost of his personal honour and good name. Indeed, one event in his career, however it be regarded, looks too sinister to be set aside; that of the ingenious escape he made from the cave at Jotapata, when all but he perished by the death compact he failed to keep. The tenor of his autobiography is marred by the complacency with which he relates such wiles. . . . *Astutia non virtute* must have been his motto who painted such wrinkles into his own portrait.' This complacency, this utter failure to view his own duplicity, cunning, and perfidy with any feelings other than pride, self-congratulation, and boasting, is condemned even more pungently by Grätz: 'It would be difficult to believe all the instances of craft and duplicity on the part of Josephus, had he not himself dwelt upon them with unexampled shamelessness.' As to the historical accuracy of the Josephan record I again feel that Grätz has hit the nail on the head: 'His version could not be perfectly truthful, seeing how far his own interests had been involved.' Perowne takes the same view, but justly emphasizes the other side of the picture: 'It is indeed well for us that, except where his own conduct is in question, he is such a comprehensive, well-informed, precise and conscientious narrator.'

There are two other matters on which I find myself in disagreement with some of my predecessors. Dr Hart writes: 'He loved his own people, and could be tender, as well as, on occasion, truly human-hearted: witness the occasion when he went with tears in his eyes to Titus and begged that three of the Jews crucified at Thecoa, whom he recognized on the cross, should be saved from that horrible and lingering death.' Readers of the *War* and the *Life* will, I think, have difficulty in finding evidence of love, tenderness, or a truly human heart. The incident of the crucified Jews makes a very different impression on one reader at least. In summarizing the story in an earlier chapter, I pointed out that Josephus showed not the slightest sympathy, regret, or pity for any of the agonized sufferers except his own acquaintances. Surely he tells the story for no other purpose than to boast of his ability to cajole Titus into granting him favours. Just previously he wrote: 'Titus Caesar urged me again and again to take whatever I liked from the wreckage of my country.' He then went on to describe how he received a gift of sacred books and was permitted to liberate such prisoners as he selected. Again, immediately after the story of the three crucified men he goes on to record the bestowal upon him of an estate in Palestine, a lodging in Rome, and an annuity, with many other marks of respect, consideration, and honour, which caused the Jews to envy him his privileged position. Is it not obvious that the one aim of the whole passage is to emphasize, in defiance of Justus, what a fine fellow he was, how highly regarded by his imperial patrons? It is proof enough of the vanity on which Hart himself comments so severely; vanity that was but the reverse side of the 'furious ambition' which Feuchtwanger finds in him.

The other matter is the gift of prophecy and inspired dreaming which Josephus claimed to possess. This claim some English commentators have taken quite seriously. Whiston, for instance, shows an ardent admiration for 'Josephus's remarkable or divine dreams, which were predictive of the great things that afterwards came to pass'; in particular 'that eminent prophetic dream of our Josephus as to the succession of Vespasian and Titus to the Roman Empire'. Many matter-of-fact writers seem to have accepted the genuineness of the famous prophecy with which Josephus hailed the two generals at that first interview. My own scepticism is based chiefly on *a priori* reasoning. Fully as I believe that God has often revealed hidden truths to those in mystical union with Him, whether they be the prophets of the Old Testament and the New, or unknown individuals to whom He makes Himself known in visual or auditory communications or in movements of the spirit within, I cannot think it possible that He would choose for such a supreme privilege a man as devoid of spirituality, humility, and disinterestedness as Josephus. If this reasoning seems too transcendental the question can be tackled on quite different lines. 'Brought before the victorious general', writes Karl Hoeber, 'he sought with great shrewdness to ingratiate himself with Vespasian, foretelling his elevation, as well as that of his son Titus, to the imperial dignity.' He certainly did display great shrewdness, but what he had to say was not something new, revealed to him alone. Tacitus and Suetonius both record that there was a firm belief long accepted in all parts of the East that at that very time— the time of the Jewish revolt—men were destined to come out of Judaea and become rulers of the world. They both add that this belief clearly foretold the elevation of Vespasian and Titus. To clinch the matter we find a third statement, this time in the Talmud, to the effect that the Rabbi Johanan ben Zakkai and certain heathen priests had also announced the same coming event. But Vespasian, though according to Josephus he had to be driven by threats of violence to accept as a duty a position for which he had no ambition, had, it seems, for many years nursed the hope of wearing imperial honours. If Suetonius is correct, the future emperor was no sooner born than his father announced that he would be Caesar. From that time on there was a long succession of portents all confirming this belief; then after his arrival in Palestine he went to Mount Carmel to consult the oracle of Baal, and was assured that any enterprise he might undertake was certain to succeed triumphantly. The priest, it would seem, was as familiar as Josephus with the prevailing belief; but perhaps Baal had sent him a prophetic dream, so that he too was inspired! Tacitus adds that this new oracle was a chief topic of conversation, and was discussed in Vespasian's presence more than anywhere else. Then, and only then, came the interview with Josephus, at which he received the seventh and almost the last intimation of his imperial destiny. There was therefore little that was new in Josephus' 'prophecy', though he undoubtedly showed great astuteness if, as he and he alone tells us, he greeted the two generals, not as emperors to be, but as emperors already.

Let us turn now to two matters on which there can hardly be any disagreement. The attitude of Josephus towards his own nation was equivocal, his loyalty questionable; but there can be no doubt of his devotion to conquering Rome, or of his whole-hearted acceptance of the people, the régime, and the family to which in middle life he was admitted. At the disposal of that people, that régime, and that family he put his brain, his voice, his pen, rendering them services which they valued highly and rewarded very richly. Freedom and citizenship, friendship with Titus, estates in Palestine, an enviable apartment in Rome, an income for life, exemption from taxation—these were recompense enough for what he had done in his own country. But in the Capital too, where he enjoyed the *otium* so dear to the heart of every cultured Roman, he continued to serve his masters, whose prestige he so enhanced by his writings that, as Eusebius and Jerome tell us, the seven books of his *The Jewish War* were not only approved and accepted by his royal patrons but placed in the public library by their command, a testimonial which must have given him the liveliest satisfaction. Last of all—whether in his lifetime or as a posthumous tribute we cannot say—a statue was erected in his honour, there in Rome, the centre and pivot of his chosen world. Our own world is full of monuments to men who have done less to deserve them!

The second matter on which there is little room for disagreement is the value of our author's contribution to knowledge, and above all our knowledge of the history of both halves of his world in the period of about a hundred and forty years ending with the final liquidation of the Jewish Revolt, one of the most critical periods in the whole history of civilized man, a period packed tight with excitement, with tragedy, and with new birth. The debt that we owe to Josephus was emphasized in the first pages of this book, and must be evident to all who have read the subsequent chapters. There is no need to dilate on it now. The greatness of the debt was recognized from the very first, and writer after writer drew on his historical record. Among them were the voluminous historian Cassius Dio and the fierce campaigner against Christianity Porphyry. Most of them, however, were prominent Christian apologists and historians, from Justin Martyr and Irenaeus through Clement and Tertullian to Origen and Jerome, who bestowed on him the notable title of the Greek Livy. Most indebted of all was Eusebius of Caesarea, who quotes Josephus over and over again, and sometimes at great length. Through all the centuries that followed till the fall of Constantinople Greek writers continued to draw upon him, and in our twentieth century he remains an authority whom no serious student of history would dare to neglect. Modern man is a hustler, and he may not find it easy to plough his way through the twenty books of *Antiquities*; but on the whole our author's works are eminently readable, and this, fortunately, is true especially of the most valuable of the four, *The Jewish War*.

In addition to its value as a first-rate source for historians, this book has provided inspiration and material for writers of fiction, who have made it the basis of a number of historical novels. Special mention must be made of Lion Feuchtwanger's *Der Jüdische Krieg*, published in German in 1932 and (by Martin Secker) in English in the same year under the title *Josephus*. It contains excellent descriptions of the background of events in Galilee and Rome, presents a fairer and more credible portrait of John and Justus, and gives an interesting, if not quite convincing, character-study of the man who so bitterly hated them. It is described by the author as 'a historical romance', and romance there is in plenty: no less than eighty-two pages—a sixth of the book—are given to Josephus' time in Egypt, which he himself described in just four words: 'I married another wife'!

But who *can* give a better and more lively or more colourful account of Josephus' life than he has given us himself? and who *can* give a really convincing character-study of the man? Josephus the writer deserves our warmest thanks: Josephus the man—not lovable, not estimable, barely tolerable—remains an enigma, but a fascinating one.

The Disputed Passages

IN THE LAST FEW CENTURIES THE QUESTION OF THE AUTHENTICITY of those sections of *Antiquities* which give brief accounts of John the Baptist, Jesus Christ, and James the Righteous has led to much argument. On the whole scholars have accepted them as genuine, with the exception of the account of Jesus himself, which the reader will find reproduced near the end of Chapter 6. Like the others, this passage is found in all extant manuscripts, and is linguistically indistinguishable from its context. The burden of proof therefore lies with those who regard it either as entirely spurious or as 'doctored' by dishonest Christian copyists. The two favourite arguments are that the passage could only have been written by a Christian, and that although Eusebius quoted it in the fourth century Origen did not quote it in the third. For myself I cannot imagine anyone less likely than a Christian propagandist to write in such a strain, having regard especially to the last sentence. The notion that only a Christian could have written it comes from misunderstanding the little sentence which I have translated as 'This man was Christ'. The fact that there is an article does not prove that the author meant 'This man was *the* Christ', i.e. the Messiah: like other Greek writers Josephus frequently puts an untranslatable article before a proper name; here the article is necessary if, as I believe, he meant 'The man I have called Jesus was the man commonly called Christ'. This is the name that appeared in the earlier passage about James: it is the name used contemptuously by Latin authors and was obviously the recognized name in non-Christian circles; and naturally so, since it was coupled, as in the last sentence of the Josephan paragraph, with the name 'Christians' for which there was no alternative. Apart from this little sentence there is nothing in the paragraph that cannot be found in other non-Christian sources, e.g. the 'reliable statements' which Klausner collected from the Talmud. As for Origen, it is very dangerous to assume that what a writer does not quote he has not read. It is argued that he would necessarily have used it as a weapon against Celsus because it proves that the writer was a Christian: surely it is safer to conclude that Origen did not take it in that sense; in any case he had plenty of other weapons in his armoury. Moreover it is hardly possible that if Origen had not read at least the first sentence of the famous paragraph he could in discussing Josephus have written 'It may be questioned whether the Jews thought Jesus to be a man, or whether they did not suppose him to be a being of a diviner kind.'

The Slavonic Version of *The Jewish War* has only been available in this century, but scholars have put forward very varied opinions about it, and especially about the references to the Baptist and to the 'miracle-worker'. Are they genuine, as Berendts believed, or interpolations as Frey argued, or in part genuine and in part forgeries, as Eisler tried to prove? I do not wish to repeat here the considerations that I put forward at the end of my translation of the *War*. The passages seem to me far more improbable as the work of a Christian than the passages in *Antiquities*; for they could not have been written by anyone even slightly acquainted with the Gospels. Nor can the writer have read *Antiquities*, which gives an account of John much more accurate than those in the Slavonic Additions. It is to be noted that in the latter John's name does not appear. Is not this because when Josephus did his first writing he did not yet know the name, or the other facts which he was to discover before writing *Antiquities*? After all, he knew so little about the decade in which Pilate was governor, and John and Jesus were active, that the whole of his information sufficed to fill only one page of the *War*. And is it credible that a Christian forger, even if he had not read the passage in *Antiquities*, would not give the 'hair-clad savage' a name?

The most recent comment on these passages that I have seen comes from R. Glover of the University of Manitoba: 'These references contain details which seem clearly based on local Jerusalem traditions of a kind that cannot long have survived A.D. 70. Indeed, they contain precisely and only such matter as might be gleaned by a man of priestly family raised in Jerusalem, which is what Josephus was.'

Manuscripts, Editions, and Translations

THE TRUE TEXT OF JOSEPHUS IS DIFFICULT TO DETERMINE, SINCE the extant MSS. show many variations. We possess only six or seven really good copies of *Antiquities* and the *War*, five of the *Life*, and one of *Apion*. Compared with our MSS. of the New Testament these are all modern, dating from the tenth to the fifteenth century. We have also two Latin versions which, since they were made in the fourth century, are probably more accurate in some places than the Greek. It is fortunate that we possess them; for the Greek of a dozen pages of *Apion* is entirely lost. It is thought that, for this book at least, the many quotations in Eusebius preserve a better text than does any MSS. that has come down to us.

The *Editio princeps* of the Greek text was that published in Basel in A.D. 1544. It is a splendid piece of work, beautifully printed, and apparently based on an excellent MS. which has since disappeared. I count myself fortunate to possess a copy. Modern editions are those of Niese (Berlin 1887) and Naber (Leipsig 1888).

The best known English translation is that of the Rev. William Whiston, a brilliant mathematician who succeeded to Newton's professorship at Cambridge but was expelled from the University for his unorthodox theology. In 1737 he published a translation of all Josephus' works, with introduction, notes, dissertations, and full index—a monumental effort. In spite of the clumsiness, long-windedness, and occasional inaccuracy of his version, his labours have been of very great service to his successors. In 1851 appeared the two volumes of a new translation (of the *Life* and the *War* only) by the Rev. Robert Traill, a devoted Irish parson who four years before had fallen 'a victim to the generous and extraordinary exertions made by him during that winter of horrors 1846-47, to alleviate the sufferings of his parishioners and neighbours'. His translation was already appearing in instalments, like the novels of Dickens and Thackeray. He had undertaken the task because he felt that Whiston's version was, 'in places innumerable, faulty', and the style 'cumbersome, crabbed, and repulsive'. His own version is certainly an immense improvement, though to our ears old-fashioned. It is accompanied by disquisitions valuable but of inordinate length, and adorned with a wealth of excellent illustrations.

Whiston was not dead yet, and his translation was reissued in 1870. Nineteen years later it made a further come-back in a new five-volume edition, revised and much modified by the Rev. A. R. Shilleto, who prefixed this severe comment: 'Whiston's translation has retained the field, not so much from its intrinsic merit as from the fact that the magnitude of the work, and the want of a good critical edition of Josephus's Greek text, has deterred scholars from the Atlantean labour of a new translation. In my revision there is, indeed, not much of Whiston left. In revising him I have amended his baldness, pruned and curtailed his archaisms, corrected his mistranslations, and generally speaking been throughout close to the text where he has been turgid and periphrastic. With regard to Whiston's notes, many of them are puerile, many irrelevant, some absolutely incorrect.' Fine words! but the revised translation is most disappointing. The archaisms remain, and there is a hotch-potch of styles. After stomaching an opening sentence one hundred and seventy-three words long, and such expressions as 'King Agrippa sendeth greeting'; 'O Josephus, thou art fond of life'; and 'As for thy country, O Justus, thou knowest . . .'; it is a shock to find 'They repaired Joppa that it might serve them as a *point d'appui*'. Evidently poor Whiston did not approve of this treatment; for when he again popped up in the Everyman edition of the *War*, his own phraseology had been restored.

For those who prefer to read the classics rendered into twentieth century English there is the bilingual Loeb edition, of which the first volume appeared in 1926 and the ninth and last is, at the time of writing, yet to come. It is the work of three men, Drs St J.

Thackeray, Ralph Marcus, and Allen Wikgren. Introduction, translation, and commentary are so good that it is impossible to praise these volumes too highly. For those who require only *The Jewish War* and who do not read Greek there is my own translation in Penguin Classics, first published in 1959.

Principal Members of the Herodian Family

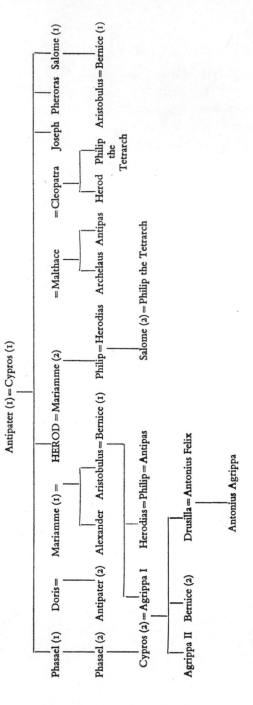

HEROD had five other wives and seven other children. Many of his male descendants married nieces, cousins, and sisters-in-law, and many were childless.

Index